Catholicism in Rhode Island
The Formative Era

Catholicism in Rhode Island
The Formative Era

Patrick T. Conley
Matthew J. Smith

Published by the Diocese of Providence · 1976

Copyright © Diocese of Providence 1976
All rights reserved
Printed in the United States of America
Library of Congress Catalog Card Number: 76-62863

No part of this publication may be reproduced or transmitted in any form or by any means, electronic or mechanical, including photocopying, recording, or any information storage or retrieval system without permission in writing from the publisher, except by a reviewer who wishes to quote brief passages for a review to be included in a magazine, newspaper, or broadcast.

Nihil Obstat: Reverend Robert C. Newbold, Ph.D.
    Censor Librorum

Design: Elizabeth Heitzmann
set in Baskerville type with Bulmer titles
Illustrations: Mildred Tilley and Patrick T. Conley

To

the Sisters of Mercy of the former St. Michael's School in South Providence,

the Christian Brothers of LaSalle Academy, Providence

and

the Dominican Fathers of Providence College

who gave the authors the training, interest and knowledge

which made this book possible

Contents

Illustrations	ix
Preface	xiii

1 Catholicism in Colonial and Revolutionary Rhode Island   1

    Roger Williams and his 'Lively Experiment'
    Catholics in Colonial Rhode Island
    The Charter Betrayed
    Our French Allies

2 Rhode Island under the Bishops of Baltimore and Boston   15

    Organizational Development of the American Catholic Church
    Rhode Island's Catholic Vanguard
    The Church in Newport
    Catholicism in Providence and Pawtucket, 1829–43
    Other Catholic Outposts
    The Dorr Rebellion and the Development of Political Nativism
    The Case of John Gordon

3 Rhode Island under the Diocese of Hartford   57

    William Barber Tyler, First Bishop of Hartford, 1844–49
    Early Educational and Social Developments

Bishop Bernard O'Reilly — A Man for the Times
The Sisters of Mercy Arrive
The Know-Nothing Movement
Growth Under Bishop O'Reilly
Bishop Francis P. McFarland — Compassionate Scholar
Rhode Island Catholics and the Civil War
The Fenian Frenzy
The Church in the 1860s
The Politics of Prejudice
The Irish Impact
The Nature of Nineteenth-Century Irish Catholicism
La langue, la foi, la patrie — The Arrival of the Franco-Americans
Portuguese, Cape Verdean and German Catholics
The New Fold and its First Shepherd

Bibliography   153

Illustration Credits   163

Index   167

Illustrations

page 2 Roger Williams

3 King Charles II of England

4 Portuguese caravel

5 Dighton Rock

Giovanni Verrazzano

8 Act of 1719

9 Colony House, Newport

10 Count de Rochambeau

11 Marquis de Lafayette

Gazette Françoise, November 17, 1780

12 French almanac, Newport 1781

British caricature of French troops

13 Act of 1783

16 Bishop John Carroll

17 Bishop Jean Louis Lefebre de Cheverus

18 Father Francis A. Matignon

19 Notice of an address by Father John Thayer

20 The Great Gale of 1815

22 Bishop Benedict J. Fenwick

23 Marker at Barney Street site of St. Joseph's Church, Newport

Fort Adams, Newport

25 Certificate of the Providence Association of Mechanics and Manufacturers, 1835

26 Old St. Mary's, Pawtucket

Mechanic's Hall, Market Square, Providence

27 The Old Town House, Providence

28 Providence to Stonington railroad line

Railroad depot and steamship docks, India Street, Providence

29 Map of Fox Point, Providence, 1849

30 Reverend John Corry

31 Reverend James Fitton

32 St. Patrick's Church, Providence

33 Tombstone from St. Patrick's Cemetery, Providence

35 Map of Woonsocket Falls, 1838

36 Michael Reddy

37 St. Mary's Church, Crompton

page 38 Notice of skilled Irish worker
40 Thomas Wilson Dorr
41 Henry Bowen Anthony
43 Native American Citizens!
45 People's Party Ballot
47 'The Paddy's Lament for Tom Dorr'
48 Big Mike Walsh
49 The Duff Petition
50 Governor Jackson and the Irish vote
52 The Sprague mill complex
53 Map of the Sprague Print Works, Cranston
General Thomas F. Carpenter
54 Court report of the Gordon murder trial
55 Rhode Island State Prison, 1845
58 William Barber Tyler, First Bishop of Hartford
60 Map of Providence, 1844
61 The First Cathedral of Sts. Peter and Paul
65 Archbishop John Hughes
67 Total Abstinence Pledge
68 Father Theobald Mathew (Close-up)
Father Mathew Preaching
69 Orestes A. Brownson
71 Bernard O'Reilly, Second Bishop of Hartford
72 Mother Mary Francis Xavier Warde
73 Mercy Convent
74 St. Xavier's Academy, music lessons
75 St. Xavier's Academy assembly room
76 Governor Philip Allen
77 'Fort Sumter' (Nast)
78 Elisha R. Potter, Jr.
79 'Don't Believe in That' (Nast)
80 The Convent Committee
82 American Handbill

83 'The Emigrant'
84 Immigrants Landing at the Battery
85 Reverend James Gibson
St. Joseph's, Fox Point
86 St. Mary's, Broadway
87 Reverend John Quinn
88 Francis Patrick McFarland, Third Bishop of Hartford
90 Rhode Island Regiment Off to War
92 Irish Militia
Father Bernard O'Reilly
93 John O'Mahony
95 Fenian cartoon
97 Charles E. Gorman
98 'Bravo' (Nast)
99 'The Ignorant Vote' (Nast)
100 The Naturalized Voter
102 'Killing the Goose' (Nast)
104 The First Church of St. Michael's Parish, South Providence
The First Church of St. Ann's Parish, Cranston
105 Immaculate Conception Church, Providence
107 St. Aloysius Home
108 The Original LaSalle Academy
109 Reverend Henry F. Kinnerney
Father Isaac Hecker
110 Reaction to Edith O'Gorman
112 Irish Cottage
113 Irish Village
114 The Priest's Blessing
115 Emigration Agent, John Whitney
116 Boy and Girl at Cahera
117 An Eviction
Famine Funeral at Skibbereen
Starving Crowd at the Workhouse Gate

page 118 The 1850 Census of Providence

119 'Paddy's Ladder'

120 'The King of A-Shantee'

121 'American River Ganges' (Nast)

'The Day We Celebrate' (Nast)

122 'The Good-for-Nothing in Dame Columbia's Public School' (Nast)

124–125 Irish Caricatures

129 The American Irish and the Pope

130 Paul Cardinal Cullen

132 Irish Religious Procession

Colleen with Rosary

134 François (Fanfan) Proulx

135 George C. Ballou

136 Clinton Cotton Mill, Woonsocket

137 A Pawtuxet Valley Mill

138 Precious Blood Church, Woonsocket

139 Father Charles Dauray

140 Father Patrick Delany

141 Notre Dame Church, Central Falls

St. John the Baptist Church, Arctic

142 St. John's Day Parade

143 Whaler's Log — Cape Verdean Entry

144 Chart of a Whaling Voyage

145 Portuguese Whalemen

German Ferry

146 Bishop William Stang

147 The First Church of St. Mary's, Broadway

149 Thomas Francis Hendricken, First Bishop of Providence

151 Providence in the 1870s

Preface

This volume — a contribution by the diocese to the state's bicentennial observance — attempts to relate the history of Rhode Island Catholicism from its colonial origins down to the formal establishment of the Diocese of Providence in 1872. This is meant to be a 'popular' history designed for the general reader who wishes to know more of our state's early Catholic heritage, but it is our hope that the book can be adapted for use in our schools.

By 'popular' history the authors mean that the work has been written with an emphasis on generalization and interpretation, with ample illustrations, and without such scholarly paraphernalia as footnotes. However, the facts and statements presented herein have been thoroughly researched and drawn from every available primary and secondary source including manuscript correspondence, diaries, newspapers, broadsides, material remains and artifacts, public documents, state, local and parish histories, published scholarly monographs and unpublished seminar papers. A select annotated listing of these sources will be found in the bibliographic essay that follows the text.

This account of the formative era of Rhode Island Catholicism differs from earlier versions which are primarily institutional in nature. We have attempted to broaden our focus to include not only the church-building process and biographical studies of bishops and prominent priests but also such topics as the religious role of the laity and their socio-economic condition, the religious factor in politics and constitutional development, the relation of ethnicity and religion, the impact of national secular and religious currents on local Catholicism, and the contributions of Catholics, both clerical and lay, to Rhode

Island's cultural, economic, social and political development.

This book is mainly descriptive but certain themes emerge — the most prominent of which is the struggle for survival waged by Rhode Island's early Catholics in the face of intolerance, nativism and discrimination. The secure, well-established and influential Church of today is the legacy of the sacrifice, zeal and dedication of its nineteenth century founders. Their efforts deserve to be recounted and appreciated.

Many people contributed their time and talent to the preparation of this volume. Reverend Robert Hayman of the Providence College History Department, Mr. Joseph Cichon, former diocesan archivist, and the Reverend Monsignor Thomas V. Cassidy, former diocesan superintendent of schools, read the work and offered many constructive criticisms. Albert T. Klyberg and his able staff at the Rhode Island Historical Society uncovered many written and graphic primary materials, and Noel Conlon of the Society copy-edited the manuscript. Professor Paul O'Malley of Providence College and Mr. Joseph McNulty of East Providence High School furnished photographic assistance. The text was typed by an able core of secretaries — Gail Gallagher, Helen S. Hodde, Jane Jackson and Barbara Jergensen. Paul Campbell and Glenn LaFantasie, the publications staff of the Rhode Island Bicentennial Commission, guided the work from typescript to finished product and performed services too numerous to recount. And Mrs. Mildred Tilley, the picture editor, made perhaps the outstanding contribution by locating, selecting and reproducing most of the illustrations in this volume. Finally, the Most Reverend Daniel P. Reilly, Bishop of Norwich, suggested the project when he was diocesan administrator in 1971 and Bishops Louis E. Gelineau and Kenneth A. Angell made the funding available for its publication. To all of these scholarly benefactors and to those pioneer Catholics who are the subjects of this book, the authors acknowledge their debt.

Patrick T. Conley
Matthew J. Smith

The Feast of St. Michael
September 29, 1976

CHAPTER 1

Catholicism in Colonial and Revolutionary Rhode Island

Roger Williams and His 'Lively Experiment'

Religion has been a potent influence in Rhode Island since Roger Williams established his settlement at Providence in 1636. Williams regarded his Providence plantation as a practical and pioneering experiment in religious liberty and church-state separation. In an age when Catholics and Protestants alike used the state to enforce religious conformity — whether in England, Spain, or Germany — Williams proclaimed religious freedom. This fiery minister was banished by the Puritan magistrates of Massachusetts Bay because he boldly condemned their use of civil power to insure religious orthodoxy.

At Providence no such interference with freedom of conscience was condoned. The initial articles of town government drafted in 1637 specifically emphasized that governmental control be exercised 'only in civil things.' A more elaborate instrument, the plantation agreement of 1640, clearly reaffirmed 'liberty of conscience.'

It is important to note that the theologically obsessed Williams sought separation of church and state not to protect the state from dominance by the church, but to free the church and the individual conscience from interference and coercions by the state. Williams made a popular statement of his view in a famous public letter: 'There goes many a ship to sea with many hundred souls in one ship whose weal and woe is common and is a time picture of a commonwealth, or a human combination, or society. It hath fallen out sometimes that both Papists or Protestants, Jews and Turks, may be embarked on one ship; upon which supposal, I affirm that all the liberty of conscience that ever I pleaded for, turns upon these two hinges: that none of the Papists, Protestants, Jews

The banishment of Roger Williams as interpreted by the nineteenth-century artist Peter Frederick Rothermel. Williams, a self-proclaimed "Seeker," founded Rhode Island primarily for religious purposes.

or Turks be forced to come to the ship's prayers or worship if they practice any.' The other 'hinge' was the safety of the crew and the security of the voyage, and for these Williams believed all should cooperate. His conclusion was that in civil matters all members of a community should obey the laws; but in religious matters individual conscience was supreme.

While Williams had no special love for Catholicism, he condemned the English persecution of Irish Catholics. He perceived that freedom of worship was a prerequisite to any permanent solution of the Irish question. In his famous tract, *The Bloody Tenent Yet More Bloody,* Williams asked rhetorically: What made the Irish 'so enraged and desperate?' His answer was 'the laws against their consciences and worships.' No wonder, he remarked, that the Irish rose to cast off their 'yokes.' If Catholics acknowledged the Pope only in spiritual affairs and pledged civil obedience, why should they be oppressed more than others, asked Williams. But the answer in that age of intolerance was not obvious to most, and those who raised the question were often regarded as dangerously unorthdox.

While Providence was still in its infancy the Narragansett region became the refuge of other nonconformists. In 1638, a group of religious exiles from Massachusetts, led by Anne Hutchinson and William Coddington, established the community of Portsmouth on the northern tip of the island of Rhode Island, now known as Aquidneck. After several months of internal dissension Coddington led an exodus to the southern end in 1639 where he established the town of Newport. Three years later Samuel Gorton, another religious dissenter, founded Warwick.

In 1643 Roger Williams journeyed to a war-torn England to secure a patent which would effect a political union of the Rhode Island settlements. He obtained such a document from Parliament, but it lacked the royal seal, because King Charles I had begun to lose power and control over English affairs. Dated March 14, 1643, this patent was the first legal recognition of the Rhode Island towns by the mother country. Its repeated use of the phrase 'civil government' gave implicit sanction to Williams's doctrine of church-state separation. Under its authority the General Assembly convened and a tenuous union of the four original towns was consummated.

King Charles II granted Rhode Island's famed charter of 1663. His religious toleration was influenced by his sympathy for the persecuted Catholics of England and his own leanings toward the Roman Catholic faith.

When the Stuart monarchy was restored in 1660 legal doubts were cast upon the adequacy of Rhode Island's parliamentary patent. As a result the apprehensive colony commissioned the able and diligent Dr. John Clarke of Newport to obtain a royal charter. After some difficulty, stemming from the desire of surrounding colonies to swallow up Rhode Island, Clarke obtained the famous charter of 1663 from King Charles II. Immediately transported to the New World, the coveted document was eagerly received by the grateful Rhode Island colonists in November 1663.

This 6,500-word corporate instrument had many significant provisions, but its most remarkable clause was that which bestowed upon the inhabitants of the tiny colony 'full liberty in religious concernments' and provided that no person 'shall be any wise molested, punished, disquieted, or called in question, for any differences in opinion in matters of religion.' This guarantee of absolute religious liberty was a vindication of Williams's beliefs and royal recognition of the fundamental principles upon which the Providence Plantation was founded — freedom of conscience and complete separation of church and state. No other colony, Maryland included, exceeded the liberality of Rhode Island. In the words of Williams, this situation stemmed from the King's willingness to 'experiment' in order to ascertain 'whether civil government could consist with such liberty of conscience.' This was the 'lively experiment' (to use the Charter's phrase) upon which the government of Rhode Island was based.

Catholics in Colonial Rhode Island

In view of the tolerant environment created by Williams and the Charter, one would expect that many persecuted Catholics sought refuge in colonial Rhode Island, but this was not the case. Although Catholicism was an influential factor in the French settlements of the Ohio and Mississippi valleys and in the Spanish regions of Florida, the Southwest, and California, Catholics were a decided minority in the original thirteen English colonies. In 1785, John Carroll, the first American Catholic bishop, conservatively estimated the Catholic population in the United States to be 25,000. Of this figure, 15,800 resided in Maryland, about 7,000 in Pennsylvania, and another 1,500 in New York. Considering that the population in the first federal census of 1790 totaled 3,939,000, it becomes most apparent that Catholicism was somewhat less than a significant force in the affairs of the original thirteen British colonies.

During 1785 François de Barbe-Marbois, a French diplomat stationed in America, estimated the Catholic population of New England at 600. He included French troops who remained after service in the Revolution, a small Irish population in and around the port of Boston, and the Catholic Indians of Maine coverted by French missionaries beginning as early as 1611. This apostolate to the Indian tribes of Maine was the only significant Catholic activity in New England during the entire colonial era.

In Rhode Island organized Catholicism was nonexistent prior to the Revolution — no Catholic church in the colony, no record of any public Mass having been said, and only one recorded visit of a priest. This clerical visitation was noted by the Reverend Ezra Stiles of Newport on March 18, 1769. Stiles recounted that he had 'spent several hours in discourse with a romish priest . . . traveling from Hispaniola

On newly-designed ships such as this caravel, Portuguese, Italian and Spanish seamen opened the New World to European settlement. The caravel was a notable advance in ship design. It was a craft of fifty tons burden and upwards, measuring from 20 to 30 meters in length and from 6 to 8 meters in breadth. It carried a crew of from 12 to 25 men. With a castle at the stern and two or three masts, it had lateen sails stretched on long poles suspended from the masthead. These sails allowed the caravel to sail windward (toward the wind). Late in the 15th century square sails were often added as in this sketch by Rhode Island artist Robert Pailthorpe. Venetian C'a da Mosto in the mid-15th century declared Portuguese caravels to be the handiest and best designed vessels then afloat.

THE FORMATIVE ERA

Dighton Rock in the Taunton River allegedly bears the carved inscriptions of Miguel Corte Real.

to Quebec,' his native province. Two weeks later Stiles again 'conversed with the romish priest' in Newport.

More numerous than references to the Catholic presence were statements of its absence. In 1680, Governor Peleg Sanford informed the Board of Trade that 'as for Papists, we know of none among us.' A generation later the learned Puritan minister, Cotton Mather, observed disparagingly that Rhode Island was 'a colluvies of Antinomians, Familists, Anabaptists, Anti-sabbatarians, Arminians, Socinians, Quakers, Ranters, everything in the world but Roman Catholics and true Christians [Congregationalists].' These facts led noted church historian John Tracy Ellis to assert that 'there is no record of a Catholic ever having been in Rhode Island during the colonial period,' but documentary evidence disproves this sweeping generalization.

From the age of exploration onward, certain Catholic laymen made their mark in Rhode Island history. Possibly one such pioneer was Miguel Corte Real. Typical of those hardy Portuguese adventurers who ushered in the era of discovery, this daring navigator left Lisbon in 1502 to explore the New World, but his ill-fated expedition was never heard from. Some scholars theorize that he was shipwrecked along the New England coast, made his way to the Mount Hope Bay region, and lived for several years among local Wampanoag Indians. According to this hypothesis Corte Real inscribed his name, the Portuguese coat of arms, the Cruz de Cristo of the Portuguese Military Order of Christ, and the date 1511 on a large sandstone boulder at Assonet Neck in the Taunton River. This 'Dighton Writing-Rock' is still preserved, but the existence and authenticity of Corte Real's inscription is the source of considerable, although inconclusive, controversy.

Until this claim can be definitely established the 1524 voyage of Italian navigator Giovanni Verrazzano stands as the first positively verifiable visit to Rhode Island by a European adventurer. Verrazzano made his famous trip in search of an all-water

Italian navigator Verrazzano, reporting to the French king concerning the exploration of Narragansett Bay, indirectly gave the state its name.

route through North America to China in the employ of His Catholic Majesty Francis I of France and several Italian promoters. After landfall at Cape Fear, North Carolina about March 1, 1524 he proceeded up the coast to the present site of New York City to anchor in the Narrows, now spanned by the giant bridge which bears his name. From there, according to his own account, he sailed in an easterly direction until he 'discovered an island in the form of a triangle, distant from the mainland ten leagues, about the bigness of the Island of the Rhodes,' which he named Luisa after the Queen Mother of France. This was Block Island, but Roger Williams and other settlers mistakenly thought that Verrazzano was referring to Aquidneck. Thus they changed the Indian name to Rhode Island, and Verrazzano inadvertently and indirectly gave the state its name.

Natives who paddled out to his ship off Point Judith were so friendly that Verrazzano sailed with their guidance into Narragansett Bay to a second anchorage in what is now Newport harbor. He remained for two weeks while his crew surveyed the Bay and the surrounding mainland, noting the fertile soil, the woods of oak and walnut, and such game as lynx and deer. Their observations on the dress and customs of their hosts, the Wampanoags, were also most revealing. In early May 1524 Verrazzano departed to press on in a vain search for a northwest passage to the Orient.

Had the Catholic French followed up Verrazzano's voyage with a claim to the lands he visited, or had Catholic Portugal persisted in efforts to explore the coast of North America, the history of the United States and of Rhode Island would have been altered markedly. But Catholicism was not destined to dominate this sector of the New World. A militantly Protestant England eventually established hegemony in this region, and that primarily accounts for the insignificance of Catholicism during the formative period of Rhode Island history.

Looking for a Catholic in the British colony of Rhode Island is like searching for the proverbal needle in a haystack, but it is possible to locate identifiable Catholic laymen. Perhaps the most important of this rare species was Charles McCarthy, a founder of the town of East Greenwich. In exile from Ireland, having departed during the persecutions which Oliver Cromwell imposed upon the Irish people in the 1650s, McCarthy first found asylum on the West Indian isle of St. Christopher but eventually made his way to Rhode Island. In 1677 he became one of a group of forty-eight settlers who received a grant of 5,000 acres — to be called East Greenwich — from the Rhode Island General Assembly, a reward for service in King Philip's War. Made a freeman or full-fledged citizen in 1679, McCarthy died in 1683. The will of this adventuresome Irishman, the first such document recorded in the probate record book of East Greenwich, gives evidence of his Catholic background. He refers to a brother in Spain, a nation in which no Protestant would seek refuge during that intolerant age, but a country to which numerous Irish Catholics were exiled.

McCarthy's status as town father and his Catholicity are persuasively documented, but this is not the case with other settlers. Thomas Hamilton Murray, noted antiquarian, has located 166 Irish surnames in those colonial records that have survived. Information on this 'Irish vanguard of Rhode Island' is scanty. It seems certain that most early Irish settlers were northern Protestants, either Presbyterian, Baptist or Quaker, but undoubtedly the list compiled by Murray included several Catholic exiles and indentured servants as well. Since these isolated individuals could not enjoy the ministrations of the clergy or the benefits of an organized church, they and their descendants drifted away from the faith.

Other normally Catholic nationalities are also discernible in the colonial population. Portugal accounted for several notable Rhode Islanders, including the famous merchant prince Aaron Lopez. Nearly all the Portuguese immigrants were, like Lopez, of Jewish ancestry. Because of the pressures of the Portuguese Inquisition they had been nominal Catholics in the Old World, but once these refugees reached America they immediately embraced Judaism. Two important exceptions were Joseph Antunes and James Lucena. Antunes — a merchant in Newport — sought citizenship in December 1750 after marriage to a Middletown girl. The Assembly accepted his petition but only 'upon his abjuring the Pope, and taking the oath of allegiance to His Majesty, and abjuration of the [Catholic] Pretender [James Stuart] before his honor the governor.' This requirement to 'abjure' the Pope, however, was almost assuredly in reference to the pontiff's temporal power.

James Lucena, also a Newport merchant, was Portuguese in nationality, Jewish in ancestry, and Catholic in religion. Even after his arrival in America, he remained in at least nominal communion with the Church of Rome. His son John Charles Lucena was baptized a Catholic and — despite a passing affiliation with the Church of England — died within the Catholic Church. The General Assembly naturalized the elder Lucena in 1760 while, oddly enough, his friends and fellow countrymen — Aaron Lopez and Isaac Elizer — saw their petitions rejected, ostensibly because they had embraced the Jewish religion.

The colonial records also reveal that Francis Ferrari, former subject of the city-state of Genoa, became a citizen in 1751. We know Ferrari was a merchant but have no evidence regarding this pioneer Italian's religion. The great majority of Italians were Catholic, but some came to early America from Italy because they had embraced some form of Protestantism, a circumstance which made their continued stay in the mother country most uncomfortable. This may have been the case with Ferrari, because he was not subjected to the rigorous requirement of 'abjuration' even though he was admitted within seven months of the Portuguese Catholic, Antunes.

Although France was predominantly Catholic, we know that Rhode Island's French pioneers ironically were refugees from Catholic intolerance. These Calvinist Huguenots settled in the southwestern sector of East Greenwich in 1686, an area now called Frenchtown. Forced from their homeland when King Louis XIV revoked the Edict of Nantes — a century-old decree which had given religious toleration to this minority group — their small colony of approximately fifty families dissolved within a generation because of disputes over title to the land these exiles occupied.

Mary Ellen Loughrey in a very able but little known study of *France and Rhode Island, 1686–1800* concludes that there was no important migration from France to Rhode Island between 1700 and 1775. Some Frenchmen, mostly merchants, did come to the colony, but after short sojourns the majority departed. Not until the War of the Revolution did French Catholics make their impact upon Rhode Island.

The Charter Betrayed

In 1719 the General Assembly enacted a statute which directly contravened the theory and practice of Roger Williams and the letter of the royal charter. This measure — the only officially proclaimed discrimination against Rhode Island Catholics during the colonial period — provided that 'all men professing Christianity and of competent estates, and of civil conversation, who acknowledge and are obedient to the civil magistrate, though of different judgments in religious affairs (*Roman Catholics only excepted*), shall be admitted freemen and shall have liberty to choose and be chosen officers in the colony, both military and civil.' This curious language meant that Catholics (and Jews as well) could not be admitted to the status of freemen of the colony. Since freemanship included the right to vote, the right to hold political office, and such other civil rights as the ability to institute court suits and to sit on juries, Catholics in effect were relegated to second class citizenship.

Early historians believe that this anti-Catholic measure was passed in 1663, but we now know that it first appeared in the compilation of laws known as the Digest of 1719 — the original published volume of the general laws. Most of the impetus for compiling the Digest came from royal officials disturbed with the actions of this troublesome colony. Rhode Island had angered these officials by its boundary conflict with Connecticut, by its unauthorized establishment of an admiralty court, and by its failure to organize the statutes of the General Assembly in a proper manner. On the last point, one critic, the Earl of Bellomont, observed: 'The people are at a loss to know what is law among them.' In response to this criticism the Digest came into being.

CATHOLICISM IN RHODE ISLAND

Anno Regni Regis Caroli *Secundi,* Decimo Sexto.   3.

An Act for Declaring the Rights and Priviledges of His Majesties Subjects within this Colony.

BE IT ENACTED By the General Assembly of this Colony, And by the Authority of the same it is hereby Enacted, That no Free-man shall be Taken or Imprisoned, or be deprived of his Free-hold, or Liberty, or Free Customs, or Out-Lawed, or Exiled or otherways Destroyed, nor shall be passed upon, Judged or Condemned, but by the Lawful Judgement of his Peers, or by the Law of this Colony; And that no Aid, Tax, Tailage, or Custom, Loan, Benevolence, Gift, Excise, Duty or Imposition whatsoever, shall be Laid, Assessed, Imposed, Levied or Required of or on any of His Majesties Subjects within this Colony, or upon their Estates, upon any manner of Pretence or Colour whatsoever, but by the Act and Assent of the General Assembly of this Colony. *No Free-men to be Imprisoned, or deprived of his Liberty, &c. But by his Peers, &c. No Tax or Duty to be raised, but by the General Assembly.*

AND that no Man, of what Estate and Condition soever, shall be put out of his Lands and Tenements, nor Taken, nor Imprisoned, nor Disinheretd, nor Banished, nor any ways Destroyed, nor Molested, without being for it brought to Answer by due course of Law; And that all Rights and Priviledges Granted to this Colony by His Majesties Charter, be entirely kept and preserved to all His Majesties Subjects residing, in or belonging to the same; And that all Men Professing Christianity, and of Competent Estates, and of Civil Conversation, who acknowledge, and are Obedient to the Civil Magistrate, though of different Judgmnts in Religious Affairs (Roman Catholicks only excepted) shall be admitted Free-men, And shall have Liberty to Chuse and be Chosen Officers in the Colony both Millitary and Civil. *No Person to be Deseised of his Lands, or otherwise molested, but by due Course of Law. All Persons of Estates, and Obedient to the Magistrate, to have liberty to Elect, and be Elected to Offices.*

This Rhode Island act of 1719 denied civil rights to Roman Catholics.

At the time the volume was being prepared a wave of anti-Catholic sentiment swept the mother country, resulting in several pieces of legislation that further restricted the religious and civil rights of English Catholics. These laws were a reaction to the forceful attempts by Jacobites in 1715–16 to place the Catholic son of James II upon the throne of England. Rhode Island lawmakers who compiled the Digest were influenced by the temper of the times and by a desire to ingratiate themselves with the king and Parliament, and these factors explain the insertion of the anti-Catholic statute into the colony's first published code of laws.

To Rhode Island's discredit this unconstitutional measure was reaffirmed by the Assembly in the Digests of 1730, 1745, and 1767. Since few Catholics lived in the colony, the law had minimal impact. It should be further noted that this law imposed only civil restrictions — at no time was freedom of worship formally impaired nor was naturalization denied to those such as Joseph Antunes and James Lucena who sought British citizenship, although Antunes was require to 'abjure' any temporal allegiance to the Pope.

Not until 1783 was the arbitrary disqualification of Catholics removed. The act that accomplished this was prompted by the liberalizing effect of the American Revolution and by a more tolerant attitude towards Catholics stemming from the assistance rendered to the United States by France and Spain during the struggle for independence.

Our French Allies

In the years 1775 to 1783 the thirteen 'original' English colonies obtained their independence from the mother country and established their identity as a free and sovereign nation. Fortunately for their cause, the American rebels had help from a most unlikely source — Catholic France.

British colonists in North America had been fearful, suspicious, and hostile toward the French settlers of Canada. A long, intermittent war for empire was fought between France and England in the years 1689 through 1763 in which New Englanders were quite active. When the British and their colonials finally prevailed in the Treaty of Paris (1763), the French were stripped of Canada and nearly all their extensive North American possessions. Removal of

The Colony House, Newport, meeting place of the General Assembly. In the south room Rochambeau's troops attended Mass during the French occupation.

this French presence, or 'menace' as British colonists called it, had a liberating impact upon the English settlements because they were no longer so dependent for protection upon the mother country. The treaty also had a profound effect on French foreign policy. From 1763 France was determined to gain revenge for the humiliation she had suffered at the hands of England during the great war for empire.

The French were well informed concerning the growing rift between the colonies and the mother country. Under the exceptionally able direction of Foreign Minister Charles Gravier, Count de Vergennes, France gave encouragement and secret aid to those Americans who sought separation from England. This covert support which began in 1775 eventually blossomed into the crucial Franco-American alliance of February 1778, by which France gave open military and naval assistance and became the first nation formally to recognize the independence of the United States. Vergennes in forging this alliance was not primarily influenced by sympathy for the United States, by interest in its novel political institutions, nor by hopes of French territorial aggrandizement in the Western Hemisphere. His policy rested on practical calculations of eighteenth-century diplomacy and a concern for the European balance of power. Since the American colonies had weighed heavily on England's scale, revenge-bent Vergennes promoted American independence to weaken and humiliate his arch-rival and to establish a European power alignment more favorable to French interests. In April 1779 Spain entered the War of the American Revolution as an ally of France in order to regain Gibraltar and check England's imperial dominance.

One of the earliest testing grounds for the incongruous Franco-American alliance was the Battle of Rhode Island. Marquis de Lafayette en route to that indecisive struggle passed through Providence in early August 1778 to rendezvous with Count d'Estaing who commanded a French fleet anchored off British-occupied Newport. The campaign was indecisive and produced some friction between Americans and their French supporters but the alliance endured.

The next major French foray came in the summer of 1780. At noon on July 11, Count de Rochambeau, commander of French land forces, came ashore at Newport with his aides. The townspeople — who had experienced more than two years of English occupation — were at first somewhat fearful and suspicious of the new arrivals. There was no rejoicing or gaiety in Newport on that eventful day. Rochambeau spent his first night in a local hotel and made arrangements on the following morning for the landing of his army, nearly 6,000 strong. He informed his host, Major General William Heath, that he had royal instructions to place himself entirely under the command of General Washington and to make the French forces an integral part of the army of the United States. Rochambeau made provisions for quartering his troops, promised that they would conduct themselves with good discipline, and offered to pay in cash for the food and services they required. These assurances were a great relief to a community that had just endured a less benevolent British army of

Count de Rochambeau, commander of the French troops in Rhode Island, as portrayed by contemporary artist John Trumbull. Rochambeau's army included a significant number of Catholic soldiers from Ireland and Poland.

THE FORMATIVE ERA

LaFayette in his earliest American portrait (1781), painted by Charles Willson Peale.

occupation and, after the agreements were made, Heath wrote to Washington that 'the inhabitants appear disposed to treat our allies with much respect. . . . For myself, I am charmed with the officers.' The French presence was strongly felt in several areas until the following June when the forces of Louis XVI departed for Yorktown and the decisive encounter with Lord Cornwallis.

When the French first arrived almost one-third of their soldiers and sailors suffered from scurvy or other disabilities. Four hundred of these afflicted troops were transported to Providence where a hospital was established for them in University Hall on the Brown campus over the strenuous objection of the college president, Reverend James Manning, and several local civic leaders. Another detachment wintered in 1780-81 in the vicinity of the present Camp Street and Rochambeau Avenue in what was then North Providence. Once the French had established themselves in Providence and its environs, public opinion became more cordial. Rochambeau himself visited the town on several occasions and was graciously received.

Another detachment was stationed at barracks which American forces had built on Poppasquash Neck in Bristol, but the vast majority of Frenchmen were garrisoned in Newport. Accompanying the army were many Catholic chaplains who ministered to the spiritual needs of the troops. After the French repaired the Old Colony House — damaged by the British — a hospital was established there and in the south room an altar was set up for the celebration of Mass and for the reservation of the Blessed Sacrament. It is generally believed that the first public Mass in Rhode Island was celebrated there after the arrival

The first issue (November 17, 1780) of the *Gazette Françoise*, the French newspaper printed in Newport.

of Rochambeau, but it is possible that this auspicious event occurred during Lafayette's sojourn in 1778.

While the French were in Newport two notable liturgical celebrations impressed the townspeople. One was the funeral of Admiral Chevalier de Ternay, late commander of the French fleet. According to a contemporary witness, Thomas Hornsby, the admiral's body was carried from Washington Street to Trinity churchyard with the coffin preceded by twelve priests who chanted the burial service at the grave. Years later Hornsby recalled that people were deeply moved by the scene, and that many were persuaded that Catholicism was 'not the vain thing which their education had taught them to believe.'

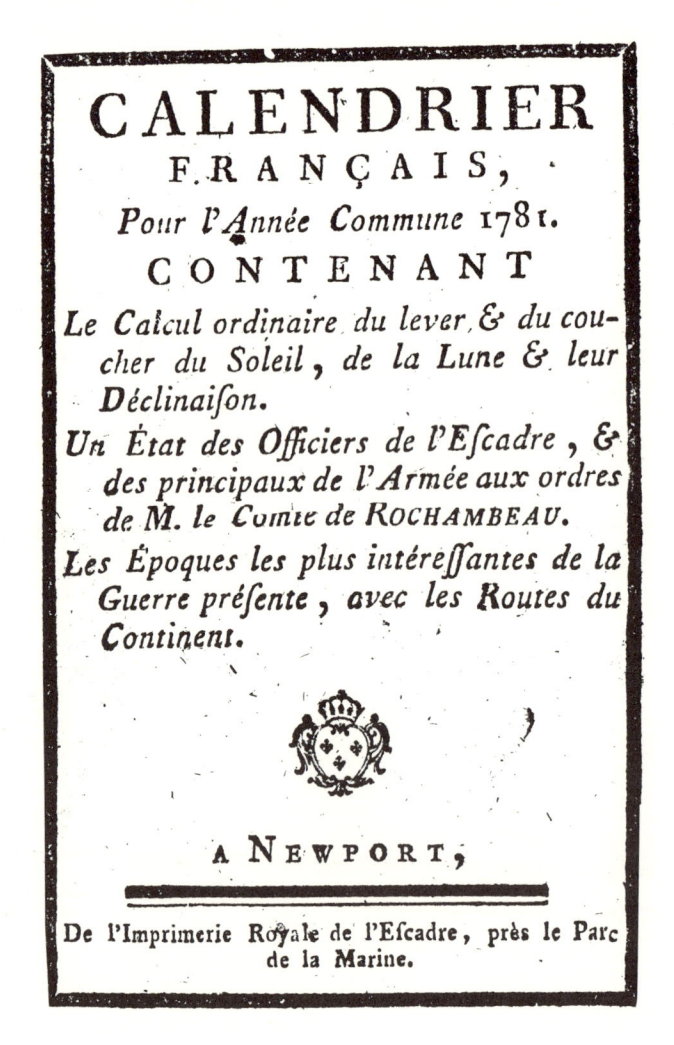

Title page of the 1781 almanac printed while the French fleet lay in Newport harbor.

The other imposing public display of faith stemmed from the long journey to Newport of several Catholic Indian chiefs from the northern frontier. These redmen and their followers had been converted by zealous and intrepid French missionaries; now they came to confer with their French allies. In response to their request to hear Mass and receive the sacraments, a great field Mass was celebrated with a large contingent of troops in attendance, followed by a military review in honor of these Indian leaders.

After a year's occupation the French received orders to move southward to assist in the campaign culminating at Yorktown. In June 1781 the main force left Newport for Providence by way of the Bristol Ferry. They camped for several days on a level, elevated area at the beginning of what is now Plain Street near the old Hayward Park. When they broke camp they headed out Monkey Town Road (Cranston Street) to Monkeytown (Knightsville), and then marched southwestward through Scituate into Connecticut and beyond.

These troops returned briefly and in triumph during mid-November 1781 en route to Boston to embark for home. Some were not so anxious to depart. Writing of the last stage of the homeward march, Count de Segur noted that he was obliged to 'keep night and day a strict watch,' because the desire of happiness

The dress and demeanor of the French troops were ridiculed in this British cartoon, but the French charmed their hosts in cosmopolitan Newport.

which liberty presented to the soldiers had created in many of them a desire of quitting their colors and of remaining in America. In several corps, therefore, the desertion was considerable. A few of these Frenchmen, enamored of America, settled in the Newport area and became the nucleus of the small Catholic community that developed there in the late eighteenth and early nineteenth centuries.

The French presence in the Revolutionary era not only contributed to the granting of equal civil rights to Catholics by statute in 1783, it also increased the attention paid in Rhode Island to French political, economic and religious thought and to the study of French language and literature. President James Manning of Brown University expressed this new spirit of cordiality and cultural rapprochement in a letter to Thomas Jefferson: 'Ignorant of the French language and separated as we were by more than mere distance of countries, we too readily imbibed the prejudices of the English — prejudices which we have renounced since we had a nearer view of the brave army of France, who actually inhabited this college edifice; since which time our youth seek with avidity whatever can give them information respecting the character, genius, and influence of a people they have such reason to admire — a nation so eminently distinguished for polished humanity.' Such sentiment was the immediate legacy of the fortuitous Franco-American alliance.

> **February, 1783.** 79
>
> *IT is further Resolved,* That the Town-Treasurer of *South-Kingstown,* who is committed to Gaol at the Suit of the General-Treasurer, be and he hereby is ordered to be discharged from Gaol.
>
> *BE it Enacted by this General Assembly, and by the Authority thereof it is Enacted,* That all the Rights and Privileges of the *Protestant* Citizens of this State, as declared in and by an Act made and passed the First Day of *March,* A. D. 1663, be and the same are hereby fully extended to *Roman Catholic* Citizens; and that they being of competent Estates, and of civil Conversation, and acknowledging and paying Obedience to the civil Magistrate, shall be admitted Freemen, and shall have Liberty to choose and be chosen civil or military Officers within this State: Any Exception in the said Act to the contrary notwithstanding. *Roman Catholics admitted to the Rights of Citizenship.*

The act of February, 1783 admitting Roman Catholics to "the rights of citizenship." This measure, passed at the Old State House in Providence, was a liberal effect of the Revolution which was prompted in part by the benevolent occupation of Rhode Island by the troops of Catholic France.

CHAPTER 2

Rhode Island under the Bishops of Baltimore and Boston

Organizational Development of the American Catholic Church

A momentous year both for the nation and for Catholicism — 1789 marked the formation of the new government under the Constitution and the establishment of an organizational structure for the American Catholic Church. The former event came with the inauguration of George Washington in April, the latter with the papal appointment of Reverend John Carroll as first Bishop of Baltimore in November.

A member of a prominent Maryland family of Irish ancestry and brother of Daniel Carroll, a framer and signer of the federal Constitution, John Carroll was active in the Revolution. In 1776 he journeyed to Canada with Benjamin Franklin and others in a futile attempt to persuade French Canadians to revolt against the Crown. After America declared independence, Rome decided to shift direct control of the missionary church in the new republic from the English Vicar Apostolic to an American clergyman. Asked by papal officials to suggest a suitable person for the post, Benjamin Franklin in Paris recommended Carroll — his companion on the Canadian venture of 1776 — and Rome responded in 1784 by appointing the Maryland Jesuit as 'Prefect Apostolic and Superior of the missions in the provinces of the New Republic of the United States of America.' This office carried some episcopal powers including power to confirm, and was a logical step in the elevation of Carroll to the dignity of first American bishop.

Baltimore, the principal city in the most Catholic state, became the mother see of the American Church. In area, the new diocese of Baltimore was co-equal with the original boundaries of the United States. As the Catholic population began to grow from the influx of Irish and French (both from France and her tur-

John Carroll, first American bishop. This portrait by the famed Rhode Island artist Gilbert Stuart was painted in 1805 at the request of an Irish gentleman in whose Baltimore home Bishop Carroll was a frequent guest.

bulent West Indian possessions), Carroll saw the need for the division of his expansive diocese. In 1806 he wrote to Rome to urge creation of at least four additional jurisdictions: one diocese in New England with the see at Boston; a second see at New York City to serve New York and East Jersey; a third at Philadelphia with control over Pennsylvania, Delaware, and West Jersey; and a fourth somewhere in Kentucky (Bardstown was the eventual choice) with jurisdiction over Kentucky and Tennessee. Carroll would retain Maryland and the four states to the south. Pope Pius VII acted favorably on this proposal. The four new dioceses were created in 1808 as suffragan sees, and Baltimore was made the metropolitan see with Carroll its archbishop.

The priest whom Carroll favored for first bishop of Boston, the direct religious superior of the Rhode Island Catholic community, was Francis Anthony Matignon. A Sulpician who had earned a doctorate in theology, Matignon had taught at the College of

First bishop of Boston, Jean Louis Lefebvre de Cheverus (1808–1823) was also portrayed by Rhode Island's Gilbert Stuart in 1823 at the request of Mrs. John Gore.

Navarre, but he fled France in 1792 to escape the terrors of the French Revolution. Bishop Carroll assigned this scholarly cleric to the small Catholic church on School Street in Boston. Matignon invited another refugee, Jean Louis Lefebvre de Cheverus, then in England, to be his assistant. Father Cheverus arrived in Boston in 1796 and thereafter the two became inseparable workers for the faith.

When Carroll offered the new Boston bishopric to Father Matignon, the humble, self-effacing priest protested strongly and even threatened to return to France. Matignon urged that his younger colleague Father Cheverus be named. Carroll honored the request and in 1808 appointed Cheverus first bishop of Boston. These two energetic clerics and their colleagues, Fathers John Thayer and John S. Tisserant, were the principal and almost exclusive emissaries to Rhode Island's small but growing Catholic community from the 1790s through the first quarter of the nineteenth century.

CATHOLICISM IN RHODE ISLAND

Rhode Island's Catholic Vanguard

From the time French troops departed in 1782 until the establishment of Rhode Island's first permanent parish in 1828, there existed a small and scattered Catholic community. Principal settlements were in Newport and the Providence-Pawtucket area, although Catholics could be found in other outposts like Portsmouth, Bristol, and Woonsocket. The best evidence of the nature of this vanguard is the entries on the baptismal register in Boston's Holy Cross Cathedral, giving information concerning the nationality of early Catholics and the identity of the priests who ministered to them. The surviving records indicate that this community was composed of several elements: a few French troops who chose to stay in America; French refugees from revolts then occurring in Santo Domingo, Guadeloupe, and other islands of the West Indies; consuls and merchants from several European nations such as France and Spain, most of whom resided with their families in Newport; and Irish who had fled oppressive conditions in their homeland.

Apparently the first Catholic priest to visit after the departure of the French army was Claude Florent Bouchard, Abbe de la Poterie, who arrived in Boston in 1788 and soon became pastor of a small congregation there. The Abbe's ambitious, imprudent conduct and administrative irregularities became a matter of grave concern to John Carroll who suspended his priestly powers in 1789. Before he returned to France, the outspoken Bouchard penned a pamphlet that criticized Carroll and caused the Church considerable embarrassment. Shortly after his suspension, Bouchard traveled through Providence where, despite the loss of his priestly faculties, he celebrated Mass on December 8, 1789 at the request of several Catholics. Bouchard's performance was a most inauspicious beginning for Rhode Island Catholicism.

The state was not visited by another priest until early February 1791 when Father John Thayer baptized a black youth — Joseph Deane — in Newport. Thayer, a New England-born Yale graduate who be-

Father Francis A. Matignon (1753–1818) pioneer French missionary to New England Catholics.

came a convert during an extended stay in Europe, made several trips to Rhode Island in the 1790s. On his second visit in October 1791, he baptized the daughter of a French officer from Santo Domingo, a West Indian island that had close commercial ties with Newport.

Santo Domingo was soon to contribute more Catholics, especially to Newport and Bristol. A Negro slave revolt in 1793 on that troubled isle forced some French Catholics to seek refuge in Rhode Island including fifty desperate exiles who arrived aboard the ship *Providence* in October 1793. The General Assembly to its credit responded in humanitarian fashion by appropriating substantial sums during 1793–95 for their support. It appears that most of the West Indian exiles resided only briefly in the state and many eventually returned to France.

Father Thayer, after a short sojourn in the South, was assigned to a ministry in New York City in 1796 but was also empowered to make missionary journeys into Rhode Island and Connecticut. There is a record of his visit to Newport in July 1798. Among those whom he baptized on this occasion was the daughter of Don Josef Wiseman, Spanish Vice-Consul, and the daughter of French Vice-Consul Louis Aracambal. On this productive stay Thayer, a militant and zealous preacher, delivered a public lecture at the Newport court house. Soon after, the polemical Thayer departed the New England scene to do missionary work for a time in Kentucky and to travel ultimately to Ireland where he died in 1815.

Thayer was succeeded by Reverend John S. Tisserant, a refugee from the Diocese of Bourges, who established residence in Wethersfield, Connecticut becoming the first resident priest in a state populated mostly by Congregationalists. Tisserant went to Newport to preach and baptize in 1802, 1803, and again in 1804, but shortly after he was reassigned to New Jersey and eventually returned to Europe.

During Father Tisserant's ministry, Rhode Island received an unscheduled visit from Bishop John Carroll who had gone to Boston to dedicate the new Church of the Holy Cross. On his return to Baltimore in November 1803 his ship became windbound after putting into Newport. Carroll seized this opportunity to go ashore. He visited the town's Catholic community and performed two baptisms.

At the turn of the century the ranks of the Catholic Irish increased. These arrivals were refugees from political turmoil, such as the abortive 'rising' of 1798, the Act of Union (1801) shifting the seat of Irish government to London, and the ill-fated rebellion of 1803 for which Robert Emmet gave his life. Their numbers at this early date were not great but this mild influx soon made them the largest group in the state's heterogeneous Catholic community.

The *Newport Mercury* printed this notice of a 1798 patriotic address by Father John Thayer.

Migration of French and Irish to the United States in the late 1790s, though very modest by mid-nineteenth-century standards, prompted the country's first national discriminatory immigration laws — the Naturalization Act of 1798 and the Alien Act — passed by the Federalist party during the Quasi-War with France. The former was designed to impede the French and the Irish from gaining citizenship and political power by requiring that the foreign-born must reside in the United States for fourteen years before applying for citizenship and then wait five additional years becoming eligible for naturalization. The Federalists resorted to this device because their British-oriented foreign policy caused newly naturalized French and Irish to ally with the opposition party, the Democratic-Republicans.

The Alien Act — even more severe in its provisions — authorized the President to deport summarily any foreigner he considered dangerous. Both laws were repealed by Democratic Republicans in 1801. It is impossible to estimate the immediate impact of this restrictive legislation on French and Irish immigration, but it appears that the direct effect was minimal. The long-term impact, however, especially on the Catholic Irish, was substantial. In the 1830s and 1840s Democratic followers of Andrew Jackson wooed incoming Irish in a variety of ways. One method was to claim political descendance from the old Democratic Republicans and to allege that the Whigs were merely the reincarnation of the anti-Irish, anti-foreign Federalist party. Such propaganda, though simplistic and historically imprecise, became one of many factors that helped to forge the traditional alliance between Catholic Irish and the Democratic party. The country's first restrictive immigration legislation — the Federalist package of 1798 — was in retrospect a cardinal political blunder both in its immediate and especially in its ultimate effects.

Following the departures of Thayer and Tisserant, Bishop Cheverus and Father Matignon became the principal clerical missionaries to Rhode Island. In September 1805 Matignon made the first of his recorded visits and repeated the practice annually through 1811, usually in the autumn. Thereafter he was joined by Cheverus and the visits became even more frequent.

The increasing preponderance of Irish names in Matignon's baptismal records indicates the slow, steady growth of that group. Industrialization in the Providence-Pawtucket area, public works projects in Newport, and the opening of a potentially rich coal mine in Portsmouth in 1809 provided job opportunities for these early immigrants. Father Matignon notes that he stopped at the Portsmouth coal pits in 1811 to baptize a child in the Kassedy family.

Providence seems to have developed a small but vigorous Catholic colony during the early years of the nineteenth century. Father Matthew O'Brien, an elderly priest from Salem, Massachusetts, who passed through in 1814 en route to New York, informed John Carroll that 'a building at Providence has been rented and formed into a church by a few Catholics who are there. A mere grain of mustard seed only eighteen months ago is now rapidly starting up, and, watered as it has been by the amiable and laborious Bishop, will soon become a tree.' The building was an old wooden school house on the north side of Sheldon Street near Benefit, first rented in 1813, then moved to another lot. Bishop Cheverus himself officiated at this Fox Point church on several occasions. Unfortunately this first Rhode Island Catholic house of worship was leveled by the Great Gale and tidal wave of 1815 — a calamity that destroyed one-fourth of the total property valuation of Providence.

The Great Gale of 1815 leveled the small wooden structure on Sheldon Street, Fox Point that served as Rhode Island's first Catholic church.

During and after the War of 1812, Bishop Cheverus came to Rhode Island more frequently as the journey from Boston became too arduous for his aging colleague. In 1817 Cheverus visited Bristol, baptized a child in the McClean family, preached at the Bristol court house, and made the acquaintance of Right Reverend Alexander Griswold, Protestant Episcopal Bishop of the Eastern District, comprising Massachusetts, Rhode Island, and New Hampshire. Bishop Griswold invited Cheverus to preach in Bristol's Episcopal church, a courteous gesture which Cheverus eventually accepted. The Bishop and his partner Father Matignon were no strangers to Bristol. Their cathedral register contains several entries of baptisms administered to children of French West Indian exiles who resided in this bustling port town.

On September 19, 1818 the Boston diocese suffered the loss of its co-founder. On the fortieth anniversary of his ordination to the priesthood, the Reverend Doctor Francis Matignon died of consumption at the age of sixty-four. Visibly shaken by the passing of one with whom he had labored for twenty-two years in the promotion of New England Catholicism, Bishop Cheverus made the entry of Matignon's funeral in the church records with feeling and sincerity — 'he died as he lived, a saint.' Cheverus continued to conduct the affairs of his diocese diligently but, lonely and weary, more and more he yearned for return to his native France.

Through 1819-23, Cheverus continued to visit his Rhode Island outposts. In June 1823 he administered five baptisms in Pawtucket, the first such event recorded in that community. Later in the year he yielded to the urging of the Grand Almoner of France and returned to his native land to accept the bishopric of Montauban. Among the factors contributing to his reluctant departure were his despondency over the death of Matignon, the declining state of his health, and the growing disposition of Rome to favor Irish bishops to administer the affairs of the American Church.

The Matignon-Cheverus era of New England Catholicism closed on September 26, 1823 when the bishop sailed from Boston harbor with France his destination. Not least of the notable achievements of these pious men was the respect they earned from the Protestant community and the ecumenical spirit they fostered. When Cheverus's departure was rumored in May 1823, 226 of Boston's non-Catholic civic leaders — including Daniel Webster, Mayor Josiah Quincy, Harrison Gray Otis, Daniel Sargent, and William Tudor — drafted and signed a memorial to the Grand Almoner to prevent the transfer of Cheverus from Boston. Perhaps Tudor, a prominent Boston editor and founder of the *North American Review,* best appraised the contributions of these pioneer French priests: 'Two individuals of great acquirements, full of charity and piety, driven from their distracted country, received the charge of this infant church. They have fulfilled the numerous parochial duties required by the Catholic religion, with apostolical simplicity and evangelical zeal, neither attempting to make proselytes nor to excite controversy: and I presume it cannot be disputed, and I hope it will not be considered invidious to say . . . that their ministry is by far the most arduous and useful in the town.'

Following the resignation of Cheverus — who was elected cardinal one year before his death at Bordeaux in July 1836 — the Boston diocese experienced an interregnum. Its vicar general, Father William Taylor, who had come to Boston in 1821, was Cheverus's personal choice to succeed him. Taylor, a young Irish-born cleric who had converted from Protestantism, served as administrator pending the selection of a new bishop. When Rome decided upon Reverend Benedict Fenwick, the disappointed Taylor announced his decision to join Cheverus in France.

Bishop Fenwick, a Jesuit from a wealthy, old-line Maryland family and a former president of Georgetown University, first appeared before his cathedral congregation in December 1825. He assumed control over a diocese with only nine churches (none in Rhode Island), four clergy (including himself), and 7,000 to 8,000 Catholics, the majority resident in Boston. Great moral gains had been made under Bishop Cheverus, but the condition of New England Catholicism in 1825 made it apparent that material progress had been slow and halting, so slow in fact that Bishop Louis Dubourg of New Orleans suggested to Rome in 1824 and again in 1825 that the sees of Boston and New York be united. But the elevation of Fenwick coincided with a sharp, almost inexorable upturn in Irish immigration. This unprecedented influx, beginning in the mid-1820s and extending through the 1850s, provided Rhode Island Catholicism with a firm and broad foundation.

The Church in Newport, 1828–44

In January 1827 Bishop Fenwick sent his cathedral assistant Reverend Patrick Byrne to Rhode Island. Byrne found on the island of Aquidneck a greater number of Catholics than he had anticipated. Large-scale construction at Fort Adams had resumed in 1824 and the Portsmouth mines had expanded their operations. These activities attracted a number of incoming Irish who went to the island in search of jobs. This influx was reflected in the itinerant Byrne's report to Fenwick that about 150 people received communion in Newport and almost another thirty at the coal mines.

As a result of this promising development and a similar increase in the Providence-Pawtucket area, Fenwick dispatched a new addition to his mission band, Reverend Robert D. Woodley, to investigate the feasibility of founding a church somewhere in the state. Although discussion centered mainly on the Providence-Pawtucket area, Newport prevailed as the most advantageous location. On his first visit Woodley had been invited to buy what he described as 'a beautiful school house, in a central situation in the town, capable of holding four to five hundred people' for $1,100, to be paid over a five-year period. The building on Barney Street had been an academy conducted by Eleazar Trevett, but just prior to the purchase by Woodley the structure had been used as a meeting place for the Tammany Society of Newport. Renovations were made immediately and the title passed in early April. The first Catholic services were held on April 6, 1828. These events marked the origin of the parish now known as St. Mary's. The following October, Bishop Fenwick came to consecrate the edifice. He said Mass, preached an eloquent sermon, and confirmed eleven persons, but he was disappointed with the deal Woodley had arranged. The bishop noted in his memoranda that although the location was excellent, the lot was too narrow, the building too shabby, and the price too high. To partially redeem what Fenwick considered a bad bargain, he urged Woodley to buy the adjacent lot, eventually acquired in 1830, to gain adequate space and frontage. This Newport edifice, which Father Woodley attended monthly, is often referred to as the first Catholic church in Rhode Island. More precisely its establishment marked the beginning of a continuous structural and organizational presence of the Church. The Providence chapel of 1813–15 must rank as the state's first Catholic church.

Jesuit Benedict J. Fenwick, second bishop of Boston (1825–1846) and the successor to Cheverus as spiritual father of the Catholics of Rhode Island.

Although Father Woodley came to attend to the needs of his Newport church only once monthly, his general responsibilities covered a wide area. In addition to Newport, he was initially charged with the care of Catholics in Providence, Pawtucket, Woonsocket, New Bedford, Fall River, Taunton, and the entire state of Connecticut during the years 1828–29 — an area now divided into five dioceses. Woodley incessantly traveled over this large area, ministered to every group brought to his attention, gathered new congregations, often saying the first Mass in many places. This young Virginian, an honor graduate of Georgetown University, maintained a roving apostolate similar to that later conducted by the more famous Father James Fitton.

Unfortunately, the dedicated Father Woodley experienced some administrative problems, chiefly of a financial nature. In addition, this native American had some difficulty relating to his Irish parishioners. These factors caused Bishop Fenwick to transfer supervision of the Rhode Island mission to Reverend John Corry in December 1830. Soon after, the discouraged Woodley returned to Georgetown, entered the Jesuits, and worked among the Catholics of Maryland until his death in 1857.

Corry, Irish-born and newly ordained, was given charge of Newport in 1830, and his seven-year ministry was productive. He built an adequate new church to replace Woodley's remodeled school house.

Until recently this monument marked the Barney Street site of St. Joseph's (as St. Mary's, Newport was originally named). Today a plaque designates this historic spot.

This enterprise required four years' effort but, on August 20, 1837, St. Joseph's Church (renamed St. Mary's in 1849) was dedicated — a handsome Gothic frame structure with an 800 seat capacity at a time when the Catholic population of Newport was estimated at 700. His purpose achieved, Corry went to Providence to perform the same function, giving St. Joseph's to Reverend Constantine Lee (1837–39) who in turn was succeeded by Father James O'Reilly (1839–44).

For a few years the affairs of the Newport church

The huge stone walls of Fort Adams are mute but enduring monuments to Newport's early Irish laborers.

proceeded smoothly. Although Newport's 'golden age' as a summer resort was in the future, it was an attractive 'watering place' for those from warm, humid, southern states and had been a vacation spot for a century. In August 1841, Bishop Fenwick's memoranda reveal that he visited the town and was hosted by Mrs. Goodloe Harper, a daughter of Charles Carroll of Carrolton and a native of Baltimore. Fenwick also noted that Sunday vespers were sung 'by some Southern ladies.'

At this time Newport Catholicism experienced one of its early cyclical declines. In 1842 the construction work that had been carried on for so long at Fort Adams was discontinued and many laborers were forced to seek work opportunities elsewhere. Depletion of the congregation caused Father O'Reilly's income from St. Joseph's to dip to eighty dollars per year in 1842. When he attempted to collect money owed for pew rent by having his sexton keep defaulters out of church, some of his parishioners took him to court. The case, however, was dismissed.

By 1843 financial difficulties forced the Newport pastor to reside with Father Edward Murphy in Fall River. Finally in March 1844 the discouraged O'Reilly was transferred to Boston and was replaced by Father James Fitton who solidified Catholicism in Newport during the ensuing decade. When this roving missionary took up permanent residence in 1846, the Catholic population had reversed its downward trend and numbered 375 according to Fitton's own count. Thereafter the famine-inspired Irish migration produced a steady increase.

Catholicism in Providence and Pawtucket, 1829–43

The most impressive growth of the Church from the late 1820s to the early 1840s was in the Providence-Pawtucket region, an area experiencing high urbanization and offering numerous job opportunities for incoming Irish Catholic immigrants. These two communities were much smaller geographically than they are today. Providence's six square miles of territory was less than one-third its current size. Present outlying neighborhoods in northern, western, and southern portions of the city (places like the North End, Elmhurst, Mt. Pleasant, West Elmwood, and South Providence) were part of the surrounding towns of North Providence, Johnston, or Cranston. Diminutive Providence boasted a population of 16,836 in 1830 and 31,747 by the city census of 1845. The rise in the foreign-born population was even more dramatic — from an estimated thirty-nine aliens in 1820, to 1,005 foreigners not naturalized in 1835, to 5,965 'foreign born' in 1845. Of this last figure nearly two-thirds were Irish and a very high percentage were Catholics as well. Father John Corry estimated the Catholic population of Providence at nearly 200 in 1830. By January 1839 a census conducted by the Hibernian Orphan Society counted 1,696 souls, all except 'eight or ten' Irish. By 1842 the total had risen to nearly 2,500, according to Father Corry's calculations.

By the time it became a city in 1832, Providence was a natural entrepôt for immigrants seeking employment and economic opportunity. The city was now entrenched as the economic leader in a rapidly industrializing state and it possessed the most balanced and diversified manufacturing economy. Already cotton and woolen production, the precious metals industry, and the base metal industry were firmly established. The city also owed its industrial primacy to superior financial resources and banking facilities, the development of steam power, and its emergence as the hub of Rhode Island's transportation network by virtue of its port facilities and its position at the southern terminus of the new Blackstone Canal. Providence was well on its way to becoming the metropolitan center of southern New England.

Pawtucket, the other nucleus of Catholic influence, did not have a separate existence as a town but was merely a populous mill village in the eastern sector of the town of North Providence. There were actually two Pawtuckets — the Rhode Island village and the Massachusetts community incorporated as a town by the General Court in 1828. Prior to 1862 the Blackstone or Seekonk River, which bisects the present city, was the boundary line between the two Pawtuckets and the two states as well.

Pawtucket first achieved fame in 1790 when Samuel Slater reconstructed a cotton spinning frame similar to Arkwright's in a mill at Pawtucket Falls. This event, which some have lavishly termed 'the beginning of Rhode Island's industrial revolution,' was at least a catalyst in the state's transformation from a mercantile and agrarian economy to one based principally upon industry, and it helped shape Pawtucket's future development.

By the end of the 1820s, the village had established itself as a pioneer in the textile and iron industries. Although its growth and importance did not equal that of Providence, it did become the home of the first Rhode Island edifice specifically constructed as a Catholic church. This distinction resulted from two factors. First, in 1828, when plans were being discussed for the erection of a church in the state, the

THE FORMATIVE ERA

Pawtucket area had a slightly higher number of Catholics (*ca.* 250) than neighboring Providence. Second, David Wilkinson — a prominent iron manufacturer and inventor, brother-in-law of Samuel Slater, and a Protestant — donated a fine lot on the south side of Pawtucket village near the Providence-Pawtucket turnpike as the site for a church. Wilkinson gave the land in hopes of satisfying the spiritual needs of his employees.

Since Pawtucket was part of the far-flung parish of Father Woodley, this energetic priest and his parishioners collected funds and awarded the building contract for $1,200 in early 1829. By November when Bishop Fenwick and Bishop Joseph Rosati of New Orleans viewed it, the 'neat wooden building, painted white, with green doors and Venetian blinds' was almost finished. Finally, on Christmas Day 1829, Father Woodley celebrated the first Mass in this new church of St. Mary's.

Hard times hit Pawtucket in 1829 in the form of an industrial depression that closed businesses and precipitated the failure of the local Farmers' and Merchants' Bank. Many Catholics lost their jobs and migrated elsewhere leaving Father Woodley with the difficult and immediate burden of paying the construction debt with a rapidly dwindling congregation.

This 1835 certificate of the Providence Association of Mechanics and Manufacturers symbolizes Providence's early industrial growth. Such industry attracted the first Irish settlers to the Providence-Pawtucket area.

This condition coupled with other misfortunes, including Fenwick's dissatisfaction with Woodley's Newport purchase of 1828, prompted Woodley's recall.

Father John Corry took charge of the entire Rhode Island mission in 1830. Corry placed primary emphasis on the congregations in Providence and Taunton, Massachusetts, although he did manage to pay St. Mary's debt by 1832. This pioneer parish was ministered to by a sizable array of priests during its first two decades. Its administration finally stabilized with the coming of Father Joseph McNamee (1847–53)

Old St. Mary's, Pawtucket, the first Rhode Island edifice constructed as a Catholic church, was completed in 1829.

and especially his successor, Reverend Patrick G. Delany, who enjoyed a fruitful twenty-six-year pastorate from 1853 to 1879.

Construction of a church in Providence had been considered by Father Woodley as early as 1828. While an edifice was in the discussion stage, Woodley secured the use of Mechanics' Hall on Market Square. Bishop Fenwick celebrated Mass there on September 14 for a congregation that included several curious Protestants, and at its conclusion he administered the sacrament of Confirmation to five persons. Sunday services in those less hectic times included morning Mass usually at ten o'clock, followed by mid-afternoon Vespers or Confirmation when the bishop came. Fenwick customarily preached at both services, but on this day, a young deacon, William Tyler (the future bishop of Hartford), spoke in the afternoon.

A few months before his departure in June 1830, Father Woodley responded to the wishes of his Providence flock by purchasing a lot on Pearl Street. In the same month he petitioned the General Assembly to allow a lottery to raise $10,000 for the construction of a large church. The Assembly, more because of increasing aversion toward lotteries than hostility to Catholicism, overwhelmingly rejected the petition. To compound the misfortune, Woodley was forced to mortgage the Pearl Street lot in November 1830 for a loan of $35, and shortly after, it was sold.

Father John Corry, young, energetic, and a great organizer, began and completed the task of establishing a physical presence for the Church in Providence. When he received his new appointment, Father Corry was also charged with the care of Catholics in Pawtucket and Taunton. His initial efforts were primarily concentrated in the latter community. He chose it as his residence and, as a result of his leadership, Taunton soon had it first Catholic church, St. Mary's, dedicated by Bishop Fenwick in October 1832.

While engaged in this successful building venture, Corry arranged the purchase of a possible church site on High Street in Providence. The land was actually bought by Francis Hye, a Catholic layman, 'trader' by occupation, and one of two naturalized Irishmen

In Mechanic's Hall on Market Square (center building) Bishop Fenwick celebrated Mass on September 14, 1828.

The Old Town House as it appeared in 1851. During the 1830s city authorities allowed Providence Catholics the use of this historic building for services and lectures.

living in Providence. Hye in turn transferred the land to Fenwick. When the seller, Isaac Mathewson, learned why Hye had acquired the property, he offered its purchase price plus a $500 bonus for return of the deed, an offer considered but refused.

Unfortunately, Father Corry, who appears to have been the ablest and most effective of the pioneer priests in the 1820s and 1830s, was relieved of his Providence and Pawtucket assignments in November 1832. His successors did not enjoy a harmonious or productive sojourn. First came Reverend Peter Connolly, a young Ulsterman with experience in the roving type of ministry. He purchased a residence near a popular tavern, the Halfway House on the main highway between Providence and Pawtucket. Connolly's stay, however, was short. On April 30, 1834, Fenwick transferred him to Lowell, Massachusetts and commissioned Father Constantine Lee to take charge of the Providence-Pawtucket area. Lee, an Irishman educated in Rome and possessor of a doctorate in theology, held the Providence post until 1837 and remained in Rhode Island until his departure for Europe in 1839.

During the early 1830s, the city authorities generously allowed Catholics the use of the Town House, at what is now the corner of Benefit and College Streets, for services and lectures. In 1835 Father Lee leased the former Tin Top Congregational Church at Pine and Richmond Streets for an annual rental of $150 and conducted services there.

Such temporary, makeshift quarters were becoming glaringly insufficient as the Irish Catholic population of Providence mounted to more than 1,000 by 1835, a five-fold increase over the 1830 estimate. Besides the lure of manufacturing, a new attraction accounted for this influx — the railroad. In 1831 the Massachusetts legislature had chartered a company to build a railroad from Boston to the Rhode Island boundary at Pawtucket or Seekonk. As the road neared completion, businessmen in Rhode Island saw that if the state were to reap full economic benefits, the line had to be continued across the Seekonk

Another evidence of the "Transportation Revolution," the Providence to Stonington, Connecticut rail line was opened in 1837. It was built with the help of Irish labor. A turn-of-the-century artist has re-created the scene at Stonington.

Immigrant Irish Catholics were important participants in the "Transportation Revolution" which brought railroad facilities to Providence such as those depicted in this mid-nineteenth century India Street scene.

THE FORMATIVE ERA

River into Providence. The Boston and Providence Railroad and Transportation Company was organized, and in 1835 the route was completed with its terminus at India Point. From there one could board a steamer to Newport or New York. Spurred on by prospects of profit from railroads, businessmen built additional lines to connect Providence with other New England cities, the first of which was a route from Providence to Stonington, Connecticut.

New England and the nation in the 1830s were caught up in what economic historian George Rogers Taylor calls 'the Transportation Revolution,' and immigrant Irish laborers were important participants in that economic upheaval. They provided much of the unskilled manpower that spun a web of turnpikes, canals, and railroads linking mid-nineteenth-century America. In Rhode Island Irish workers were involved in building the Blackstone Canal (1825–26) and participated to a much greater degree in the construction of the railroad from Boston to Providence.

Wages on such projects were often low, working and living conditions were incredibly bad, and fevers and sickness of all kinds were prevalent.

It was quite common for laborers to remain where they were when the route was completed, either 'squatting' on vacant land or securing cheap rentals in the area. The Catholic population in Providence was augmented by the arrival of construction workers in 1834 and 1835. The old Irish community in Fox Point, near the railroad's terminus, seems to date from this time; a rise of land in that neighborhood was soon dubbed 'Corky Hill.'

This influx of Irish laborers caused Father Lee to request an assistant in September 1835. The responsive Bishop Fenwick dispatched Father Michael Lynch who was soon replaced by Reverend Patrick McNamee. The needs of the growing congregation now made a church imperative, so in July 1836 a foundation for an eighty-by-forty-foot church was laid on the lot purchased by Father Corry on High Street.

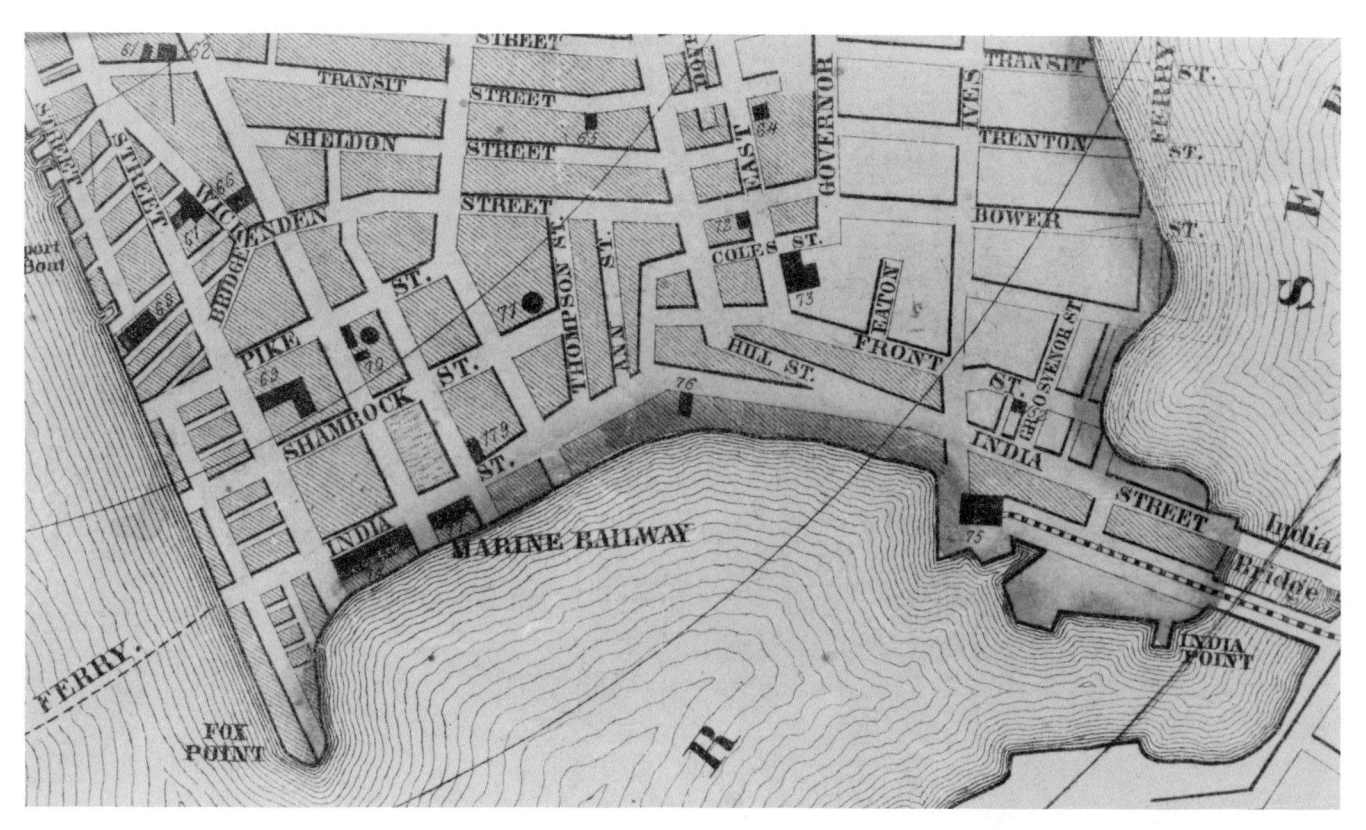

Shamrock Street on this Providence street map of 1849 is evidence of Fox Point's early Irish community. Sheldon Street, the site of the state's first Catholic church, is three blocks north.

Reverend John Corry (above) and Reverend James Fitton (right), Rhode Island's two most notable pioneer Irish priests.

Construction did not progress smoothly. The congregation quarreled among themselves over building and other matters, they also argued with their priests and sent petitions and delegations to Bishop Fenwick. Lee and McNamee proved incompatible; at one point Lee's domestic servant sued McNamee for slander. Carpenters and masons placed a mechanics' lien on the property because their wages were in arrears.

Father Michael Mills, a native of Dublin, was added to the Providence staff in 1837 to assist in resolving such difficulties. Shortly after, Lee's ministry was limited to Pawtucket, and McNamee received his *exeat* from the diocese, so Father Mills took charge of church construction.

Conditions did not brighten — the city became more firmly mired in the economic depression known as the Panic of 1837. The new church was again threatened by the congregation's inability to pay its labor costs. For the second time the Bishop himself undertook to arrange payment. Then Father Corry came to the rescue. When Fenwick visited Newport on August 20 to dedicate the new St. Joseph's that Corry had built, the Bishop reappointed this trouble-shooting cleric to Providence. Corry accepted his new charge eagerly. His restless energy provided an impetus to construction, and a visitor reported to the Bishop on November 13 that a roof had just been added to the structure. On December 10, 1837, Father Corry celebrated the first Mass in the still unfinished edifice.

During 1838 Corry encountered several problems. His responsibilities increased when Pawtucket was added to his assignment and his difficulties intensified when several members of his Providence flock, led by John McCarthy, a calico printer, rebelled against his leadership. Finally on November 4, 1838, Bishop Fenwick dedicated the finished church to the patronage of Sts. Peter and Paul. Within six years it would become the cathedral church of the newly formed Diocese of Hartford. During its first decade (1837–47), over 2,200 baptisms and nearly 600 marriages were performed there.

Relieved but disgruntled, Father Corry wrote at the head of the church's baptismal register: 'It is not to be found in History that ever was there a Catholic Church built with so much opposition on the part of the Catholics as this.' Regardless of the accuracy of this assertion, the castellated Gothic structure of slate-stone covered with cement, eighty by forty feet, and built at a price of nearly $12,000, assumed its place as one of the largest and most expensive Catholic churches in New England. Whatever toil and anguish it had cost, its erection was no small credit to a congregation of only 1,600 persons, made up almost exclusively of very recent immigrants and largely composed of poor 'railroaders' and 'factory hands.'

The tower was still incomplete when the structure was dedicated, and the church lacked a bell, a deficiency soon remedied when prominent civic leader and future Democratic Governor Philip Allen donated a fine Spanish bell. Allen, a Protestant uncle of the famous reformer Thomas Wilson Dorr, then owned a calico print works which employed many of the parishioners of Sts. Peter and Paul.

In July 1840 Father Corry asked Fenwick for a short leave because of ill health. Only eight days after the Bishop made a notation of Corry's request in his memoranda, he recorded the cryptic phrase, 'Great trouble in Providence.' So began a heated three-and-one-half-year controversy that had considerable impact on the Catholic community. The exact nature of the 'trouble' remains obscure, but the contest pitted Father Corry against an old nemesis John McCarthy and Henry J. Duff, an associate of Thomas Wilson Dorr. In a subsequent public letter in 1843, Duff declined to discuss causes of the dispute, but he said of the priest 'that one-half of his congregation disliked him and he returned their indifference with a cordial hatred.' It seems that in Duff's mind at least the basis of the division lay in the strong-willed Father Corry's authoritarian attitude toward his Providence parishioners.

In October 1840 Corry organized a *Catholic Temperance Society,* the first such agency in Rhode Island.

At the dedication of St. Patrick's Providence in July, 1842, Bishop Fenwick celebrated the first pontifical high mass sung in Providence.

Members of the group pledged not to use 'ardent spirits, strong beer, or porter, nor wine or cider when they are offered for sale,' in other words, not to drink in public places. The society enrolled between 1,300 and 1,400 members by 1841, but the dissident leaders did not join.

When the Repeal Movement came to Rhode Island in early 1841 in response to Daniel O'Connell's plea to abrogate the Act of Union joining England and Ireland, two groups sprang up in Providence. The first, headed by Patrick O'Connell and Duff, was condemned by Corry who denounced those joining a group led by his personal opponents. The forceful priest responded by founding a Repeal Association of his own that eventually prevailed.

The increasing size of the Catholic population in Providence and North Providence and the rift in the congregation prompted Bishop Fenwick to lighten Corry's load in January 1841 by sending Reverend William Fennelly to Pawtucket to assume the direction of St. Mary's. This move gave John McCarthy the notion to lighten Corry's load still further. In February 1841 the disaffected layman wrote to Fenwick inquiring about the possibility of building a second church in the northern sector of the city. Fenwick gave encouragement despite Corry's objection, and the movement for a second Providence parish got underway at a meeting held in Washington Hall on March 13. This gathering acted favorably towards the project and elected a church committee with the familiar names of John McCarthy and Patrick O'Connell as president and secretary respectively. In about a month a site was selected in the Smith Hill-Jefferson Plains area overlooking the old cove. Fenwick approved its $2,000 purchase and Father Fennelly agreed to take charge of the new parish and to superintend the construction of the church. Its cornerstone was laid in July 1841 and on Christmas Day a Mass was celebrated in the unfinished structure by Father Dennis Ryan who had replaced Fennelly both at Pawtucket and in the new church for reasons that are obscure. Ryan's stay was also short-lived, for Fenwick called Father William Wiley from Taunton

Many early Irish settlers of Providence were buried in St. Patrick's Cemetery on present-day Douglas Avenue adjacent to the Chad Brown housing development.

in January 1842 to supervise the final stages of construction. In July 1842, during the uneasy period of martial law proclaimed in the aftermath of the Dorr Rebellion, the church was dedicated under the patronage of St. Patrick by Bishop Fenwick, who celebrated the first recorded Pontifical Mass sung in Providence. John Hughes, the powerful and controversial bishop of New York, preached at this tense ceremony.

Father Wiley, a convert from upstate New York who had spent his early years in an orphan asylum, became St. Patrick's first pastor. His new church, designed by Major Russell Warren, was impressive — ninety-three feet long, fifty-six feet wide. The spacious church could seat 800 and boasted an imposing tower whose bell had been purchased in large part through Philip Allen's generous donation. Its total cost was also impressive — $18,217. St. Patrick's stood as a physical expression of the sacrifice and devotion of its poor Irish founders. In 1844 ten acres of land were purchased within the parish for the burial of Catholics. This plot off Douglas Avenue, designated St. Patrick's Cemetery, is the resting place for many of Providence's early Irish settlers.

On the other side of town things were not well with Father Corry, who apparently lost favor with Fenwick because of the rift in the community. This estrangement was evidenced by Fenwick's cordial visit to the home of John McCarthy in March 1842. So long as internal controversy remained dormant, Fenwick was not disposed to act. When the dispute flared up again in mid-1843 over the leadership of the local Repeal movement, Corry was removed from his post at Sts. Peter and Paul.

Corry's followers protested vehemently to Fenwick, and a thirteen-man committee of laymen seized possession of the church's books, keys, and other property. For this impetuous act they were apparently threatened with interdict. To relieve tension Fenwick dispatched the able Father James Fitton to the scene. He made a forceful statement to the parishioners and received their acquiescence.

Father Corry, who had performed so ably in Taunton, Pawtucket, Fall River, Newport, and Providence, was thoroughly disgusted by the turn of events. He secured his *exeat* from the diocese and journeyed to the wilderness of Arkansas to help build the infant diocese of Little Rock. After five years he returned north to New York State where, as pastor in Greenbush (now Rensselaer), he died in 1866.

Several months before his departure Corry had written historian William R. Staples who was gathering information for his *Annals of the Town of Providence*. The letter, dated January 10, 1843, contained Corry's estimates of the growth of Catholicism in Providence. The increase in this era prior to the Great Famine was impressive: from 150 to 200 in 1830 to 1,696 in 1839 and to a point in 1843 where Sts. Peter and Paul had approximately 1,200 to 1,400 souls in its congregation, while St. Patrick's had 800 to 1,000. This steady growth, coupled with the appearance of new Catholic communities elsewhere in the state, suggested to Bishop Fenwick the need for a division of the Diocese of Boston.

Providence was definitely emerging as the center of Catholicism in southern New England. At St. Patrick's in November 1843, Rhode Island's first regular parochial school opened to accommodate the girls of the city. In the same year the state's first Catholic newspaper, the *Catholic Layman,* published two diminutive issues before expiring. Recognition of this vibrant growth came in 1844 when the city acquired its own bishop-in-residence. Spiritually Providence had come of age.

Other Catholic Outposts

Mention has been made of the pioneering Catholics of Newport, Portsmouth, Bristol, Pawtucket, and Providence, but the Church was not confined to these areas in the period before creation of the Diocese of Hartford. There were also outposts in such places as the Fall River section of Tiverton, Woonsocket, the Pawtuxet Valley, and the Sprague mill complex in Cranston — all associated with the expanding textile industry to which the Irish came as unskilled operatives.

The most notable increase in any of these outlying mill settlements occurred during the 1830s in the village of Fall River, which at that time was located partially in Massachusetts and partially in Tiverton, Rhode Island. This growth began in 1822 when Patrick Kennedy, accompanied by his wife Helen and five children, arrived in the area. Father Woodley was the first priest to make regular visits to Fall River, commencing in 1828, but it was the ubiquitous John Corry who guided this village's Catholic community towards the construction of their first house of worship, the church of St. John the Baptist established in August 1837. Corry continued to minister to the 200-member Fall River congregation from his Providence base until Father Richard Hardy began his brief pastorate in 1839.

Geographically, St. John's church was curiously situated. After its enlargement in 1840, it rested squarely on the old boundary line between the two states. Its altar and the first six pews were in Rhode Island with the remainder of the church in Massachusetts.

In 1840 St. John's acquired its most famous administrator, Father Edward Murphy, called by many the 'Grand Old Man' of Fall River. During Murphy's forty-seven-year career in the 'City of Spindles,' Catholicism grew prodigiously. The boundary was moved two miles north in 1862 during the land swap which made eastern Pawtucket and East Providence a part of Rhode Island and transferred all of Fall River to Massachusetts. By that time Murphy had replaced the small and 'decaying' St. John's with the larger and more imposing St. Mary of the Assumption, established in 1855 on the same site.

In this formative era, encouraging signs of growth continued in northern Rhode Island. This growth was especially apparent in the mill village of Woonsocket, a settlement — according to the vastly different political divisions of the time — located partly in the town of Smithfield and partly in the town of Cumberland. Bisected by the Blackstone River at its falls, this village was a prime site for the development of water-powered manufacturing and eventually became a magnet for immigrant laborers.

According to tradition, the earliest Catholic residents of the Woonsocket area were several French

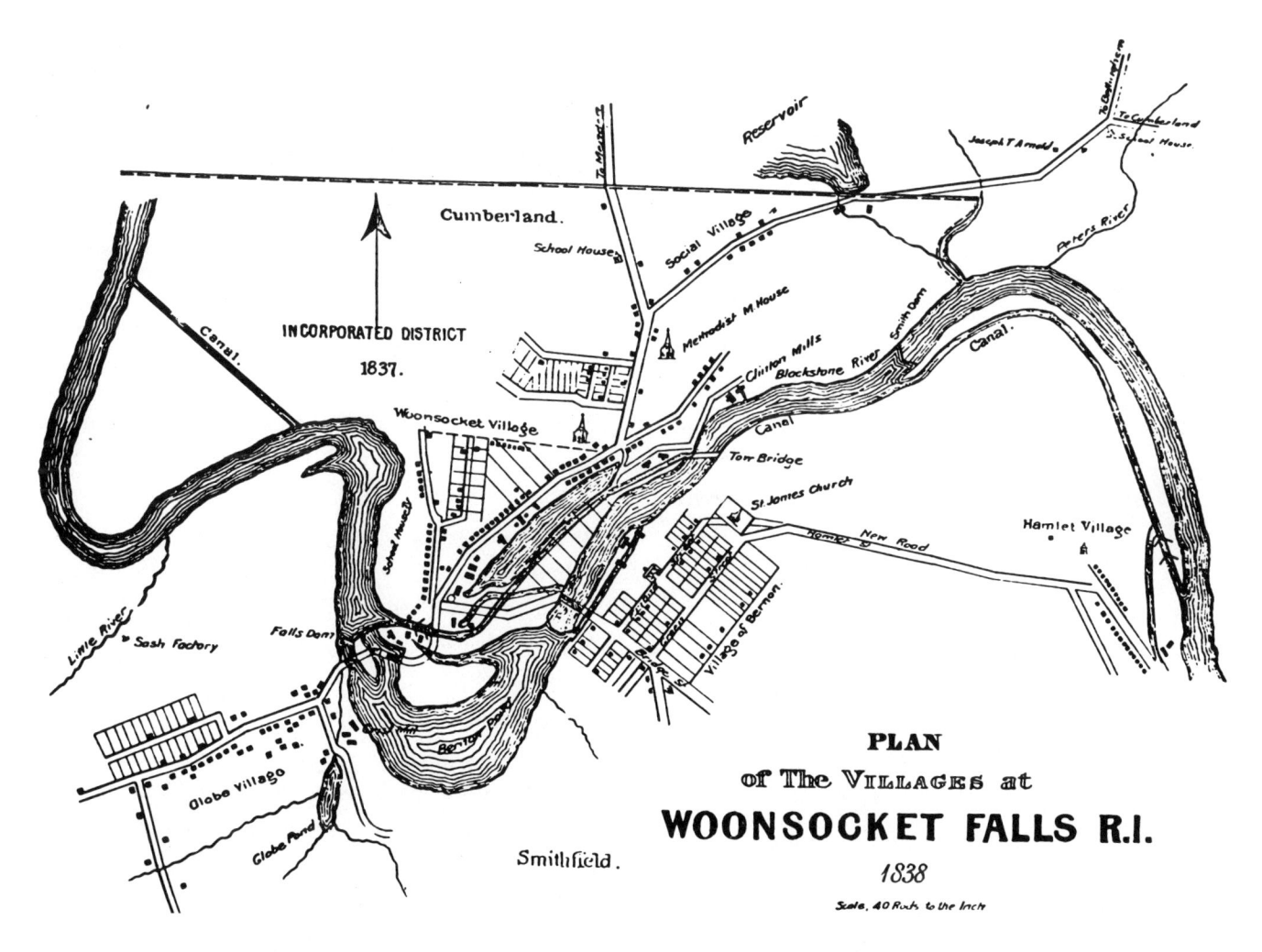

In 1838 when this map was drawn, Woonsocket Falls was merely a collection of mill villages (Hamlet, Globe, Bernon, Social and Woonsocket) situated on the banks of the Blackstone River. Cumberland owned the east bank and Smithfield the west. The separate, incorporated town of Woonsocket was created from these two communities in 1867.

families who settled there during 1815–21 in the wake of the War of 1812, the first of which was the family of Francis Proulx. Unfortunately there are no church records relating to these individuals and no evidence that Cheverus or Matignon ever included this settlement in their itinerary.

The Irish made their appearance in the mid-1820s. The first Gael to call Woonsocket his home was Michael Reddy, a tall, athletic man who worked on the Blackstone Canal. Construction of the waterway from Providence to Woonsocket was completed in 1826, and here young Reddy and several Irishmen who worked with him decided to establish a residence. The register of baptisms in the Boston Cathedral shows that Father Patrick Byrne performed such a ceremony on February 14 in Rhode Island at 'Smithfield, on the Canals' — an adequate description of the unincorporated village of Woonsocket.

In 1828 when Father Woodley was dispatched to Providence, Reddy sought him out and brought him to the northern part of the state for a visit. During his brief stay Woodley celebrated for a congregation of ten men what is reputed to have been the first Mass in Woonsocket (unless Father Byrne said one in 1826) at the home of a generous and liberal Quaker, Walter Allen of Union Village. In gratitude for Woodley's effort the ten men took up a collection among themselves and gave the itinerant priest the substantial sum of fifty dollars to assist him in conducting his missionary work.

At least four different traveling clerics made their appearance in Woonsocket during the period 1828–34. In the latter year Father Fitton assumed the distinction of becoming the first priest to establish a system of regular visitation for Woonsocket. When he began his ministry the Catholic population of the entire area was only thirty, but it grew rapidly in the next decade. During the late 1830s Mass was celebrated in Mr. Reuel Smith's tavern. When the size of the congregation reached significant proportions in the early 1840s, a more permanent and dignified assembly place was necessary. A church was completed in 1844 at North Main and Daniels Streets at

Michael Reddy, laborer on the Blackstone Canal and the first Irish Catholic settler in the Woonsocket area.

the site of the present St. Charles' Church, and on October 12 of that year Father John Brady came from Providence to perform the first baptism and first marriage ceremony in the new edifice.

Father Fitton retained Woonsocket on his mission circuit until 1846 when the Reverend Charles O'Reilly became the parish's first resident pastor. Originally from County Cavan, Ireland, O'Reilly had arrived in Rhode Island from the West Indies where he served as a missionary. At the time of his appointment, a census of Woonsocket and its environs, conducted by S.C. Newman, identified 666 persons of Irish birth. Newman's statistics also disclosed the existence of the first sizable community of French Canadians in Rhode Island. Two-hundred-and-fifty natives of French Canada had settled in the place that they eventually came to dominate. The parish of St.

Charles achieved true stability under the expert administration of Father Michael McCabe who came to Woonsocket in 1855 and remained, except for a three-year interval (1866–69), until his death in 1893.

Another significant area of early Catholic activity was the Pawtuxet Valley section of Warwick in what is now the town of West Warwick and the villages of Crompton, River Point, and Clyde. Irish had been moving into the valley since 1834 when Michael Carroll, his wife, and his brother Edward came from Ballybay, County Monaghan to work in the Green and Pike Bleachery at Clyde. These three harbingers of Catholicism were followed by friends and neighbors, and within a few years a sizable community of Irish had developed. Most of them came from the same town, Ballybay, but there were a few representatives from County Roscommon.

In 1838 Michael Carroll is said to have brought the first Catholic priest to the valley to celebrate Mass in Carroll's home at Birch Hill. There is some uncertainty over the priest's identity, but Father Corry or Father Fitton are the two most probable visitors. The Providence Cathedral records do not indicate that Father Corry baptized in Warwick in 1838.

Until 1844, if Valley settlers wished to attend Mass on Sunday they had to walk to Sts. Peter and Paul in Providence, a distance of approximately ten miles. Even in those days when walking was more common, a ten-mile hike was still quite a chore. Since a church in the Valley was needed Father Fitton acquired a parcel of land in Crompton in September 1844 with the aid of twenty-eight-year-old Mary Doran, the wife of a calico printer at the Crompton Print Works. On October 15, Fitton witnessed the placement of the cornerstone for a church, and on January 4, 1845, the small building, fifty by thirty feet, was completed. In July it was dedicated to Our Lady of Mount Carmel by the new Bishop of Hartford, William Tyler. Today it is Rhode Island's oldest Catholic church still in use.

Crompton was a mission station served by priests from the Cathedral in Providence during the first five years of its existence. In 1850 it became the separate parish of St. Mary's, and the Reverend Daniel Kelly was appointed first pastor. Father Kelly, after a nine-month tenure, was succeeded by Reverend James P. Gibson, a Yankee convert, who ably served St. Mary's parish until his death in 1892.

Known today as St. Mary's, this Crompton structure dedicated to Our Lady of Mount Carmel in 1845, survived a 1926 fire to become the oldest Roman Catholic church still in use in Rhode Island.

Rhode Island in 1845, on the eve of the Great Famine migration, contained seven churches, counting the Fall River edifice it shared with Massachusetts. The Woonsocket and Crompton structures were the first to be completed after the state's inclusion in the new Diocese of Hartford.

Last of the noteworthy early settlements, but one that did not receive a mission church until 1858, was the area in Cranston around the Sprague Print Works. Father Woodley made a baptismal visit there in the late 1820s, but little is known of the growing Irish *rect* Edition.

☞ NOTICE.

JUST arrived from the Metropolis of Ireland, a Person perfectly skilled in the Cotton Manufactory, having been regularly bred to the same, and carried it on for his own Account several Years very extensively, as he can shew.—He can manufacture all Sorts of Fustians, Jeans, Cantoons, Royal Ribs, Rib Delure, Stockinet, Thickset, Corduroy, Velveret, Velvetteen, Calicoes and Nanquins, Chequers and Furnitures, &c. &c. He can also dye, press, dress and finish the above Goods; can direct and assist in making Looms, Frames, and several other Parts of the Machinery wanting in said Business, together with the Spring Shuttle, Springs, &c. He would engage with a Company of Gentlemen to conduct the Whole, and take a Partner's Share of Profit as a Compensation for his Skill and Knowledge.

N. B. He will colour any Kind of Cotton Goods, for Town or Country, equal to those imported from Great-Britain or Ireland, giving Security for such as may be committed to his Care. He will teach any Branch of the Art, likewise the Cutting of Corderoys, the Use of the hot and cold Callender, and measure Land, &c. on very reasonable Terms.—Enquire at General Thayer's, or for the IRISH ARTIST near the Baptist Meeting-House.

Providence, Oct. 3, 1789.

THE Subscribers to this GAZETTE, who contracted to make Payment in Grain, Wood, or other Articles of Country Produce

The earliest Irish immigrants were relatively skilled and educated as indicated by this notice in the *Providence Gazette*, October 31, 1789.

community at the mill complex prior to the killing of Amasa Sprague, an event that precipitated the famous Gordon murder trial in 1844. It is estimated that nearly 500 Irish Catholics had clustered in the area of the Print Works by 1843. They also commuted to Sts. Peter and Paul if they wished to hear Mass regularly.

By the time the Church in Rhode Island entered a new stage in its development with the creation of the Diocese of Hartford, Catholicism had achieved fairly wide dispersement. Only South County and the remote western hill towns had been unaffected by the Catholic influx, principally because of their agrarian nature and the absence of job opportunities. But even there, within the next decade, the Church would plant its roots, principally in Wakefield and Westerly.

The spread of Catholicism during this formative era corresponded to the general observation made by Thomas T. McAvoy in his analysis of American Catholicism: 'Church history tends to concentrate on clergymen, but in the history of the Church in the United States the laity generally have preceded the clergymen in most localities so that the problem of the Church in this country has always been to gather into congregations the scattered flock that was already there and to build for them churches, meeting halls, and, where possible, schools.' It is a tribute to both the laity and the clergy of nineteenth-century Rhode Island that this task was so successfully accomplished.

The Dorr Rebellion and the Development of Political Nativism

During the nearly sixty years from the arrival of the French in 1780 until the latter part of the 1830s, Catholicism was not only tolerated in Rhode Island, it was often cordially received. The friendly posture of Rhode Islanders toward the French troops, the concern of the General Assembly for the Guadeloupe refugees, the ecumenism of Episcopal Bishop Griswold, the generosity of David Wilkinson and Philip Allen, and the hospitality of city officials of Providence were positive developments in the early history of Catholicism in the state.

There is further evidence of this truly Christian spirit. In the wake of the tragic burning of the Ursuline convent by a Charlestown, Massachusetts mob in 1834, several Providence newspapers including the *Providence Journal* labeled the incident a disgrace. No echoes of the violence rumbled through Rhode Island. A number of Newport citizens wrote Bishop Fenwick inviting him to relocate the convent in their city. Three years later, when Father Corry was leaving Newport to assume direction of the church-building project in Providence, he wrote to a fellow Newport clergyman, Reverend Mr. Ross, praising the toleration of Newport's citizens. 'Our church stood for two years with its windows unprotected by blinds, and during that time not one pane of glass was broken,' observed Corry. At Providence's first public banquet in honor of St. Patrick in 1839 at the City Hotel, about 100 Irish and several natives including Philip Allen were in attendance. Of the many toasts offered, one praised 'the virtuous and liberal Americans of Providence, who spurn bigotry and tyranny with the spirit of Emmet and Fitzgerald.'

A most notable statement of this early spirit of tolerance and Christian brotherhood was contained in a public communication from Thomas Wilson Dorr to Father Thomas J. O'Flaherty concerning the latter's lengthy 'discourse in explanation and defense of the Catholic faith' delivered at the Providence Town House on April 18, 1833. Young Dorr praised O'Flaherty's efforts and observed that 'the higher clergy, especially, of this denomination, are distinguished among us for learning, piety, and usefulness; and are everywhere entitled to a high degree of respect.' The future leader of the Dorr Rebellion contended: 'It is quite time that a better state of feeling should prevail, and that narrow, illiberal prejudices should be discarded. Whatever good the division into sects may have done, it is time that they should overlook the party lines behind which they have entrenched themselves, and extend to each other the

Thomas Wilson Dorr, patrician reformer, from an early daguerreotype.

Dorr's arch-rival and Rhode Island's leading nativist, Henry Bowen Anthony, governor (1849–51), United States Senator (1858–84) and editor-publisher of the *Providence Journal*.

hand of fellowship. If men cannot agree in religious opinions — and from the constitution of the human mind such an agreement can never exist — they certainly can agree to differ peaceably. There is a common ground of good will and charity on which they can and ought to meet as brethren.' Dorr concluded his enlightened essay by urging 'the cultivation of kind, cordial, affectionate, and benevolent feelings toward the division of the Christian Church.'

The records of the 1840s and 1850s reveal no similar reaffirmations of this spirit of ecumenism. Instead the inflammatory rhetoric of nativism and the clandestine intolerance of the Know-Nothing party dominate the attitudes expressed in the written accounts.

When and why did this change in attitude occur?

Historian Thomas N. Brown, a former Rhode Islander and a leading student of Irish-American nationalism, cites the career of Dublin-born Matthew Carey of Philadelphia to illustrate the drift from acceptance to antagonism towards the Catholic Irish. Carey — a brilliant and eloquent author, printer, pamphleteer, and an economist universally esteemed by his contemporaries — was representative of the relatively skilled and educated Irish Catholic immigrants who composed a substantial portion of the early migration. By the mid-1820s the educational and socio-economic levels of Irish immigrants declined while their number dramatically increased. These changes had an adverse effect upon the native American population. As the new Irish became social liabilities, economic competitors, and threats (however remote) to the religious and political dominance of natives, resistance toward these 'low Irish' stiffened.

Professor Brown believes the death of Carey in 1839 at least symbolically brought to an end the first period of Irish-Catholic life in the United States. The era of acceptance had expired and the age of antagonism was at hand. Even the reasonably cordial relations that had existed between Protestant and Catholic Irish broke down. As one authority puts it; 'the Protestants ceased being Irish. For a while they became "Ulster Irish" but before long they blended into the composite native American stock that had already claimed the Scots.'

The watershed in the relations between the Catholic Irish and the native Americans was probably Henry Bowen Anthony's accession to the editorship of the *Providence Journal* in July 1838. In that year Joseph Knowles and William L. Burroughs bought the once liberal *Journal* and retained the young and bigoted secretary of the Whig state committee as their editor. From his accession to his death as United States senator in 1884, Anthony compiled a record nearly unmatched in the annals of American nativism.

In August 1838 Anthony launched his public vendetta against enfranchisement of the 'foreign vagabond.' Frequently, he compared the 'purity' of Rhode Island's elections to those of the 'immigrant-infested' city of New York where Irish Catholics had gained a foothold in the Democratic party, and he bitterly assailed the Equal Rights Democrats or 'Loco-focos' of the metropolis for their support of universal suffrage.

The seeds of intolerance, insularity, and prejudice that Anthony planted in the late 1830s and early 1840s had an appreciable effect upon his own Whig party and upon the native Rhode Island community generally. When Thomas Wilson Dorr and his associates attempted to enfranchise this 'rabble' in 1842, these seeds bore bitter fruit.

Thomas Dorr's equal rights crusade of 1841–42, popularly styled the Dorr Rebellion, greatly influenced Catholic and especially Irish Catholic history in Rhode Island. Many historians regard Dorr's insurrection as the most important single episode in the state's development. The origins of the controversy reach back to the first generation of Rhode Island's existence; some of its effects linger into the present. The current state constitution is one of its legacies; so also is the strong connection between Irish Catholics and the local Democratic party and the persistence of political nativism in Rhode Island down through the first quarter of the twentieth century. Distortions and omissions of earlier historians, notably Arthur May Mowry (author of the standard study *The Dorr War* published in 1901), have served to obscure the importance of nativism as it related to this controversy.

The Dorr Rebellion grew out of a movement to replace the royal charter of 1663, a document that had survived the American Revolution as the state's basic law. Although this charter had ranked among the most liberal instruments of government produced during the sevententh century, both the concept of liberalism and Rhode Island itself had changed markedly by the mid-nineteenth century. Rhode Island in 1842 was obviously not the pristine, wilderness refuge of Roger Williams, and the once progressive royal charter appeared starkly reactionary compared with the basic laws of Rhode Island's sister

NATIVE AMERICAN CITIZENS!
READ AND TAKE WARNING!

A SHORT SERMON.

LET EVERY SOUL BE SUBJECT TO THE HIGHER POWERS. *Romans*, 13, 1.

Christians, like all other men, have the right to protect themselves against oppression. They have also the right to aid in the protection of others, but our Savior said, "MY KINGDOM IS NOT OF THIS WORLD," and thus taught his followers that it was inconsistent with their duty to him, and with their respect for his doctrines, to mingle in the strife for power. Paul, in the above quoted text, did not intend to teach his brethren that they should submit, with degrading servility, to tyranny, cruelty, and oppression, when they could remove the evil without producing another equally great. But his frequent exhortations, as well as those of his DIVINE MASTER, fully show that they considered it the indispensable duty of CHRISTIANS to submit to existing governments for the sake of peace, until oppression became too cruel to be borne, or until the evil could be remedied without unnecessary violence; and that, in ALL CASES, for the HONOR of the CHURCH, the SUCCESS of the GOSPEL, and the PEACE of the COMMUNITY, CHRISTIANS should "be subject to the HIGHER POWERS," as *long as forbearance would be a virtue.*

CHRISTIAN PROFESSORS OF RHODE ISLAND, I put to you a plain question—Will you answer it as on the ALTAR of GOD, to HIM AND YOUR OWN CONSCIENCES? Does it appear that the Constitution to be voted on for adoption or rejection, on the 21st, 22d, and 23d, inst. is of such a character as to threaten danger to your rights and privileges, or those of others? Is it oppressive in its provisions or bearings? Would you be justified in rejecting it, and in adopting another which will place your government, your civil and political institutions, your PUBLIC SCHOOLS, and perhaps your RELIGIOUS PRIVILEGES, under the control of the POPE of ROME, through the medium of THOUSANDS of NATURALIZED FOREIGN CATHOLICS? Does the honor and prosperity of the church require it? Do the peace, welfare, and prosperity, of the State require it? Yet, reject the Constitution now presented to you, and you show your preference for another, which, *should it ever be adopted,* WILL PLACE THE BALLANCE OF POWER IN THE STATE, IN THE HANDS OF THOSE PEOPLE. The event can readily be predicted. Would you defend yourselves and your church against the operations and predominance of such a power, and preserve the State from anarchy and ruin? Would you preserve peace, and thereby avoid violence and bloodshed? Would you pay that respect to the CONSTITUTED AUTHORITIES WHICH THE GOSPEL DEMANDS? Would you keep a conscience pure and undefiled, by pursuing a course on which you can hereafter look with approbation, and for the correctness of which, you can CONFIDENTLY APPEAL TO HEAVEN IN THE HOUR OF DEATH, AND AT THE DREAD TRIBUNAL HEREAFTER? Then, and I must suppose such to be your wish, array yourselves on the side of the "HIGHER POWERS," in a quiet and peaceable manner, GIVE YOUR VOTES FOR THE CONSTITUTION ON MONDAY NEXT. Show those who act in the opposition only to carry out their will, that you value too highly your CHRISTIAN PROFESSION, your CHRISTIAN CHARACTER, and your CHRISTIAN PRINCIPLE, to countenance sedition, and to endanger the peace of an entire community, only to defeat the benevolent object of the existing government, and to give encouragement and support to a spirit of violence and disorder. Tell those who would allure you to aid them in the work of strife. 'WE HAVE NOT SO LEARNED CHRIST.'

REV. WILLIAM S. BALCH.

The above gentleman, late Pastor of the First Universalist Church in this city, and who, while *here, did much for the party* which have made and voted for the "*People's Constitution*," was requested by that party to lecture during his visit here this week from New York. He very properly refused to do so; and said he *would not were he now a resident here*; for the reason, that the *party have carried the thing too far,* and are *now making a political affair of it, and he would have nothing to do with it.* This is valuable testimony from one of the *ablest* and *fastest friends of the suffrage cause.*

AN EXAMPLE.

In a "Short Sermon" puplished in our extra sheet, the writer alluded to the possibility that, should a constitution like that called the "People's Constitution" be adopted, the naturalized foreign Chatholics might exercise a pernicious influence on our political, civil, and religious institutions, and on our public schools. We have a case in point. The CATHOLIC BISHOP HUGHES, of New York, at the last election in that city, ARRAYED UNDER HIS CONTROL, some THREE THOUSAND FOREIGN CATHOLIC VOTERS, after an effort of a few days, to sustain at the BALLOT BOX his own views on the question of public schools, for the purpose of diverting to the use of the CATHOLIC CHURCH, a portion of the common school fund of the State. With a longer period for the purpose, it is probable a body of foreign naturalized Catholics might have been organized, and will hereafter be organized, in that city and State, under PAPAL ECCLESIASTICAL INFLUENCE, *to carry out their views.* The excitement on the question still continues. The Bishop and his party are determined to succeed in their efforts. The native citizens have become alarmed. And meetings have been held to prevent the abhorred attempt from becoming successful.

On Wednesday last, a meeting was held in the Park, New York city, on the question. And during the proceedings, a band of foreigners broke in upon the assemblage, and by means of violence, broke up the meeting. A New York paper says, "Our cheeks are suffused with shame and indignation as we write about this matter; for so gross an insult to our rights as Americans, we have never seen or heard of before. Bands of filthy wretches, whose every touch was offensive to a decent man, drunken loafers; scoundrels who the police and criminal courts would be ashamed to receive in their walls;· coarse, blustering rowdies; blear eyed and bloated offscourings from the stews, blind alleys and rear lanes; disgusting objects bearing the form human, but whom the sow in the mire might almost object to as companions—these were they who broke into the midst of a peaceful body of American citizens—struck and insulted the chosen officers of the assemblage, and with shrieks, loud blasphemy, and howling in their hideous native tongue, prevented the continuance of the customary routine. We saw Irish priests there—sly, false, deceitful villains—looking on and evidently encouraging the gang who created the tumult. We noticed two or three tavern bullies strike on the head a presiding officer—one of the most aged and respectable men of our city. We beheld the whole body of those officers forced, at length, from their seats, and driven, with jibes and blows, from the stage. And these officers were native Americans—men with grey heads—men known for long years among us, as gentle men of reputation, philanthropy and exalted worth!

And is New York to utter no loud voice of abhorrence towards this transaction? Is this hypocritical scoundrel Hughes, and his minions, to drill ranks of ignorant and vindictive followers—and send them forth to act as those wretches acted—and shall no note be taken of it? It is a blot and an insolent violation of our dearest and most glorious privileges. The whole city—the whole state—ought to rise up as one man, and let these jesuitical knaves, and their apt satellites, know what it is to feel the blast from an injured and outraged country."

RHODE-ISLANDERS—Read this. Ponder seriously on it. Say—are you prepared to witness such scenes enacted in your little, and hitherto peaceful and prosperous State? Are you prepared to see a Catholic Bishop, at the head of a posse of Catholic Priests, and a band of their servile dependents, take the field to subvert your institutions, under the sanction of a State Constitution. If not, vote for the Constitution now presented to you, which is well calculated to protect you from such abuses. ROGER WILLIAMS.

This March, 1842 broadside graphically reveals the ethnic and religious opposition to Dorr's campaign for "equal rights."

states of the Jacksonian era.

Constitutional reform was necessary because the charter was unable to meet the demands of a diversified, urbanized, and expanding commonwealth. It even lacked provisions for its own amendment or replacement. In addition, there existed a number of specific governmental abuses the statutory correction of which had become increasingly improbable — true because in the political system which prevailed the ultra-conservative General Assembly was virtually omnipotent. Composed of and elected by landholders under a system of apportionment that had become grossly inequitable, this body was a bulwark against reform. As the chance for redress of grievances by the legislature diminished, demand for constitutional reform intensified.

Ranked in a probable order of urgency, the four major goals of the insurgents in 1842 were the extension of suffrage through elimination of the $134 freehold qualification (this became the crux of the Irish question); the reapportionment of the House of Representatives to eliminate the 'rotten borough' system in which rural towns were overrepresented; a constitutional bill of rights; and the removal of the judiciary from Assembly control. Other grievances included the harsh penal code, a court system which discriminated against non-freeholders, and the requirement that non-voters do service in the militia.

Because the General Assembly resisted these demands both by failing to pass necessary legislation and by refusing to consent to substantial charter revision, the reformers had no alternative but to seek change through abrogation of the charter and adoption of a new constitution which would incorporate the desired changes and place proper limitations on the power of the Assembly.

During the constitutional crisis of 1842 and in the decade preceding the Dorr Rebellion, reform of suffrage appears to have been the vital issue. The suffrage question actually had its origins in the colonial charter of Charles II. This royal document conferred upon the General Assembly power to determine those citizens who would be eligible to vote. The legislature in the years following 1663 had exercised its prerogative by establishing a statutory freehold (*i.e.* a real property) qualification for voting. This qualification fluctuated during the eighteenth century and was finally set at $134 worth of real estate in 1798.

There was no significant effort to remove this voting requirement until the late 1820s when pressure for reform mounted as the growth of industry and the slowly rising tide of immigration swelled the ranks of the landless and voteless population. Unfortunately, the General Assembly's resistance to reform hardened as it became more apparent that the mounting industrial population would be composed less of native stock and more of 'undesirable' Irish Catholics. Native Americans of the small towns, regardless of party affiliation, began to resist suffrage reform because it involved the enfranchisement and the increase in political power of a group that did not share their values and interests and that in the course of time seemed destined to become more powerful politically. For similar reasons of political self-preservation the farming element opposed redistribution of seats in the lower house of the legislature and abolition of the 'rotten boroughs' primarily because these changes would increase the power of urban and industrial groups in state affairs.

Increased vigor and cohesiveness marked the movement for constitutional reform in the early 1830s and eventually led in 1834 to the formation of the Constitutional party, composed chiefly of members from the expanding northern and eastern towns. One of the leaders of the Constitutional party was Thomas Wilson Dorr, a nephew of Philip Allen, and a man of intelligence, courage, and determination. Dorr made his debut in the arena of governmental reform by writing in behalf of his new-born party the *Address to the People of Rhode Island,* a logical and concise repudiation of the charter regime.

Agitation in 1834 pressured the General Assembly into calling a constitutional convention but it was composed of freeholders elected by freeholders and, as might be expected, no reforms would be conceded by that entrenched, landed minority. After sitting two

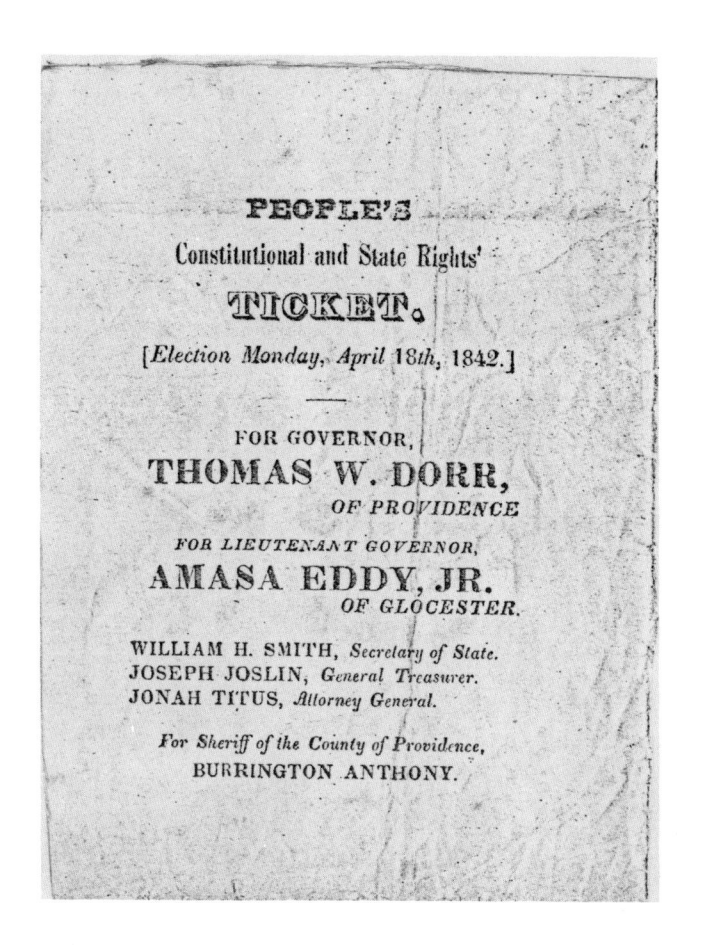

The "prox" or ballot of the People's Party in the April, 1842 gubernatorial election.

weeks the farcical convention recessed and never reconvened. Because the Constitutional party was comprised mainly of freemen and held a moderate position on the issue of suffrage reform, it made little progress enlisting the active support of the entire disfranchised class, and the organization evaporated during the economic depression of 1837.

The hectic 'Log Cabin and Hard Cider' presidential campaign of 1840 resurrected the reform cause and precipitated the rise of the radical Rhode Island Suffrage Association. With the previous litany of frustrations in mind many advocates of suffrage extension became convinced that only revolutionary measures would achieve the desired reforms. Emulating the novel political techniques used with such success by 'Tippecanoe and Tyler too' — parades, mass meetings, and torchlight processions — the Association launched a vigorous and spirited campaign to eliminate governmental abuses.

This militant suffrage crusade, like the Constitutional party movement of the 1830s, was nonpartisan, at least technically. It differed from its predecessor in several respects. Its membership was overwhelmingly drawn from the urban wing of the Democratic party, and its rank and file was composed mainly of non-freeholders. The party advocated *universal manhood suffrage* and denounced real and personal property qualifications for voting on political as distinguished from financial questions. Significantly, it was willing to utilize extra-legal methods to achieve reform by ignoring or intimidating the legally constituted charter government.

Once again reformist demands prompted the General Assembly to authorize a constitutional convention, this one scheduled for November 1841. Agitators correctly assumed that the Assembly's act was insincere and opportunistic, merely designed to sap vitality from the Association's cause, and no more intended to be the vehicle of change than previous 'do-nothing' conventions summoned to appease the disfranchised in 1824 and 1834. As a result of this belief they decided upon an extra-legal course to attain their ends. Drafting Dorr to lead them, they exhorted the adult male citizenry to disregard the landholding qualification and go to the polls to elect delegates to a 'People's Convention' in October 1841. Within six weeks the reformers' convention presented the fruit of its deliberations to the white male populace for ratification.

Drafted principally by Dorr, this liberal document (the 'People's Constitution') remedied many abuses which had persisted under the charter regime. The most notable and controversial departure from the charter system was in the area of suffrage. The statutory $134 freehold requirement was repudiated by a clause which extended suffrage to adult white male citizens with one year's residence in the state. Other significant features of the People's Constitution were its reapportionment provision that increased the House representation of Providence and other urbanized centers, its secret ballot clause, a bill of rights, and a general diminution of the power of the legislature by providing for clear separation of powers on the three-branch principle.

A three-day popular referendum beginning on December 27, 1841 was held on this proposed constitution. Disregard for the landholding requirement swelled the turnout to nearly 14,000. Only fifty-two votes were cast against the People's Constitution because charter adherents boycotted the election. Dorr claimed that the constitution had been ratified by a majority because 13,944 of the state's estimated 23,142 white adult citizens had voted their approval. The possibility of fraudulent voting was high — as for any election in that age — and undoubtedly a number of bogus ballots were cast but, when the results were in, the reformers insisted that the People's Constitution had supplanted the charter as the paramount law of the state.

Such reasoning was totally unacceptable to charter adherents but the old guard realized that they must give ground. The constitution which their Landholders' Convention had begun to draft at their first session in November 1841 was so reactionary that it had ignored nearly all the reformers' demands. This remarkable display of 'standpattism' coupled with the impressive December referendum gave a temporary advantage to the Dorrites.

Dorr's opposition, mainly comprised of urban Whigs, industrial interests, and rural Democrats from South County and the western hill towns, had every intention of asserting their legal authority, and in the early months of 1842 they made a determined bid to undermine the revolutionaries' position. Their attack on the Dorrites was four-pronged. One weapon was their enactment of the so-called Algerine law which imposed severe penalties upon those attempting to exercise power or hold office under the People's Constitution.

Another extremely potent maneuver was the Charterite appeal to sectional, class, ethnic, and especially religious sentiments of Rhode Islanders. The Law and Order party, as Charter adherents were called, played upon the fears of native-born Protestants by warning them that the liberal suffrage clause of the People's Constitution would pave the way for the political ascendance of Irish Catholic immigrants swarming into the state in ever-increasing numbers. The most unyielding exponent of this political nativism was Henry B. Anthony's influential *Providence Journal*. During the crisis its pages were replete with impassioned diatribes against the Irish Catholic immigrant 'menace.'

A third offensive by Law and Order forces consisted in an appeal to President John Tyler for federal protection to preserve the status quo. The Chief Executive, after some ambivalence, promised aid if violence erupted.

The fourth and decisive machination of charter adherents was the reversal of the reactionary stand taken at the first session of the Landholders' Convention. Their about-face in February 1842 produced a document known as the Freeman's Constitution. Its concessions stole the thunder from the Dorrite cause by driving a wedge between extreme and moderate reformers. The Freeman's document contained a guarantee of individual liberties, made moderate improvements in the system of House apportionment and, most important, extended the franchise to all adult white male *native-born* citizens. This concession produced many defections from the ranks of the Dorrites by the native-born during the spring of 1842.

Despite resolute efforts of the Law and Order faction to squelch the insurgents, Dorr tenaciously held his ground. When the Freeman's Constitution was placed before the people for approval in March 1842 he exhorted the citizenry to vote it down. They responded by the ominously narrow margin of 8,689 to 8,013. Ironically the negative vote of the ultra-conservative faction of the Law and Order party, those opposing any reform whatever, temporarily won the day for the Dorrites; the vote of the reformers alone would not have been sufficient to defeat the Freeman's Constitution.

In the campaign over the Freeman's Constitution nativistic rhetoric became especially inflammatory. One broadside told natives that the People's Constitution would 'place your government, your civil and political institutions, your PUBLIC SCHOOLS, and perhaps your RELIGIOUS PRIVILEGES, under the control of the POPE OF ROME, through the medium of thousands of NATURALIZED FOREIGN CATHOLICS.' This widely disseminated leaflet further advised that support of the Freeman's Constitution was essential unless the native-born wished 'to see a Catholic Bishop, at the head of a posse of Catholic Priests, and a band of their servile dependents, take the field to subvert your institutions under the sanction of a State Constitution.' As one suffragist complained in a letter to Dorr, 'men were called upon not to vote for a constitution but to vote against Irishmen,' while a contemporary broadside expressed the exaggerated opinion that 'every Roman Catholic Irishman in Rhode Island is a Dorrite.'

The *Providence Journal* activated the acid pens of Henry Anthony and William Goddard on the eve of the referendum on the Freeman's Constitution to succinctly state its case:

> The balance of power rests in the hands of the Senators from the agricultural areas of the state. Where will the balance be under Messrs. Dorr, Brown and Company ... Where but among 2,500 foreigners and the hundreds more who will be imported. They will league and band together, and usurp our native political power ... Their priests and leaders will say to a political party as they say in New York City, give us by law every opportunity to perpetuate our spiritual despotism. At the feet of these men will you lay down your freedom ... Foreigners still remain foreign and are still embraced by mother church. He still bows down to her rituals, worships the host, and obeys and craves absolution from the priest. He cannot be assimilated ... Now is the time to choose between the two systems, the conservative checks or foreigners responsible only to priests.

Conversely, the American Irish press lined up with Dorr. 'It is our own Home Rule question in Rhode Island,' asserted the *Truth Teller* (New York) in an article upholding the cause of the Dorrites. Clearly the

This poem, printed in the *Providence Journal*, March 30, 1843, satirizes the defeat of Dorr and the cause of the Irish immigrant which he espoused.

The Paddy's Lament for Tom Dorr.

Air—Widow Malone.

'TWAS that swate little lump of Tom Dorr,
That so nately could break through the law,
　　And could raise such a row
　　By the wag of his pow,
And such crowds at his heels he could draw
　　　　　　With his jaw,
Och a swate chap was Governor Dorr.

He knew how to govern a state
In a way that was new and first-rate,
　　And the votes in his day
　　Were all our own way,
And the way we did brag was so great,
　　　　　　Och t'was swate,
When we and Tom Dorr ruled the state.

And to please the dear people—that's us—
He kicked up a beautiful fuss,
　　Och we'd plenty of mobs
　　And some swate little jobs
To rob Algerines in the muss,
　　　　　　And no worse,
Though for law we did not care a curse.

Then he mustered us all in his ranks,
And promised us "beauty and banks,"
　　But Algerines came
　　With guns, swords and flame,
And our hero he took to his shanks,—
　　　　　　Small thanks
Did we get 'stead of "beauty and banks."

Still Tom is a hero full grown,
And dear to the hearts of his own,
　　He's been true as steel,
　　As we all of us feel,
For when he was balked of his fun—
　　　　　　Why he run,
Just as any of us would have done.

Shure Tom is a broth of a boy,
The Spartans and Buttenders joy
　　And we'll flog him gentailly
　　With fist or shillala,
Who finds in his doings a flaw,
　　　　　　Then hurrah!
For our jewel is Governor Dorr.

Irish Catholic issue was an essential aspect of the 1842 controversy, despite its suppression by Arthur May Mowry and its subsequent neglect by Marvin Gettleman, George Dennison and other historians of the Dorr War.

After the Freeman's Constitution was narrowly repudiated, the revolutionaries staged an election on April 18 under the People's Constitution from which Thomas Wilson Dorr emerged as the 'People's Governor.' Dorr and those elected with him proceeded to establish a skeleton government in violation of the Algerine law. The 'People's Governor,' in the eyes of his apprehensive opponents, had now committed treason against the state.

Then, on May 18, after an unsuccessful effort to win the backing of President Tyler, Dorr intemperately tried to solidify his position by seizing the state armory. Fortunately his two antiquated cannon misfired during the 'attack,' so bloodshed was averted, and Dorr unceremoniously left the field.

The arsenal fiasco was the death knell of the Dorrite cause; use of violence was a tragic blunder, the step which many reformers less zealous, less headstrong and more cautious refused to take. Except for a few diehard supporters, Dorr stood alone. On the morning following the incident the 'People's Governor' fled across the state line into exile with charter forces at his heels.

The strategy of the Law and Order party had carried the day; the reform movement was stymied. The Charterites' propaganda campaign had been a stunning success, their Algerine law intimidated many insurgents, and their appeal to President Tyler undermined the reform cause. Furthermore, and of great importance, their concession of suffrage to the native-born caused many defections from the ranks of the Dorrites. Previously disfranchised natives realized that their agitation had been sufficient to improve *their* lot, and few of them were altruistic enough to risk their future by pressing for enlargement of suffrage to include the naturalized Catholic Irishman. Many native-born reformers deserted the People's Constitution when they became convinced that their political status could be raised by compromising with the charter forces.

Despite the seeming hopelessness of his cause, Dorr persisted in his endeavors to establish the People's Constitution. On June 25 he returned to Rhode Island and encamped on Acote's Hill in the village of Chepachet with a tiny band of New York volunteers led by Mike Walsh, an Irish agitator, and less than 200 loyal suffragists. His mere presence in the state sent Governor Samuel Ward King into another frenzy.

Big Mike Walsh, shown here in 1843 at Tammany Hall, was with Dorr at Acote's Hill. The Irish-born journalist and politician, a master in the techniques of political organization, was instrumental in opening Tammany to Irish participation. He served in Congress as a Democratic representative from 1853 to 1855.

To the Hon. General Assembly of the State of Rhode-Island, at their May Session, A. D. 1846.

The undersigned, Citizens of the United States, resident in the State of Rhode-Island and Providence Plantations, respectfully set forth,

That under the Constitution and laws of the United States, the naturalized citizens of the United States, resident in Rhode-Island, have renounced all allegiance to any foreign power or government, and have been duly admitted to the rights and privileges of American citizens. And yet, your petitioners have to complain, that, by the existing Constitution of the State of Rhode-Island, the great majority of them are debarred from the most important political right, that of partaking, as voters, in the choice of their Representatives and other officers; inasmuch, as by a provision in said Constitution, no citizen of the State, born out of the U. States, can exercise the right of suffrage without being possessed of real property, which is impossible to many to obtain, and is a degrading brand placed upon all naturalized citizens, setting them apart as a peculiar, unworthy and disqualified class, to be shackled and held in suspicion, and continual objects of insult and derision.

The undersigned would further represent, that to render more marked the stigma which is thus affixed to naturalized citizens in Rhode-Island, the colored population of this State are allowed to exercise the right of suffrage, as freely as it is accorded to, any white native citizen of the United States, thereby degrading naturalized citizens below the colored population.

The undersigned do not wish to be understood by this allusion to envy the colored population; on the contrary, they believe they have received nothing but what they are in justice entitled to: but, as the impression is abroad, that the colored race is inferior to the white and shaded population, the insult is more piercing.

The undersigned are not aware of anything in the character or conduct of naturalized citizens to warrant this illiberal, unjust and insulting distinction. They are useful members of the community; they contribute by useful labor and industry, to the prosperity of the community in which they live, as is evident to every unprejudiced mind; they do their full part in supporting institutions of government, learning and religion. They are ever ready, like the LAFAYETTES, STEUBENS, MONTGOMERIES, DE KALBS, KOSCIUSKOS, ST. CLAIRS, GATES and GALLATINS, on whom the success of American Liberty was so largely indebted in 1776 and 1812, and on all occasions of danger (as testified to by the most eminent Americans) to engage in the defence of the country and the home of their choice and adoption; and the undersigned challenge an investigation to show when and where naturalized citizens ever proved faithless to the confidence reposed in them, or shrunk from danger, or in what respect they are unworthy to exercise *all* the rights of American citizens.

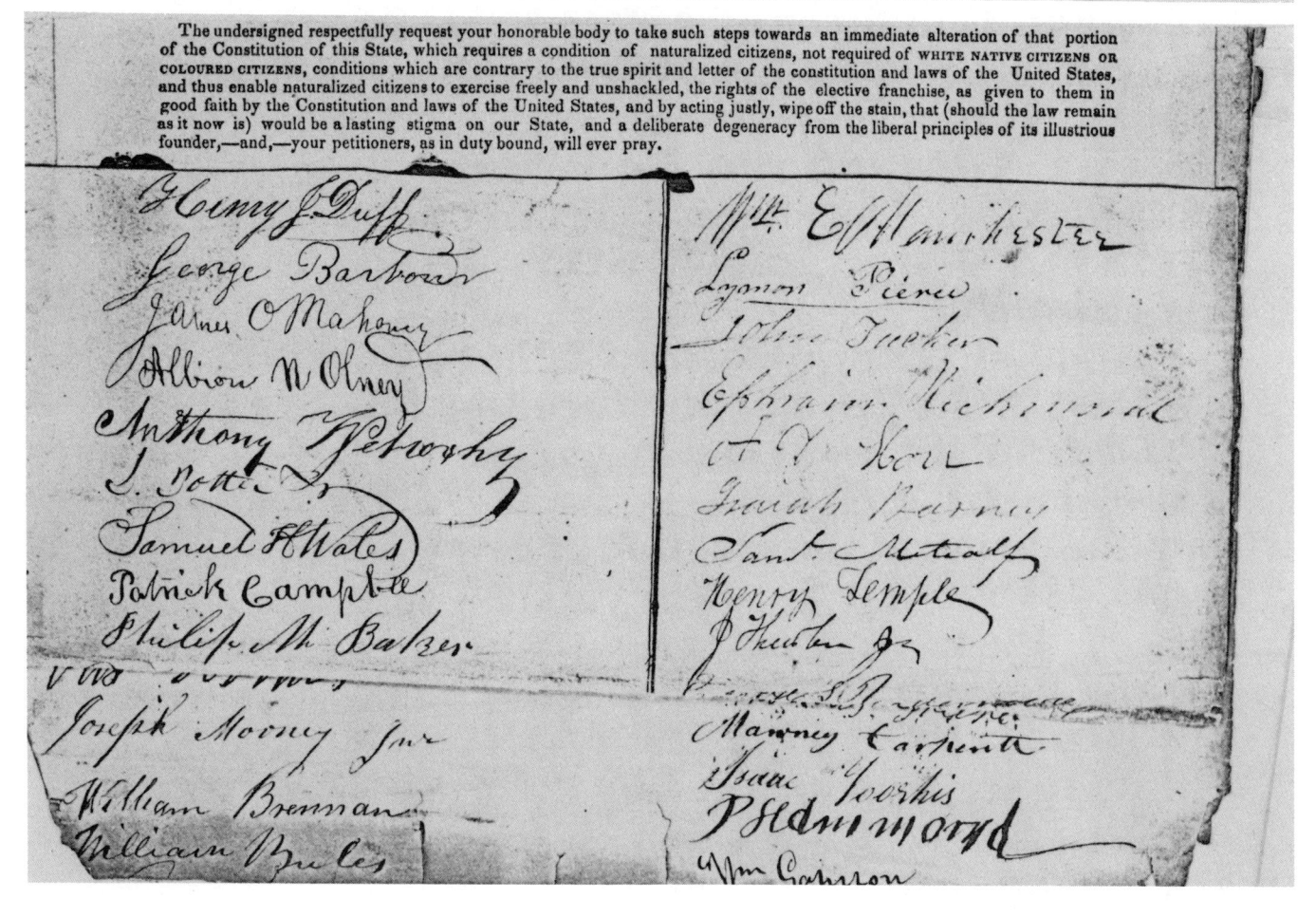

The undersigned respectfully request your honorable body to take such steps towards an immediate alteration of that portion of the Constitution of this State, which requires a condition of naturalized citizens, not required of WHITE NATIVE CITIZENS OR COLOURED CITIZENS, conditions which are contrary to the true spirit and letter of the constitution and laws of the United States, and thus enable naturalized citizens to exercise freely and unshackled, the rights of the elective franchise, as given to them in good faith by the Constitution and laws of the United States, and by acting justly, wipe off the stain, that (should the law remain as it now is) would be a lasting stigma on our State, and a deliberate degeneracy from the liberal principles of its illustrious founder,—and,—your petitioners, as in duty bound, will ever pray.

This 1846 petition by Henry J. Duff was the first of many formal attempts to remove the nativistic suffrage provision from the 1843 state constitution.

FRIENDS OF GOV. JACKSON, READ THIS!

IRISH VOTERS!!!

We have just been informed that the Country towns are flooded with *Infamous Handbills*, misrepresenting the views of **GOV. JACKSON** as to the *Qualification of Foreign Voters!*—It is well known that Gov. Jackson PROPOSED the *FREEHOLD QUALIFICATION* in the CONVENTION. The whole story that *Gov Jackson* is in favor of ABOLISHING that qualification is *utterly* and *totally without foundation!* It is manufactured by SAMUEL CURREY, a *Naturalized Foreigner* from NOVA SCOTIA, who has been HIRED to *MISREPRESENT* the views of GOV. JACKSON *and his friends.*

People of *Rhode-Island* believe not these INFAMOUS LIES manufactured by this *HIRED TOOL* of the Providence ARISTOCRACY!—They are *INTENDED to DECEIVE you*, and thus prevent the election of GOV. JACKSON AND HIS PROX. They dared not *circulate* one of them in Providence, for they *knew it would be refuted forthwith!*

Friends of CHARLES JACKSON, are you willing to see *him* crushed by the FALSEHOODS and *MALIGNITY* of his bitterest enemies?—— *We know you are NOT!*

MANY WHIGS.

The militia was summoned and the following day 2,500 armed troops assembled in Providence. Bolstered by this show of strength the charter government declared martial law throughout the state. On June 27 a march on Chepachet from Providence was begun. Upon hearing the size of the force arrayed against him, Dorr dismissed his men and once again departed for safer regions.

After Dorr's second flight the triumphant Law and Order party convoked another constitutional convention in late 1842 which framed the present state constitution. To a degree the demands of reformers were met: this new document contained a bill of rights, paved the way for eventual establishment of an independent judiciary, slightly diminished the power of the General Assembly, and provided for a fairly equitable system of House apportionment.

Arthur May Mowry, an historian of the Dorr War, calls this instrument 'liberal and well adapted to the needs of the State,' but his appraisal glosses over one important item — the 1842 constitution established a $134 freehold suffrage qualification for naturalized citizens, and this restriction, not removed until 1888, was the most blatant manifestation of political nativism found in *any* state constitution in the land — a matter that cannot be overemphasized. It furnishes the central theme in Rhode Island political history from 1842 until passage of the twentieth amendment to the state constitution in 1928. The stranglehold on the senate which the 1842 document gave to the rural towns is also of paramount importance and remained so at least until the 'bloodless revolution' of 1935.

This constitution, overwhelmingly ratified in November 1842 by a vote of 7,024 to 51, became effective in May 1843. Despite the margin of victory, the turnout was meager for there were more than 23,000 adult male citizens in the state. That the opposition in mute protest refrained from voting explains in part the constitution's apathetic reception.

Adoption of the nativistic suffrage clause coupled with the gubernatorial triumph of Dorr's arch-rival, James Fenner, crushed the spirit of the exiled reformer who returned to Providence in October 1843 to surrender. Immediately arrested and jailed until February 1844, he was indicted under the Algerine law for treason against the state. In a trial of less than two weeks he was found guilty by a jury composed entirely of political opponents. A new trial was denied him and he was sentenced to hard labor in solitary confinement for life. He served one year in prison before Governor Charles Jackson, elected on a 'liberation' platform, authorized his release. A Democratic General Assembly, during the governorship of Philip Allen, restored Dorr's civil and political rights in 1851 and in 1854 reversed the treason conviction. These gestures did little to cheer the vanquished reformer whose spirit and health were broken. He died disillusioned in December 1854, in the midst of the local Know-Nothing campaign directed against immigrant Irish attempts to secure the vote.

No tempest in a teapot, the Dorr Rebellion had national repercussions and has enduring significance. The most important and controversial domestic occurrence of the Tyler administration, it eventually involved the President, both Houses of Congress, and the Supreme Court. Of even greater significance, the Rhode Island controversy inspired substantial contributions to theories of suffrage, majority rule, minority rights, and constitutional government by John C. Calhoun, John L. O'Sullivan, Orestes Brownson, John Quincy Adams, Daniel Webster, Horace Greeley, George Bancroft and others of similar stature.

The rebellion's central figure — a man of integrity, intelligence, and lofty ideals — Thomas Wilson Dorr must be ranked among the greatest American reformers. His rash act at the armory should not obscure the multitude of positive contributions to his fellow men. Champion of educational reform, outspoken foe of slavery, Dorr initiated notable banking reforms and made the cause of the immigrant his own.

The opponents of Governor Charles Jackson, who had liberated Thomas Dorr in 1845, tried to engineer the governor's defeat in 1846 by alleging that Jackson favored the repeal of the real estate qualification for naturalized voters. In this broadside the "friends of Gov. Jackson" assure native citizens that this claim is a "falsehood" and an "infamous lie."

Certain refinements should be made concerning Dorr and his solicitude for the Irish Catholic community. There is no evidence from Dorr's voluminous papers that he waged his campaign *primarily* to benefit the Irish immigrant. His basic concern was 'equal rights,' but Irish and other immigrants would have been beneficiaries of this concern had Dorr succeeded. He was definitely aware that his suffrage plan would have a dramatic and beneficial impact on the landless factory operative of Irish birth. One of his associates, the knowledgeable Henry J. Duff of St. Patrick's, informed him in precise terms of the rapid growth of the Irish Catholic community at the very time Dorr was drafting the suffrage article of the People's Constitution. Fully cognizant of the impact that his document would have upon the political structure of the state, Dorr staunchly stood by his principles and by the immigrant to the end.

The Rhode Island Irish Catholic community was well aware of the injustice perpetrated against them by the new constitution. The appeal to the United States House of Representatives in April 1844 by Henry Duff and seventy-five others (many of whom were naturalized Irish), the creation of the American Citizens Association in 1845, and the rejection by the General Assembly in 1847 of Duff's petition requesting equality for naturalized citizens, were only the initial incidents in a litany of immigrant protest that convulsed Rhode Island politics until passage of the twentieth amendment in 1928. Such was the legacy of the Law and Order party and the lament of immigrants denied full privileges of citizenship in their adopted state by the constitution of 1843.

The Case of John Gordon

Before the nativistic tide engendered by the Dorr Rebellion had receded and while Dorr himself awaited trial, Amasa Sprague was brutally bludgeoned to death on December 31, 1843. The gory incident touched off the Gordon murder trial, an event that became the Rhode Island version of Sacco-Vanzetti, but here the defendants were Irish Catholic immigrants rather than Italians.

A powerful, wealthy, and influential man, Amasa Sprague, as administrator of the A. & W. Sprague industrial empire, personally supervised the Cranston complex at Sprague's Village in the manner of a feudal baron with several hundred Irish men, women, and children in his employ. He and his brother William, a United States senator from Rhode Island and a former governor, arrayed themselves with the Law and Order faction during the Dorr Rebellion. The Spragues had a disdain for 'low Irish' but not to the extent of penalizing their own interests by drawing an

The Sprague mill complex in Cranston, idyllically portrayed on a textile label.

ethnic barrier against willing and hard-working Celts who toiled for meager wages in their textile mills.

A strong and forceful personality, Amasa Sprague owned the plant, the company houses, company store, and the farm which supplied that store. He even owned the church where Protestant workers worshipped; the Irish walked to Sts. Peter and Paul.

On that fateful Sunday afternoon, forty-six-year-old Amasa left his mansion adjacent to the print works and began his mile-and-one-half walk to a large farm that he owned in the neighboring town of

Johnston. Between dusk and darkness, Michael Costello, handyman in the Sprague household, took the same route and came upon Sprague's bloodied body, shot in the right forearm and then brutally beaten.

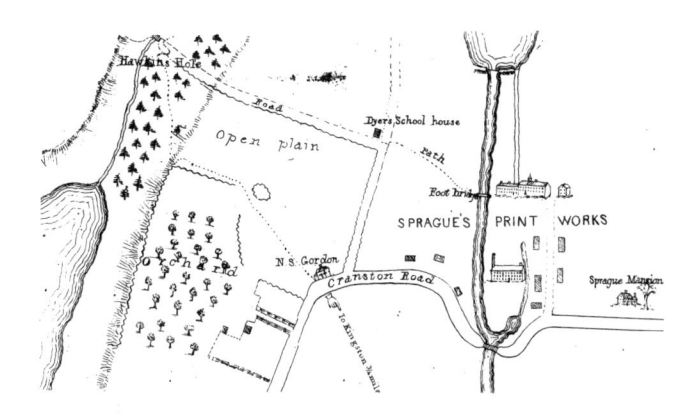

A detailed map of the Sprague print works by S.B. Cushing (1844) showing the location of Nicholas Gordon's store.

Sixty dollars found in the victim's pocket seemed to eliminate robbery as a motive and made the murder appear to be one of hatred or revenge.

Suspicion immediately centered on the Gordon family, a clan particularly hostile towards the strong-willed Yankee industrialist. In the mid-1830s Nicholas Gordon had emigrated from Ireland and settled in Cranston. He opened a small store near Sprague's Village where he sold groceries, notions, and miscellaneous items, and then expanded his business by obtaining a license from Cranston town officials to sell liquor. The popularity of this new commodity in the dreary mill village enabled Nicholas in 1843 to finance the migration to America of his aged mother; his sister; three brothers, John, William, and Robert; and a niece. But Gordon's liquor sales also produced a confrontation with Amasa Sprague who felt intoxicating brews were adversely affecting the productive capacity of the factory hands. Sprague used his considerable political weight to block renewal of Nicholas Gordon's license in June 1843. Tempers flared, harsh words were exchanged, and upon Amasa's death the Gordon brothers became prime suspects. One might say that public opinion convicted them immediately. It appeared to many that this heinous crime was an instance of the infamous 'Whiteboy' outrages that Irish peasants had visited upon their opponents throughout the early nineteenth century.

Three of the brothers were promptly indicted on circumstantial evidence — John and William for murder, Nicholas as accessory before the fact, the implication being that he instigated the murder in revenge and even imported his brothers for that purpose. Nicholas received the lesser charge because an investigation proved he was in Providence on that day, first at Mass and later at a christening.

The Irish communities in Providence and Cranston rallied to support the Gordons and raised money to employ able counsel. Several colleagues of Thomas Dorr accepted the challenge to defend the accused Irishmen and did so without fee. One was General Thomas F. Carpenter, unsuccessful Democratic candidate for governor in 1840 and a leading member of the Rhode Island bar, whose Catholic sympathies

General Thomas F. Carpenter, Democratic gubernatorial candidate in 1840, Dorrite, and legal defender of John Gordon.

would lead to his conversion in 1850. Another attorney assisting the Gordons was the well-known reformer Samuel Y. Atwell, who later in the year would serve as chief defense counsel in Dorr's trial for treason.

The Yankee community was far from monolithic in its intolerance as Dorr, Carpenter, and Atwell illustrated, but the climate of native opinion in this year of the bloody Philadelphia riots was decidedly anti-Catholic and anti-Irish, and John Gordon would feel its oppressive weight. The trial, conducted before the spring 1844 term of Superior Court with Chief Justice Job Durfee presiding, lasted from April 8 to 17. At the outset William definitely established that he was elsewhere when the crime was committed, so Attorney General Joseph M. Blake zeroed in on the hapless twenty-one-year-old John, who could not prove his whereabouts. From then on the trial was a mockery of justice. The evidence, which was entirely circumstantial and conflicting, consisted primarily of the fact that the murderer had a shoesize and stride similar to John's, that a broken gun was found that allegedly belonged to Nicholas (though Nicholas produced a gun he said was his), and that a blood-stained coat belonging to the Gordons was found in the vicinity (the 'blood' turned out to be madder dye). The Gordons proclaimed their innocence, and the defense suggested that another laborer called 'Big Peter' was the real culprit. Peter disappeared from the village immediately after the killing, but no serious attempt was made by the state to determine his whereabouts.

When the testimony was concluded, Chief Justice Durfee, who later presided in partisan fashion over the trial of Dorr, gave a charge to the jury in which he drew a distinction between the testimony of native-born witnesses and that of the Gordons' 'countrymen.' The jury apparently took Durfee's injudicious advice; it left the box at 6:30 on the night of April 17 and returned one hour and fifteen minutes later with a verdict of guilty for John Gordon and freedom for William. Sentenced to death, John was confined to the old state prison on the cove in Providence to await execution. An appeal made to the October session of the court was rejected, so Gordon then petitioned the General Assembly for reprieve and commutation of sentence. The petition — debated by the House on January 14, 1845, with Law and Order chieftain Wilkins Updike of South Kingstown leading the opposition — was rejected by a vote of thirty-six to twenty-seven, but the narrowness of the margin indicated growing doubts concerning the fairness of the trial.

Time was running out for John Gordon, and Governor James Fenner, Dorr's arch-rival, was not sympathetic to the Irishman's plight. Hanged in the yard of the state prison (where Dorr was also an inmate) on February 14, 1845, John Gordon maintained his

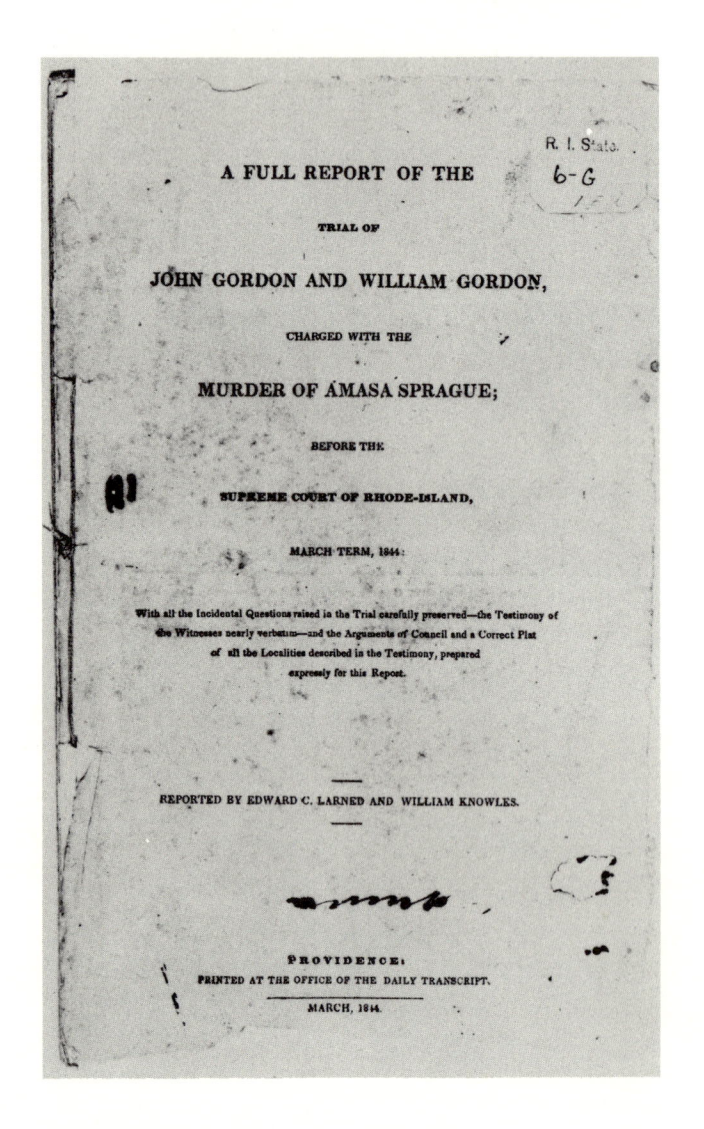

The 1844 court report of the Gordon murder trial.

Rhode Island State Prison, located on the old Cove (site of the present Providence municipal parking lot below the State House). This sketch was made in 1845 at the same time that the facility was occupied by Thomas Dorr and John Gordon.

innocence to the end. Father John Brady who attended him was quoted as saying: 'Have courage, John — you are going to join the noble band of martyrs of your countrymen who have suffered before at the shrine of bigotry and prejudice.' John Gordon's funeral was attended by Irish from miles around, some journeying from Massachusetts and Connecticut. According to observers, mourners in the procession took thirty minutes to pass a given spot.

The trial left many questions unanswered, but the compelling attitude, which even some of those who thought John guilty came to share, was that the young man had been convicted on insufficient and unsatisfactory evidence which fell far short of the required standard of reasonable doubt. The hanging of John Gordon disturbed the conscience of Rhode Island, and it had a slight influence on the 1852 statute abolishing capital punishment (except in cases of first degree murder by someone already under a life sentence). Governor Philip Allen (1851–53) and his Dorrite supporters enacted this legislative change. An obscure and poor Irish immigrant thus served a humane end by his death.

Nicholas Gordon, who was released after two juries deadlocked on the question of his guilt, never recovered from the personal calamity of John's execution or from his own ordeal in a damp, vermin-infested prison. Broken in health he took to excessive drink and died at an early age.

CHAPTER 3

Rhode Island under the Diocese of Hartford

William Barber Tyler, First Bishop of Hartford, 1844–49

Early in 1843 Bishop Fenwick compiled some statistics on the growth of the Diocese of Boston. They revealed a total Catholic population of 68,133. Fenwick's figures show that Massachusetts had 47,941 Catholics with Rhode Island a distant second at 5,074. Connecticut with 4,753 ranked fourth behind Vermont. Because Fenwick's New England-wide diocese had grown to such considerable proportions, he decided to recommend its division. In view of future growth projections he also determined that the first subdivision of the Boston diocese should comprise Connecticut and Rhode Island, but for some unknown reason he chose Hartford over larger and more important Providence as the see city. His selection for bishop of the new entity was his favorite companion and constant associate William Barber Tyler. Fenwick presented this proposal at the Fifth Provincial Council of Baltimore in May 1843. His fellow bishops accepted and submitted the plan for final approval to Pope Gregory XVI.

In February 1844 the appropriate papal bulls arrived in Boston and on March 17, in the cathedral at Baltimore — still the metropolitan see for the Boston diocese — Fenwick consecrated Bishop Tyler. One week later at Georgetown he elevated the brilliant John B. Fitzpatrick to the rank of coadjutor bishop of Boston. Then he and his two young colleagues journeyed north to Hartford where thirty-eight-year-old Tyler was installed on April 14.

The sixty-two-year-old Fenwick because of advancing age had decided to divide his diocese and select a coadjutor. Unfortunately his apprehensions concerning his declining vigor were soon confirmed. By the end of 1845 it was clear that he suffered from a heart

William Barber Tyler, first Bishop of Hartford (1844–49).

ailment and dropsy. Experiencing a rapid decline, he died on August 11, 1846.

Fenwick's episcopate, according to historian Robert Lord, marked the great turning point in the fortunes of the Church in New England. Through his superb organizational ability Fenwick helped transform a feeble diocese into one of the strongest in the American Church. He built up a sizable body of clergy, made great strides in marshalling the laity behind varied social projects, and championed the cause of education. With Father Fitton he helped found the first New England Catholic college — Holy Cross in 1843 — and backed the establishment of the area's first Catholic newspaper, the *Pilot* in 1829 (originally named *The Jesuit,* or *Catholic Sentinel*). These accomplishments had a great long-range impact on the Rhode Island Catholic community. If the heroic Father Matignon and Bishop Cheverus were the true founders of the Diocese of Boston, Bishop Benedict Joseph Fenwick more than any other deserves to be called its organizer.

Fenwick's protégé, William Tyler, also had an impressive if short episcopacy. He was a native Vermonter and a son of a prosperous farmer. His mother was a daughter of Daniel Barber and the sister of Virgil Barber, who were noted Congregational ministers until they entered the Catholic Church and eventually its priesthood. In 1821, a year or so after her father and brother converted, Mrs. Tyler followed their example together with her husband, four daughters and three sons, including fifteen-year-old William. In August 1826 young Tyler went to Boston to study for the priesthood under Fenwick. His fellow students in the bishop's household included James Fitton and William Wiley. By 1829 Tyler completed his theological studies, was ordained, and eventually selected vicar general of the Boston diocese.

According to his colleague, Bishop John Fitzpatrick, Tyler's 'talents were not brilliant nor was his learning extensive, though quite sufficient. But he possessed great moderation of character, sound judgment, uncommon prudence and much firmness.' He gave not one hour 'to idleness nor vain amusements or visits. He was methodical in the distribution of his time. . . . Zeal for the glory of God and the salvation of souls, true humility, total indifference to popular favor and applause, and a perfect spirit of poverty, were his peculiar virtues.' In short, his temperament was much more akin to Matignon's and Cheverus's than to Fenwick's or that of irascible Bernard O'Reilly, second bishop of Hartford.

A further insight into Tyler's character can be gleaned from his simple life style. He looked upon gifts he received from his people as a contribution to the Church, and was most reluctant to use the little money he obtained for purposes not intimately connected with 'religion.' As a result he dispensed with most of the luxuries that befitted one of his high station. He had no carriage and traveled the streets of Providence on foot. His house had only the most necessary articles of furniture and was without carpeting. His table was common and his meals plain. Tyler was a common man for the common people he served.

In 1844, at the time of Tyler's elevation, Hartford contained about 1,300 inhabitants. Of this number 500 to 600 were adult Catholics, compared with approximately 2,500 Catholics in Providence. Because of the disparity of the two cities in size and significance, and because Providence possessed a superior church building in Sts. Peter and Paul, Tyler — after consultation with Fenwick — decided to move to Providence and establish his cathedral there. He also wished to make Providence the see city. Rome granted permission for Tyler's change in residence but declined to make any other alteration in the original structure of the diocese.

Tyler first visited Providence in June 1844 and took up residence at Sts. Peter and Paul, despite the fact that it was built on a narrow piece of ground and had stables on both sides that the new bishop termed 'very offensive in warm weather.' His coming to Rhode Island had its personal compensations, for Tyler was able to join his former classmates, Father Fitton and Father Wiley, the pastor of neighboring St. Patrick's. Of this illustrious trio, Wiley and his bishop were converts. From the outset of his administration

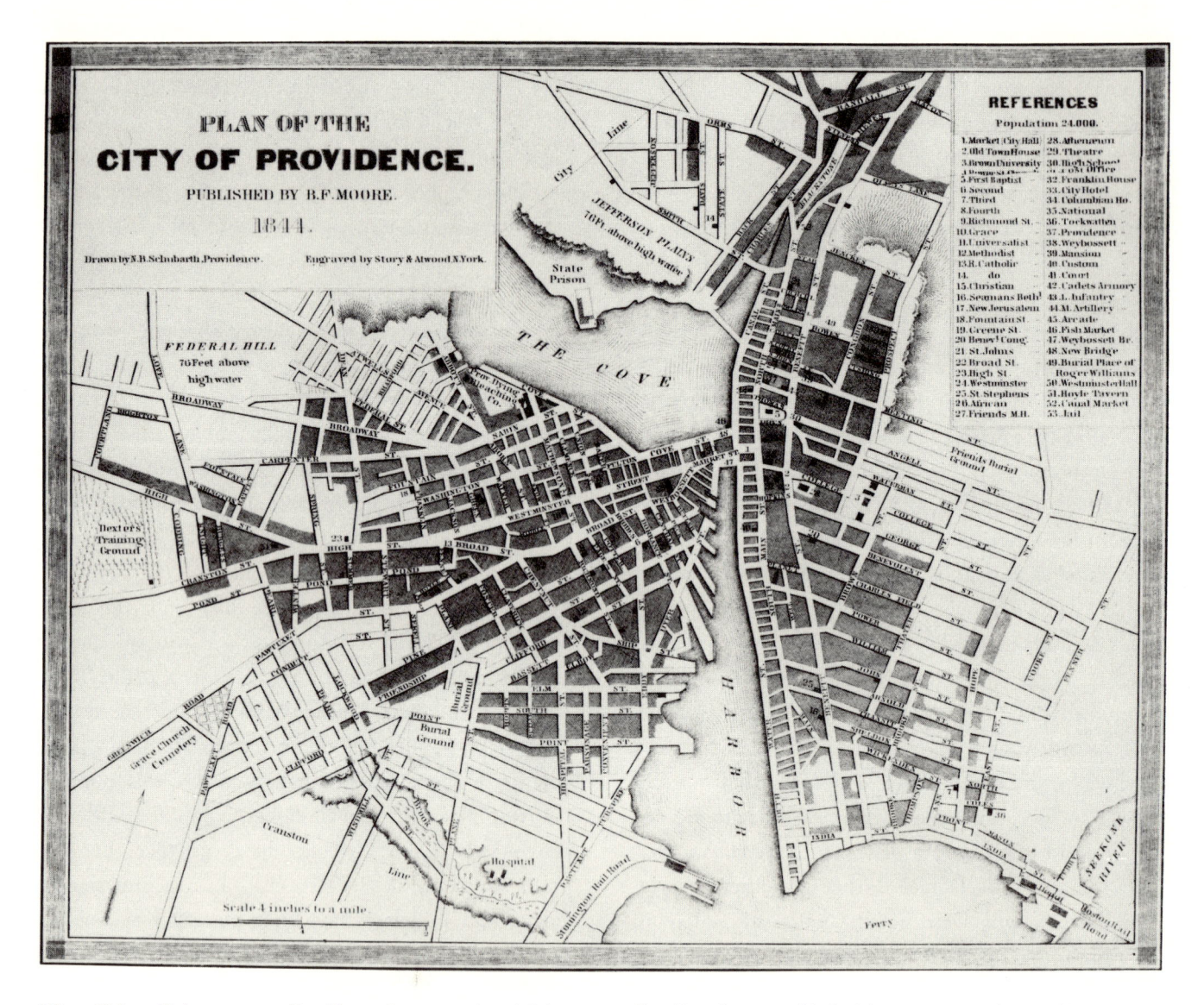

When Bishop Tyler came to Providence it was a city of 6.1 square miles (less than one-third of its present area). As this 1844 map indicates, sections such as the North End, Wanskuck, Elmhurst, Mount Pleasant, Silver Lake, Elmwood, South Providence and Washington Park belonged to the surrounding towns of North Providence, Johnston or Cranston.

the frail Tyler showed signs of what his physician, Edward P. LeProphon, called 'latent consumption,' and this disability brought about the bishop's premature demise, but not before he left an indelible impression on Rhode Island Catholicism.

One problem that plagued Tyler was the shortage of clergy. Other than Fitton and Wiley, there was only one additional priest in the entire state, Father William Ivers of St. Mary's, Pawtucket. To compound the difficulty, Ivers — a scholarly, contentious, and seemingly restless man — left the diocese in July 1844.

To supply the needs of the faithful, Tyler was forced to assume parish duties at Sts. Peter and Paul, and Fitton embarked once again on a roving ministry.

To remedy this scarcity of priests, Tyler looked toward Ireland and the missionary college of All Hallows in Dublin, opened in 1842 to train young men for the foreign missions. The bishop wrote to the institution's founder, Reverend John Hand, a Vincentian, requesting young recruits. 'This diocese,' Tyler wrote, 'has a peculiar claim upon you, in as much as all the Catholics here are Irish with very few exceptions.' Within the next few years All Hallows sent at least eight young men who served the Hartford diocese as priests, though the tenure of some was brief.

The type of man Tyler sought was much like the bishop himself. In one of his missives to Father Hand, Tyler informed him that 'it is not great learning that is required in priests on the mission here so much as solid piety, a spirit of poverty, and sincere zeal for the salvation of souls.' Tyler also trained and ordained several native-born priests, at least three of whom were converts. One of these, the Reverend Edward Putnam from New Hampshire, became the first priest to receive Holy Orders in Rhode Island when Tyler ordained him on Trinity Sunday 1845.

The bishop's recruitment campaign had only limited success. At the time of his death there were just thirteen priests in the entire diocese, and the Catholic population of Rhode Island alone had grown to approximately 17,000. Unfortunately Irish families had not yet acquired sufficient means to spare their sons for priestly duty. The need for extra pay from the mills was more compelling. Tyler noted in an 1848 sermon that there was not a 'man in the whole diocese who was educating his son for the Church.'

Despite the need for clergy, the bishop lacked funds to maintain any more clerical students than the seven he was already supporting. The great harvest of vocations for which the Rhode Island Church is famous had to await a rise in the socio-economic status of the laity and an improvement in the financial resources of the Church itself.

So poverty-stricken was the diocese under Tyler that he was forced to make continual pleas for foreign aid. The Leopoldine Mission Society of Vienna, Austria, formed primarily to aid Catholic German immigrants, responded first with a sizable gift — a most unselfish act since the census of 1850 listed only one Austrian-born resident in Rhode Island, though there was a German colony in New Haven. By 1846 a Leopoldine survey revealed that the organization had donated 19,000 florins to the Diocese of Hartford (a florin was worth slightly less than fifty cents).

Tyler's main effort was directed toward the Society for the Propagation of the Faith in Paris (the 'Propaganda'). In his letters to the Propaganda, he wrote of the poverty of his Irish flock: 'They all came here poor. Their wages are generally low, and of course they must live poor; yet by their contributions they have supported the priests who have served them, and built all the churches we have without any help from abroad.' The Rhode Island Church was also destitute. 'The diocese wants for everything,' reported Tyler, 'my only chalice is brass and I have but one other at the Cathedral and only four or five more in the whole diocese.'

Under Bishop Tyler, the first Sts. Peter and Paul church in Providence became the cathedral of the newly-formed diocese in 1844.

In January 1847 the bishop listed his most pressing needs: funds for the enlargement of the Cathedral to accommodate his rapidly growing congregation, aid to the poor children of the diocese, and money to establish new mission stations for the expanding Catholic community. The Propaganda, it seems, was not overly generous, but Tyler was at least able to build a wing on the Cathedral. This addition, completed in 1847, prompted a rededication ceremony at which Bishop Fitzpatrick said the Mass and Father James Ryder, S.J., president of Holy Cross, preached to an overflow crowd.

At Newport, another important building project undertaken during Tyler's tenure was directed by Father Fitton. Since his return to the mission circuit in 1844, this clerical dynamo had completed the construction of churches in New London, Norwich, and Crompton. Then, with the arrival of several new priests in the diocese, Fitton was given the Newport pastorate where the Catholic population was again growing steadily as a result of the famine migration (from 375 Catholics in 1846 to 560 in 1848). This influx, coupled with the deterioration of St. Joseph's, prompted Fitton to propose a more elaborate structure. The result was the Holy Name of Mary, Our Lady of the Isle, popularly known as St. Mary's — one of the state's historic churches. The purchase price for the land was supplied by Mrs. Goodloe Harper, daughter of Charles Carroll. Plans were drawn by the soon-to-be famous church architect, Patrick C. Keely, and construction assistance was provided by soldiers from Fort Adams under Lieutenant William S. Rosecrans, later a leading Union general who came close to being named Lincoln's running mate in 1864. This all-star cast produced a splendid brownstone Gothic edifice. Begun in August 1848, St. Mary's was finally dedicated on July 25, 1852.

Early Educational and Social Developments

Under Tyler's leadership the Rhode Island Church made its first significant strides in education and social work. In November 1843, just before the bishop's arrival, Father Wiley and his parishioners at St. Patrick's had established the first parochial school in the state. Prior to the completion of St. Patrick's day school, the only facility providing Catholic lessons was located in the basement of Sts. Peter and Paul, but this was only used on Sundays for catechetical instruction. St. Patrick's initial schoolhouse, thirty-six by twenty-four feet, constructed near the church, cost $500. At first only girls enrolled because most boys, from the time they reached school age, had to help support their families by toiling in the factories.

With the arrival of Tyler a priority was placed upon the expansion of Catholic educational efforts, but inadequate finances hampered this project. The bishop invited that branch of the Sisters of Charity founded at Emmitsburg, Maryland by Mother Elizabeth Seton, to staff his proposed school. Tyler was quite familiar with their work since they had opened a school in Boston and two of his sisters were members of the order. The response from Emmitsburg was an acceptance on condition that the bishop would build a convent for them before they arrived. Tyler could not raise the money locally for such a structure, and the Society for the Propagation of the Faith was not responsive to his appeal for funds, so his bid for the Sisters of Charity fell through.

Next he made inquiries regarding the Sisters of St. Joseph — a French order that had come to America in 1836 at Bishop Rosati's request and established a mother house at Carondelet, near St. Louis, Missouri. These overtures also came to naught.

While Bishop Tyler was bargaining with the various religious orders, a school was founded under Catholic auspices at St. Mary's in Newport in 1846, under the direction of a lay teacher. Tyler also turned to the laity and established a parish school in the basement of his enlarged cathedral in 1848. One room under the older section of the church became the boys' area. Although considerably smaller than the room occupied by the girls, it was more comfortable because the girls' area had only five small cellar windows to let in light and air. Classes commenced in October 1848 with Mr. and Mrs. Hugh Carlin serving as teachers, the former earning $400 per year and his wife $3 per week. Mrs. Carlin also devoted one evening a week to catechetical instruction for adults of the parish. During the first year, operational expenses came out of general church funds, a practice which disturbed Tyler who looked to the parents to underwrite the costs of educating their children.

Father Wiley of St. Patrick's — not to be outdone by the rival crosstown parish — made arrangements to accommodate male students in December 1848. The boys' class, with an initial enrollment of thirty-five, started under the tutelage of John Coyle who received $300 annually. At St. Patrick's those parents who were able paid $1.25 for each pupil and provided their books. Any deficiency was made up by a semi-annual parish collection. From such crude and inauspicious beginnings in the 1840s the imposing parochial school system of the diocese began. From the outset the laity played a major role.

The reasons for the creation of a Catholic school system at this time were numerous and involved. The earliest argument in support of Catholic education stemmed from the conviction that moral values and religious truths could best be taught and retained throughout life by an education which combined secular and religious instruction. A theme of Bishop John Carroll's first national pastoral letter in 1792, it remains a primary reason for the existence of Catholic education. The first three provincial councils that met at Baltimore in 1829, 1833 and 1837 all reenforced this view.

Beginning in the late 1830s and the early 1840s the Church also had to guard against a current of active hostility toward Catholicism reflected in many areas of American life — including public education. The educational decrees of the provincial council of 1840 were more defensive in nature and manifested an awareness of the anti-Catholic crusade that was beginning to gather momentum. The clergy were admonished to see that Catholic children were not forced to read non-Catholic versions of the Bible or books imbued with Protestant doctrines. In the pastoral letter issued at the council's conclusion, the bishops asserted that the 'great evil' of common school education was that the 'imperfect' religious instruction the children received undermined their faith. Compulsory reading of the King James Bible, a lively topic of debate in New York during this era, did not become an issue of great consequence in Rhode Island owing especially to the enlightened stand taken by education commissioner Elisha R. Potter, Jr. (1849–54).

Protestant influence over public education was another matter. Quite naturally, public schools in early nineteenth-century Rhode Island had a distinctly Protestant character. The population had been almost exclusively Protestant, and the schools mirrored this tradition. The typical attitude was that expressed by state commissioner of education Robert Allyn when he asserted in his official report of 1856 that public education was necessary to make the people 'homogeneous' — the 'aim of our common republican Christianity.'

In Providence, which had the state's only public school program between the repeal of the free school act of 1803 and the refunding of education by the General Assembly in 1828, each of the town's four school districts was under the special supervision of a Protestant minister from 1816 to 1828. The school act of the latter year put control of public schools even more beyond the reach of the Catholic immigrant. Its most significant feature was to prohibit state money from being allocated for the support of schools controlled by private agencies. The law further authorized the creation of a school committee in every town to be elected by freemen. Since the real estate qualification for freemenship was retained for naturalized citizens in the state constitution of 1843, the influence of the foreign-born in the selection of school committee personnel was rendered negligible.

There were, of course, members of various local committees who were sympathetic to the Catholic position. Thomas Wilson Dorr — the driving force on the Providence School Committee from 1834 to 1842 — was one conspicuous example, but he was joined on that thirty-member body by arch-nativists Henry

Bowen Anthony and William Goddard, and by Thomas C. Hoppin, relative of the future Know-Nothing governor.

Alarming as the bias of some school committeemen was the bias of textbooks used in the public schools. Many texts were notoriously anti-Catholic and anti-Irish. The following are excerpts from Parley's *Common School History,* then widely in use:

> From this time forward the Popes rapidly acquired power.... Their pride was equal to their power, and neither seemed to have any bounds. ... No other tyranny had ever been like theirs, for they tyrannized over the souls of men.... If any person denied the Pope's authority he was burned alive.
>
> Abbies and monasteries became seats of voluptuousness.
>
> To this day they [the Irish] consider St. Patrick as in Heaven, watching over the interest of Ireland. They pray to him, and to do him honor, set apart one day in the year for going to Church, drinking whiskey and breaking each other's heads with clubs.

Noah Webster's *Elements of Useful Knowledge,* a text prevalent in Rhode Island schools, had this observation regarding Catholic Spain:

> The manners of the nation are corrupted by the superstitions which have been engrafted upon the Christian religions, and which, by enjoining celibacy upon the clergy, have introduced the most immoral customs.

Equally objectionable was the ecclesiastical history that took every opportunity to emphasize the alleged 'corruptions' of Catholicism, depicted missionary efforts as mere schemes of papal ambition, and used such phrases to describe the Church as 'the Scarlet Lady of Babylon.' The presence of such books in a public school system receiving state support was certainly a justifiable source of consternation among Catholics.

Additionally, Catholic schools began in nineteenth-century Rhode Island and elsewhere because of the national background of the bishops, clergy, and laity. Throughout the century from the time of Fenwick onward, every bishop having direct jurisdiction over Rhode Island Catholicism was an Irish immigrant or the son of one except for Bishop Tyler. The same was true for many other dioceses. Unquestionably the situation in Ireland influenced educational policy in the United States and, during the same generation in which American parochial schools were founded, leading Irish prelates were attacking the state-supported system of national education on the primary level created by Lord Stanley's education bill of 1831. These Irish national schools offered non-denominational education in secular subjects, but allowed the various sects to supplement this program by giving religious instruction to children of their own faith.

This system was reasonable in principle, and at first most Catholic leaders welcomed it as a means to raise the cultural level of the Irish people. In practice, however, the national schools became denominational. In Catholic districts the local priest became head of the school board, and in predominantly Protestant areas the parson performed that function. By mid-century the Catholic hierarchy led by Archbishops Paul Cullen of Dublin and John MacHale of Tuam condemned the national schools; Cullen proclaimed them instruments of Protestant proselytism, while MacHale considered them agents of British rule.

These beliefs were not without foundation. In its early years the so-called national system, under the guidance of Anglican Archbishop Richard Whately of Dublin, was indeed aimed at the conversion of Ireland. As Whately confided to a friend, 'the education supplied by the National Board is gradually undermining the vast fabric of the Irish Roman Catholic Church.' Later the Anglican prelate stated the Protestant posture: 'I believe that mixed education is gradually enlightening the mass of the people, and that if we give it up, we give up the only hope of weaning the Irish people from the abuses of Popery. But I cannot venture openly to profess this opinion. I cannot openly support the Board of Education as an instrument of conversion.'

In the 1840s MacHale also led the fight against the Queen's Colleges that attempted to apply this principle of 'mixed education' on the college level. MacHale's conservative view that 'nothing but separate grants for separate education will ever give satisfaction to the Catholics of Ireland' was a position shared by a considerable number of those Irish missionary priests who labored in America. Such an attitude and tradition obtained also, as we shall see, with the second great wave of Catholic migrants to Rhode Island — the French Canadians who valiantly maintained the separate identity of their church schools in English-dominated Canada.

Finally, then as now, the Catholic school was valued because it exerted behavioral controls over its students. This function was ably described by John Francis Maguire, Member of Parliament, in his 1868 treatise *The Irish In America:*

> The [Irish] youth of the country rapidly catch the prevailing spirit, and thus become impatient of restraint at a period of life when restraint is indispensible to their future well being. This is peculiarly observable in the youth who are trained in the Public Schools. The boy who is trained in these institutions is apt to disregard, if not altogether despise, that authority which is held so sacred in Ireland; and once this first and holiest of all influences is lost, on goes the headlong youth, reckless of consequences, and the slave of every impulse. . . .
> The Catholic Schools, on the contrary, inculcate obedience to parental authority — respect for the head of the family — reverence for holy things — for what is great and good and noble. . . .

This combination of factors influenced the creation of the Catholic school system in Rhode Island during the 1840s. Anti-Catholic attitudes then prevalent gave this project priority and special urgency. Archbishop John Hughes, the metropolitan for the province in which Rhode Island was located, emphasized this contemporary concern in an 1850 circular letter. 'I think the time has almost come,' he warned, 'when it will be necessary to build the school-house first, and the church afterwards.'

The Catholic school system created in response to these attitudes generally succeeded in its primary pur-

John Hughes, Archbishop of New York and head of the ecclesiastical province in which Rhode Island was located, led the fight for public aid to parochial schools.

pose of defending and promoting the faith. But the parochial school also helped institutionalize the religious and secular differences dividing Catholic and Protestant America, and the issue of its support involved the Church in a long-standing political battle that has endured into the present. Hughes spearheaded the drive for public funding in New York during the 1840s, and John Coyle of St. Patrick's began the Rhode Island crusade in 1853. Unfortunately the principal result these early proponents of public aid achieved was to inflame popular fear and distrust of Catholicism.

Bishop Tyler and his flock also engaged in some pioneering social action. The *Hibernian Orphan Society,* apparently the state's first Catholic social agency, was established in the late 1830s to ensure that Catholic children who had lost their parents would be raised in the faith. The only activity of this society known to us is the census it conducted in 1839 showing 1,696 Catholics in Providence. In 1841 rival repeal associations were formed by Father Corry and his antagonists, but these had more political than religious orientation as did the earlier *Hibernian Relief Society* established in Providence in 1827, just before the passage of O'Connell's Catholic Emancipation Act.

Under Tyler new organizations were formed primarily for benevolent and charitable purposes. The bishop established in May 1847 a *Confraternity of the Blessed Virgin Mary to Befriend Children,* to effect 'the increase of piety in its members and the spiritual and corporal welfare of the children of the congregation.' Specifically the confraternity provided catechetical instruction and supervision for the youth of the parish and helped 'provide suitable clothing for very poor children, who now remain away from church on account of being destitute in this respect."

Across town, Father Wiley established in 1848 a *Young Catholic Friends Society* — modeled on one founded in Boston thirteen years earlier — 'for the clothing of poor children and otherwise assisting in providing for them spiritually and corporally.' A large number of men attended the organizational meeting and about seventy enrolled as members. At a subsequent session they chose John McCarthy president. Emulating their Boston archetypes they organized annually a series of public lectures that became important events in the intellectual life of Rhode Island's Catholics.

Admission fees from these talks, assessments levied upon the society's members, and contributions from the public, furnished funds to provide poor boys with clothes, schooling, and other necessities. The society generated such enthusiasm in St. Patrick's parish that its members voted in March 1848 to extend operations to the entire city. At its annual meeting in January 1849 a motion urged the establishment of a female society to act in unison with it. This proposal, though not immediately implemented, led in 1851 to a metamorphosis by which the group was transformed into the *Providence Roman Catholic Orphans' Asylum and School Society,* the association that eventually established St. Aloysius Home. Because of these early beginnings St. Aloysius — now based in Greenville — ranks as the oldest continuous social welfare agency in the diocese.

St. Patrick's under the energetic Wiley also developed a *Rosary Society* that enrolled 350 women in 1849 and a *Purgatorian Society,* but such purely religious or devotional sodalities were not nearly so numerous in the mid-nineteenth century as in later times. Perhaps they were not so much needed by that generation of destitute Catholics, who were accustomed on Sunday to attend with almost equal fidelity morning Mass and afternoon Vespers, and to hear a long sermon at both services.

Among those associations dedicated more to social improvement than to charity, the most important were the temperance societies of which Rhode Island Catholicism had its share in the decade of the 1840s. Temperance proved a leading concern to this generation. Both Protestants and Catholics were active in the movement, although they did not always cooperate in the crusade against 'Demon Rum.' In neighboring Massachusetts there occurred a brief period of 'fraternization' and joint action against drink, but in Rhode Island the evangelical nature of the non-Catholic agencies and the tensions generated by the Dorr Rebellion and the Gordon trial seem to have prevented mutual cooperation between the several Protestant-led organizations and those under Catholic auspices. Many native reformers considered the Irish the most intemperate of groups — an attitude that further discouraged fusion.

The moderate *Catholic Temperance Society* formed on October 4, 1840 enrolled 1,300 to 1,400 members within a year, but its leader, Father Corry, was undermined by a rift in the Providence Catholic community. After Corry's angry departure, Fathers Fitton and Wiley established the city-wide *Catholic Temperance Confraternity* of Providence in November 1843 to arrest the alarming increase of intemperance. This new society was more stringent than Corry's agency because it required its members to abstain totally from drink, not merely from consuming it in public places. Only July 4, 1844 the confraternity marched 1,500 strong to a picnic grove on Smith's Hill.

Tyler, a strict temperance man, approached the problem of drink both by calling on his people to swear off liquor and by attacking those who sold it. Although the Church actively promoted temperance societies in the parishes, it challenged the right of the state to legislate on the matter, because the Irish harbored an ingrained fear that the state could be used — as it had been in Ireland — for strengthening secular against religious influences. This, in essence, was also a factor contributing to the Irish suspicion towards compulsory public education. From the 1830s through the remainder of the century as the temperance movement waxed and waned, the Church emphasized personal choice and the 'Catholic pledge' rather than government-imposed prohibition as the proper way to combat the evils of drink.

The highlight of the local Catholic temperance movement of the 1840s was the visit in 1849 of Father Theobald Mathew to Rhode Island. This humble, self-effacing and unworldly Capuchin friar, had conducted a remarkable total abstinence crusade in Ireland beginning in 1838 and had risen in stature among the Irish second only to Daniel O'Connell. After his enormous success in Ireland, this 'Apostle of Temperance' launched an American crusade in late July 1849 and stayed two years and four months. His reception by Protestants was generally enthusiastic. When he visited Washington the House and Senate voted him an honorary seat in Congress. Up to that time General Lafayette had been the only foreigner to be accorded such a distinction.

During his tour he visited most of the states east of the Mississippi and gave the total abstinence pledge to an estimated 500,000 to 600,000 people. Rhode Island's turn came in September 1849 when Mathew stopped in Providence and Woonsocket. In the former community the mayor, several Protestant clergymen, and many civic leaders gave him an official welcome, and a large number of citizens took his pledge. In Woonsocket the *Father Mathew Benevolent Total Abstinence and Aid Society* — formed in his honor just after his visit — continued its work intermittently for the remainder of the century.

The long-range influence of Mathew's crusade was substantial. In later decades his spirit was recalled and his principles invoked. Father Stephen Byrne, who compiled a handbook for Irish immigrants in 1873, wrote of Mathew's impact: 'Millions now living, if not in opulence, at least in independent circumstances and enjoying the comfort of peaceful homes, are indebted to him for all they possess.' While Byrne is perhaps guilty of hyperbole, even the most dispassionate scholars admit that Mathew wrought a moral revolu-

> "Be sober and watch, because your adversary, the devil, as a roaring lion, goeth about seeking whom he may devour."—2 Peter V., 8.
>
> **ST. PATRICK'S CHURCH**
> **Valley Falls, R. I.**
>
> **Copy of Total Abstinence Pledge.**
>
> *I...*
>
> *firmly promise, by the aid of God, to abstain from all intoxicating drinks from this the ....day of ....191....until the..........day of............191.... and to avoid as much as possible all company that will lead me to intemperance.*
>
> *Rev...*
>
> N. B.—To Persevere in this Pledge: Repeat it in the hour of temptation; pray for strength; frequent the Sacraments, avoid temptations.

In the nineteenth and early twentieth centuries the Church emphasized the voluntary "Catholic pledge" rather than government-imposed prohibition.

Father Theobald Mathew, following successes like this London meeting of 1843, brought his total abstinence crusade to Rhode Island in 1849 under the banner of "temperance and religion." At right is a close-up of this famed Irish priest.

tion, especially among the Irish at home and in America.

Other inspiring Catholic visitors traveled to Rhode Island in the 1840s. Two of the most notable were converts — James A. McMaster, outspoken editor of the *New York Freeman's Journal,* and Orestes A. Brownson, polemical editor of *Brownson's Quarterly Review.* Both participated in the *Young Catholic Friends Society* lecture series of 1848. No stranger to Rhode Island, Brownson made several trips from his base in Boston to address the local Catholic community.

Brownson's background was indeed remarkable. Like Tyler he came from native Vermont stock, but his road to conversion was far more circuitous. His journey from Congregationalism included detours as a Presbyterian, a Universalist preacher, an anti-Christian 'World Reformer,' a liberal Unitarian, and a

THE FORMATIVE ERA

Transcendentalist. Finally in 1844 he became a Catholic, and there he remained — faithfully if not always easily — until death.

The irrepressible Orestes expounded a stern, austere, uncompromising Catholic orthodoxy; he was a defender of papal supremacy and a political conservative. One of his self-imposed missions was to harmonize Catholic doctrine with American democratic principles — a task he shared with convert Isaac Hecker.

Brownson espoused this cause at a time when his fellow natives were alleging the incompatibility of 'monarchical Papism' and democracy. He argued that democracy entrusts government to the people, but religion is necessary to condition them to direct and administer government properly; and that religion must be above the people and control them; that Protestantism, based on individual conscience, was insufficient since it would eventually produce a condition of anarchy where individual liberties would be violated. The Roman Catholic religion, however, was necessary to preserve popular liberty, affirmed Brownson, 'because popular liberty can be sustained only by a religion free from popular control, above the people, speaking from above and able to command them.' Brownson's contention that only the Pope could make America safe for democracy brought many natives to the verge of apoplexy, but it instilled in his immigrant Catholic audiences, such as those in Providence, a sense of pride and belonging.

Brownson was the most famous but not the only local Catholic to attempt a defense of the faith. During the 1840s Fathers Fitton, Corry, and Ivers all broke into print with public letters or books justifying their beleaguered Church. Although still a small minority, Catholics made their presence felt.

In retrospect the 1840s loom as extraordinarily eventful and precedent-setting years in the history of Rhode Island Catholicism. Unfortunately the bishop who presided over them did not survive this turbulent decade. Although in his letters the sickly Tyler spoke optimistically of improvements in his health, he knew by early 1849 that he would no longer be able to carry on the responsibilities of his office. He decided to ask his fellow bishops at the upcoming seventh provincial council to approve a successor. The prelates at Baltimore, rather than accept Tyler's resignation, recommended that the Reverend Bernard O'Reilly, then vicar general of the Buffalo diocese, be named coadjutor. O'Reilly's selection was no doubt influenced

Convert Orestes Brownson, a noted author, editor, philosopher and lecturer made several visits to Rhode Island to address its Catholic community on religious and social topics.

by Bishop John Hughes of New York, a rising power in the American Church.

Among several items approved by the council was a proposal to petition Rome for three new metropolitan sees — New Orleans, Cincinnati, and New York. When the Pope consented to this arrangement, Hughes became archbishop and the Hartford, Boston, Albany, and Buffalo dioceses were included in the new archdiocese of New York.

Tyler, despite his weakened condition, attended the

Baltimore conclave and on his return slept in a cold, damp bed aboard the steamer that plied between New York and the railhead at Stonington, Connecticut. He contracted an illness from the ordeal that Dr. LeProphon diagnosed as 'rheumatic fever.' Tyler slipped into a coma for three weeks and then died in the presence of his colleagues Bishop Fitzpatrick and Father Fitton on June 18, 1849. He was only forty-five, but the stress of the times and the arduous nature of his mission took their toll. Many of those who knew Bishop Tyler well used the adjective 'saintly' when they wrote of him in later years. His remains now repose beneath the present Cathedral of Sts. Peter and Paul.

Bishop Bernard O'Reilly — A Man for the Times

At mid-century the Diocese of Hartford received its second bishop, Reverend Bernard O'Reilly, officially appointed by Pius IX in October 1850 after news of Tyler's death had been received by the Holy See.

The new bishop was born in County Longford, Ireland in 1803, the son of Thomas and Catherine (Sheridan) O'Reilly. Little is known of his early years, but at the age of twenty-two he informed his parents of his desire to become a priest. Detesting British subjugation of Ireland, he decided to leave for America 'to minister at the altar that's free.' Arriving in 1825, the young seminarian studied at St. Mary's in Baltimore, and under the Sulpicians at Montreal. He was ordained in New York City by Bishop Francis P. Kendrick of Philadelphia on October 13, 1831.

For the next eighteen years Father O'Reilly served the Diocese of New York. His first pastorate coincided with a devastating cholera epidemic that swept the nation's largest city in 1831–32. The strength of purpose and self-sacrifice he was to manifest later in Providence was shown by his tireless efforts among the sick of his largely immigrant flock in Brooklyn. Twice contracting the disease, he labored on until the ravages of the epidemic had subsided.

In 1842 he was assigned to St. Patrick's Church in Rochester where an immigrant population had settled in the Genesee River valley. The parish and its missions extended as far west as Niagara Falls. Much of O'Reilly's time was spent traveling in the rugged frontier area. His success at Rochester led to his appointment in 1847 as vicar general of the newly created Diocese of Buffalo under Bishop John Timon. Among his various duties was that of serving as rector of the diocesan seminary. Three years later, he reluctantly accepted his election to the titular see of Pompeiopolis and coadjutor bishop of Hartford, confiding in his diary: 'I will, God helping, labor faithfully in this awful office. I have nothing at heart but God's glory in it.' In mid-November 1850 O'Reilly assumed full direction of the Hartford see.

The Diocese of Hartford in 1850 was a missionary church valiantly attempting to meet the needs of an ever-increasing number of immigrant Irish Catholics spread among the cities and villages of Connecticut and Rhode Island. Bernard O'Reilly's tenure was a brief five years, but during that interval he accomplished much of enduring significance. Acting simultaneously in the areas of education, social welfare, vocations and clergy recruitment, he attempted to serve a flock that had been swelled by the post-famine immigration. Beginning in December 1850 with a pastoral letter that exhorted the laity to frequent the sacraments, safeguard the education of their children, and care for orphans, the new bishop launched his episcopacy with zeal and confidence.

The most pressing need in his sprawling diocese was for clergy. With only thirteen priests in the entire two-state region Bishop O'Reilly estimated that at least thirty were needed to serve the faithful adequately. His first ordination in December 1850 was Daniel Kelly, a native of Ireland, whose studies at Holy Cross College had been supported by Bishop Tyler. In an effort to increase the supply of priests, the energetic prelate, utilizing experience gained in Buffalo, opened the first seminary in the diocese, St. Mary's, in September 1851, at his Cathedral in Provi-

Bernard O'Reilly, second Bishop of Hartford (1850–56).

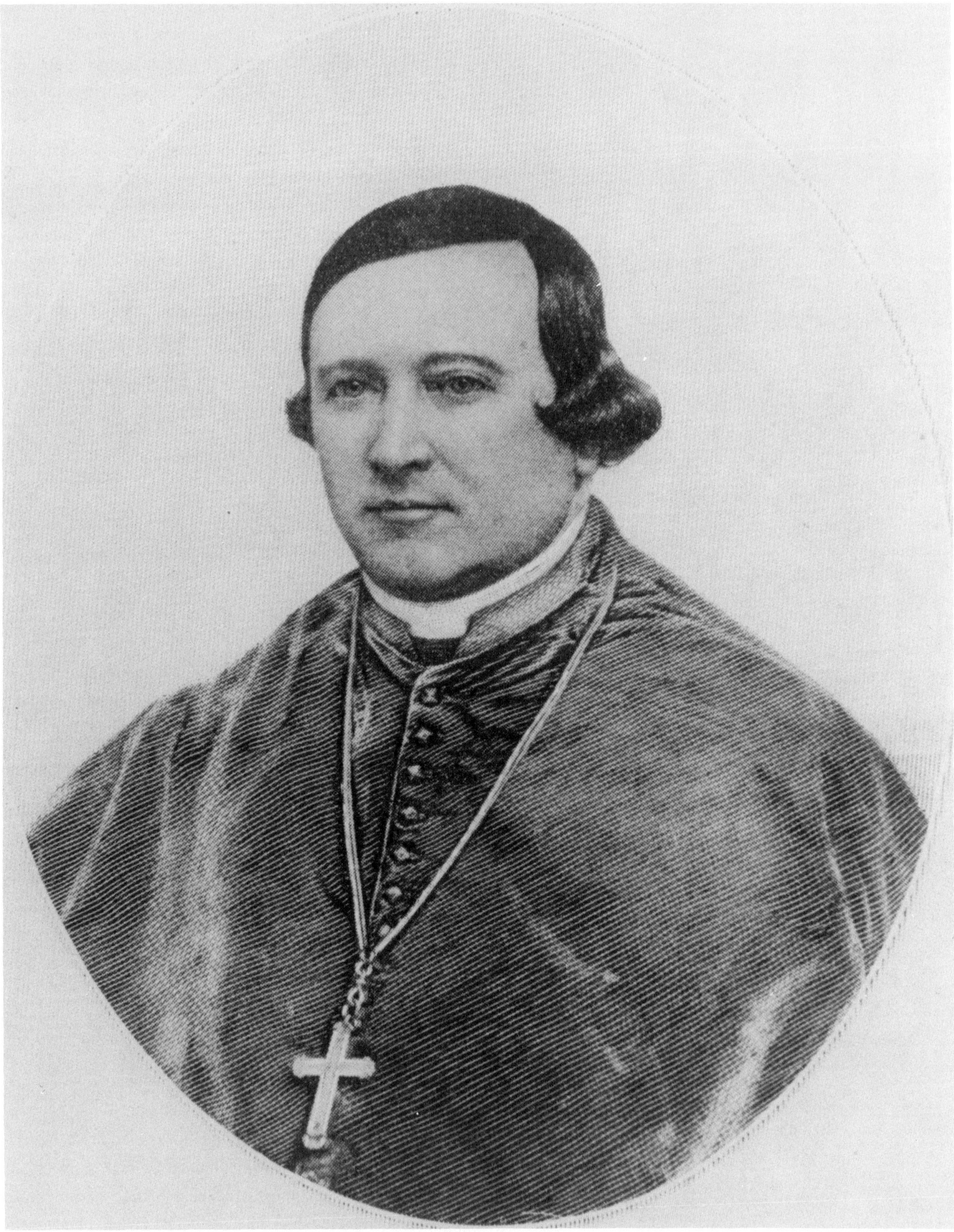

dence. Here the bishop with Fathers Hugh Carmody and Patrick Lambe, both products of All Hallows in Ireland, taught theology and philosophy to a student body that grew to eight by 1853. But this pioneering effort could not be sustained, for the diocese was too poor. Even a special diocesan collection instituted in 1852 was unable to save the institution. Most of the students were sent to other seminaries where the bishop supported their studies. The *Metropolitan Catholic Almanac* of 1855 reports that Bishop O'Reilly had '22 young men studying for the priestly state.'

The most important sources of priests for the diocese were the Irish seminaries at Maynooth and All Hallows, Dublin. O'Reilly's letters to the superiors of these institutions had a constant theme: 'I am sorely distressed for the want of priests.' Sometimes requesting two clerics for his American mission, at other times pleading for four, Bishop O'Reilly steadily increased the number of priests in his diocese, but he was not always satisfied with the products he received. Demanding absolute obedience and dedication, he could not understand why 'I have to labour at the Cathedral with one priest, where four were required, whilst my young priests were taking what is called recreation.' During his tenure, this fiery prelate removed at least five pastors for various reasons ranging from mismanagement of parish affairs to lack of obedience. Courageous and indefatigable, O'Reilly was a man of and for the times. His tense and stormy episcopacy coincided with an era of crisis for the Church of Providence, and he met that crisis well.

The Sisters of Mercy Arrive

Early in 1851 the Sisters of Mercy accepted O'Reilly's invitation to his diocese. This was to have a beneficial and enduring effect upon the Church in Rhode Island. The bishop's motives were clear. Faced with a public school system with strong Protestant overtones, he sought an alternative that would provide a Catholic value-oriented education. In addi-

Mother Mary Francis Xavier Warde, American foundress of the Sisters of Mercy.

tion, he had a special desire to aid the orphans of the diocese, who, through the untimely death of their parents or as a result of abandonment were sometimes placed in Protestant homes. The bishop hoped to expand the *Young Catholic Friends Society* founded at St. Patrick's in 1848 into an ongoing orphanage. For this dual purpose — education and social welfare — the Sisters of Mercy came to Rhode Island.

Their order was young. Its first house was founded in 1831 by Mother Catherine McAuley in Dublin. The first sister to arrive in the United States, Mother Mary Francis Xavier Warde, came in 1843 to Pittsburgh at the urging of Bishop Michael O'Connor. It appears that O'Connor suggested the Order to his friend Bernard O'Reilly, a fortunate recommendation indeed. Mother Xavier Warde, the 'American foundress,' and four sisters arrived in Providence on March 11, 1851 while Bishop O'Reilly was visiting parishes in Connecticut. He had made tentative arrangements for their stay by purchasing a small house on High (Westminster) Street. Upon his return, he attempted to obtain the home of a Providence jeweler on the corner of Broadway and Carpenter Streets, which would be large enough for a combination convent, school, and orphanage. Neighbors of the embarrassed merchant raised such a cry against the proposed sale that the bishop withdrew from the bargain 'not wishing to disturb the peace of any neighbor.' In May he purchased the Stead estate at the corner of Broad and Claverick Streets with a frame house on the adjacent lot, now the site of Saint Xavier's High School.

Within a year the Mercy community had expanded to thirteen. The sisters took over the schools at the Cathedral and St. Patrick's in 1851, and those at St. Mary's (Newport) and St. Joseph's (Providence) in 1854. In addition, they assumed the care of nineteen female orphans at the Mercy convent. To support their constantly expanding ministry to the orphans, the sisters instituted an annual Orphan's Fair that received the widespread support of both Catholic and Protestant communities. In 1852 these commendable efforts were extended to New Haven and Hartford where new orphan asylums were soon opened.

The Mercy Convent at Broad and Claverick Streets, Providence in 1851. This was the site of the Know-Nothing demonstration against the "female Jesuits" in 1855.

Catholic education, the principal function of the sisters, was a prime concern of O'Reilly. During the 1850s, the bishop provided the impetus for the expansion of Catholic schools in Rhode Island. His report on education in 1855 was a forerunner of the position that would be officially adopted later in the century by the Third Plenary Council. Reflecting on the attitude of his fellow bishops he said:

> It is hoped that in a little time every congregation in the diocese will have its school. If we wish to save the rising generation to religion and God, we will, even at sacrifice, give them a thorough Catholic education; nothing short of this will protect youth against error, and save them to religion.

The entire Catholic community responded to this exhortation. The Sisters of Mercy over the next decade undertook the education of most young women in parish elementary schools. Their efforts were augmented by a dedicated group of laymen who taught those young men not forced by family circumstances to work long hours in the factories. Parents also recognized the importance of Catholic education by tolerating the inferior physical plants that passed for school buildings in this early period. A pioneer Mercy nun reminisced on this cooperative attitude:

> They are convinced that any of the inconveniences of heat or cold, or uncomfortable school furniture which the children will have to endure, cannot do them any material harm, as it will continue on for a comparatively short time, and they think it is sufficient compensation to have their children receive a Catholic education.

This enthusiasm for education manifested by Rhode Island's Catholic community resulted in the establishment by 1860 of seven elementary schools and one high school.

During the O'Reilly years, the original schools founded under Bishop Tyler continued and new ones were opened at St. Joseph's in Fox Point (1852), and St. Mary's in Pawtucket (1855). These early institutions were always under severe financial strain. St. Joseph's had to be closed twice before the parish was able to find sufficient funds to maintain the enterprise. Another constant problem was finding qualified teachers. Both St. Mary's in Pawtucket and St. Charles' in Woonsocket (established in 1859) solved this by securing lay personnel until Mercy nuns were available to operate their schools. In the case of the Woonsocket institution, it was not until 1869 that the Mercy faculty was available to replace its lay counterpart.

In 1855 Bishop O'Reilly opened the largest parochial school in the state in his Cathedral parish. Located on Lime Street near downtown Providence, this three-story frame building was built with money raised on three-penny contributions that the bishop often collected in person on the front steps of his Cathedral. It was originally intended as an elementary and secondary school for boys.

The first Catholic 'academy' or high school for male students in Rhode Island was housed for a brief period in the Lime Street structure. It was founded by O'Reilly in 1852, and its initial classes were held in the Cathedral basement. When the new school was completed the first floor was used for elementary instruction and the second was devoted to the boys' academy. The third floor, which was originally designed as a hall for school entertainments and dramatic presentations, was taken over by girl students almost immediately because of overcrowded conditions at the Mercy convent. This parish-sponsored boys' high school, which was run by priests and laymen, was forced to close in 1858 after O'Reilly's ill-fated mission to secure the Christian Brothers to staff it, so the girls took over the second floor of the Lime Street

Lessons in voice, piano, guitar and the harp were provided by the sisters to these early students of St. Xavier's Academy.

building as well.

There are few enrollment records available for the early Catholic schools. However, Americo L. Lapati, the historian of Catholic education in this state, provides figures on some of the parish units. From his estimates it appears that the total Catholic school enrollment by 1860 was 1,900 students. In addition to those formally attending Catholic institutions were the large numbers of children who participated in parish Sunday schools. While O'Reilly labeled these schools 'feeble auxiliaries to Catholic education," he recommended their continuance, since funds for building regular schools were lacking and because so many children were employed in factories. Catholic education made a formidable beginning in the years before the Civil War. A firm foundation was established for

High school assembly room of St. Xavier's Academy, the first Catholic secondary school in Rhode Island, fifty years after its founding.

the great expansion of teaching orders and parish institutions that occurred in later decades.

The quality of education in these first schools compared favorably with their public school counterparts. Much of the credit for this condition rests with Mother Mary Francis Xavier Warde, R.S.M., founder of the Mercy order in this country and its superior general until 1858. One of the foremost Catholic educators of the nineteenth century, her system for elementary schools was quite comprehensive compared to present approaches. The typical day consisted of two learning sessions separated by a two-hour break for lunch and recreation. The three-hour morning session and the two-hour afternoon period were devoted to mathematics, reading, writing, spelling, and English grammar, alternated with history, geography, English literature, and bookkeeping. At the core of this program was a thirty-minute daily catechism lesson based upon the illustration of religious truths by stories and examples rather than by mere recitation. Included in the curriculum were lessons on etiquette, hygiene, and character building. Sewing, mending, and knitting were also offered for the girls.

Under Mother Warde's supervision, St. Xavier's, the first Catholic secondary school in the state, opened in 1851. A boarding and day school combined, it served as a novitiate for postulants and as a finishing school for girls of families with sufficient means. It was first housed in the cottage on High Street and then in the Stead mansion, before moving into a newly built brick building on Claverick Street in 1856, the capacity of which was doubled nine years later. St. Xavier's curriculum expanded upon the traditional elementary subjects and placed added emphasis on conversational French, basic Latin, and the fine arts. Lessons in voice, piano, and guitar were included at additional cost. In 1874 the boarding department was transferred to the newly established St. Mary's Academy, Bay View.

The short-lived boys' academy on Lime Street, before closing in 1858, offered a double track curriculum for students desiring classical or commercial education. Because of O'Reilly's death on a mission to staff it, a permanent secondary school for boys would not become a reality until 1870 when the Fountain Street Academy opened. In 1871 the Christian Brothers came to Providence to man that facility, eventually called LaSalle Academy.

The Know-Nothing Movement

During the 1850s American Catholics experienced the most intense attack upon their faith ever mounted in this nation's history. The emotional phenomenon known as 'Know-Nothingism' swept the land like a prairie fire threatening to extinguish the Church and its immigrant flock. These flames of intolerance singed Rhode Island.

The Know-Nothing party originated in 1849 when Charles B. Allen of New York formed the secret and chauvinistic Order of the Star-Spangled Banner. Its object was to advance political support to nominees of the Whig and Democratic parties that were anti-immigrant and anti-Catholic in outlook. Like the later American Protective Association of the 1890s and the revived Ku Klux Klan of the twentieth century, their members feared the Catholic Church's allegiance to the Pope and the immigrants who carried this faith. The Order evolved rapidly into a political party called 'Know-Nothing' because of the secretiveness of its members. By 1854 the party was a potent force in American politics. Throughout the country Know-Nothing governors, legislators, and congressmen were

Industrialist Philip Allen, uncle of Thomas Wilson Dorr, benefactor of the churches of Sts. Peter and Paul and St. Patrick, advocate of equal voting rights for naturalized immigrants, and Democratic governor of Rhode Island from 1851 to 1853.

elected, and former president Millard Fillmore carried the organization's banner in the national election of 1856, receiving twenty-five percent of the popular vote.

The roots of the Know-Nothing or American party in Rhode Island rest in the Dorr War. The nativistic harangue of the 'Law and Order' men did not die out after the suppression of the quasi-rebellion. The increase of Irish immigration in the late 1840s and early 1850s produced an increasing fear of the foreign-born and their religion that lay just beneath the surface of Rhode Island affairs. The catalyst for the revival of nativism occurred in 1851 when Thomas Dorr's uncle, Philip Allen, was elected governor. Allen and his followers represented the liberal, urban branch of the Democratic party in the state. Strongly advocating the extension of suffrage to naturalized immigrants on the same basis enjoyed by native citizens, these Jacksonians made several abortive attempts to achieve this reform during their brief period of ascendancy. The victories of these Allen supporters over a split Whig party in 1852 and again in 1853 revived the old anti-Dorr sentiments as demonstrated by a *Providence Journal* comment on the danger of removing the suffrage restriction: 'Rhode Island will no longer be Rhode Island when that is done. It will become a province of Ireland: St. Patrick will take the place of Roger Williams, and the shamrock will supercede the anchor and Hope.'

When the Democratic-controlled legislature offered a referendum in 1853 on calling a new constitutional convention to liberalize the suffrage, the issue became clear-cut. The Whig party, which had begun to divide over the slavery question, moved steadily toward the Know-Nothing position and the referendum was soundly defeated. By 1854 nativist Whigs realigned themselves with those rural Democrats from South County and the western hill towns who feared the liberalism of their party's urban wing. This coalition was similar to the Law and Order faction that had vanquished Dorr. It was supplemented, however, by many native-born newcomers to politics from the working-classes who were restless and disgusted with the existing leadership of the two major parties. The novelty of the emergent American party, its chauvinistic nativism, the chance it offered the common man for participation in the decision-making process, and its repudiation of the political establishment made it

This illustration depicts Irish Catholic priests and laity firing the "ecclesiastical canon" from "Fort St. Patrick" at the United States Public School System. It represents the ongoing Catholic effort, pioneered by John Hughes in New York, to get public funds for private schools, thereby making less money available for public education. This demand particularly incensed *Harper's Weekly* cartoonist Thomas Nast.

an attractive alternative for these disgruntled voters. By 1855 the Whig party disintegrated and the Democrats were eclipsed by a combination of antislavery and nativist factions that built separate organizations but nominated almost identical state tickets. These factions — the antislave Republicans and the nativistic American party — were politically dominant during the 1850s. Gradually they fused under the Republican label with suffrage restriction a common bond.

Anti-Catholic feeling was further fanned by controversies over education which developed in the 1851–54 period. Questions of Bible reading in the public schools and government aid to Catholic schools became burning issues when volatile Archbishop John Hughes of New York demanded separate Bibles for Catholic students in public schools and financial aid to church institutions. The spin-off from this New York affair was felt in Rhode Island when a Providence Catholic who taught at St. Patrick's, John Coyle, advanced these demands locally in 1853. The question of financial aid, of course, received no hearing, but Elisha R. Potter, Jr., state commissioner of education, and the influential *Providence Journal* agreed that it would be inconsistent with the state's religious heritage not to allow Catholic school children the use of their own version of the Scriptures. Potter contended that 'the reading of the Bible or conducting other devotional exercises at the opening or closing of schools is neither forbidden nor commanded by law, and rests with the teacher, who should respect his own conscience and the consciences of his pupils and their parents.' This enlightened view was not held by many, and the intolerant majority continued to demand that the Protestant Bible be exclusively retained.

Opponents of Catholic education also used the truancy device to combat the growth and influence of parochial schools. In 1853 two bills dealing with truancy were introduced into the Rhode Island legislature. The proposed legislation empowered towns and cities to provide by ordinance for the punishment of truant children between the ages of five and fifteen. Under the terms of these measures, successfully opposed by Commissioner Potter, students not attending *public* schools would be regarded as truants and subjected to disciplinary action. Both bills passed the House but died in the Senate.

After the nativists gained control of the state in 1855 a series of articles from the Know-Nothing mouthpiece, the *Providence Daily Tribune,* inflamed a debate in the state legislature over the tax-free incorporation of Bishop O'Reilly's infant asylum. These essays accused the Sisters of Mercy of kidnapping a child and holding her in their convent. While the tax exemption measure gained approval in the lower

Elisha R. Potter, Jr., an opponent of the Dorrite movement in 1842, drafted an enlightened statement on Bible-reading in the public schools in 1854 while he was state commissioner of education. In 1861 Potter, as state senator, sponsored a bill to give equal voting rights to naturalized citizens who fought for the Union cause. This able historian and civil servant was also a United States congressman (1843–1845) and an associate justice of the Rhode Island Supreme Court (1868–1882).

house, the Senate refused to act upon it until an anti-Catholic bill was passed that would allow local school committees to visit and inspect tax-free institutions (the so-called 'Nunnery Bill'). The Senate remained adamant on this question so both acts were passed but only after the incorporation bill was amended to lower the amount of tax-free valuation on the asylum from $100,000 to $50,000.

This Thomas Nast cartoon in *Harper's Weekly* shows rowdy "Irish Roman Catholic children" kicking the King James' Version of the Bible out of the public schools.

The legislative debate spilled over into the community where the scurrilous *Daily Tribune* repeated its kidnapping charge under the title 'Mysterious Disappearance — Probable Abduction.' A situation was developing not unlike that which preceded the Ursuline Convent burning in Boston two decades before.

The spirit of native intolerance was further inflamed by the issue of 'Rum and Romanism.' Temperance reform for Protestants and Catholics was a leading concern in this era, and since the 1840s interested citizens and groups worked to rid the state of 'Demon Rum.' The Catholic Church's stand, however, had traditionally left moral regeneration to the individual conscience rather than to state enforcement as Protestants demanded. As a result of these conflicting views, the temperance cause in the state became another storm center of controversy that was further clouded by nativism.

The urban Democrats under Philip Allen were lax in enforcing the 1852 'Act for the Suppression of Drinking Houses and Tippling Shops,' a half-way prohibition measure directed against small grog shops, many of which were run by immigrants (such as Nicholas Gordon) and frequented by the working class. Of course, the Yankee mill worker drank as much as the Irish mechanic but, as one scholar puts it, the 'Irish were louder' and more boisterous. This more conspicuous Irish intemperance furnished additional ammunition for nativists in the mid-1850s.

Know-Nothing strength increased throughout 1854 and 1855 in proportion to the anti-Catholic sentiment raised by the local issues of suffrage reform, Bible reading in public schools, aid to Catholic education, and temperance. It was further augmented by the incongruous currents of antislavery and bigotry that were sweeping the land. State elections in 1855 brought a resounding Know-Nothing victory. The *Providence Journal* commented upon the electoral results:

> The election passed off very quietly, the result being a foregone conclusion. The vote is light, but the majorities are enormous. Our returns embrace the entire state, except Cumberland and the two island towns, and the Know-Nothings have carried all but two, Gloucester and Foster.... All other members of both Houses are Know-Nothings. We have classed them as Whigs or Democrats, so far as we are acquainted with their politics, but we suppose that the distinction will not be raised.

Fortunately, the Know-Nothing ascendancy of 1855 did not produce any serious legislative assaults upon the local Catholic community, although the party flirted with a measure that would have required twenty-one years of residence before a foreigner could apply for citizenship. The most formidable Know-Nothing threat came not in the General Assembly but

A contemporary cartoonist ridicules the activities of inspecting committees created under anti-Catholic "nunnery bills" such as that passed by the Rhode Island General Assembly in 1855 at the height of the Know-Nothing movement.

outside the Mercy Convent on Broad Street in March 1855.

Pitted against this rise of anti-Catholicism in Rhode Island was the strong-willed Bishop O'Reilly, derisively called 'Paddy the Priest' by some local natives and their children. Like his counterpart in New York, John Hughes, the bishop never backed down from a fight. As vicar general in Buffalo, he had used the pen to defend the Sisters of Charity in a newspaper joust with a local Protestant minister. When Know-Nothing sentiment increased, O'Reilly escalated his defense to meet it.

In 1851, using the pseudonym 'Roger Williams,' he had denounced the imprisonment of Catholic soldiers from Connecticut at Fort Columbus, New York because they had refused to attend Protestant services. Two years later a series of articles appeared in the *Providence Journal* signed by 'Sentinel' projecting the Know-Nothing line that the Church of Rome was the most serious threat to the civil and religious liberty of the world. This assault led to a war of articles with the Catholic position strongly defended by 'Vindex.' The identity of 'Vindex' has not been conclusively established, but there is reason to believe he was the pugnacious O'Reilly. The popularity of 'Sentinel's' rhetoric prompted the *Journal* to give prime space to his diatribes and on one occasion to expand its edition to six pages to accommodate his lengthy articles.

This rise of anti-Catholic feeling was noted by O'Reilly in a letter to the superior at All Hallows: 'Bigotry is greatly on the increase here and throughout the length and breath of this land . . . the good Providence of God has protected us so far, yet there may be at any moment an avalanche outburst of Protestant hatred against us. . . . This city and state is eminently puritanical and exceedingly hostile to Catholicity. Ask your religious community to pray for the triumph of religion in this diocese.'

Even O'Reilly could not repudiate every attack upon the Church, for the times were too turbulent and the state virtually inundated by anti-Catholic lectures and literature. In the 1852–54 period Rhode Island was visited by a series of malcontents. Two apostate priests, Fathers Gavazzi and Leo, lectured against the 'popish church,' 'Claudius Petrat' commented upon his book *The Jesuits Unveiled,* and an itinerant stump-speaker thrilled audiences by recounting his part in tarring and feathering a priest in Maine. These visits, augmented by the dissemination of traditional anti-Catholic literature such as the tales of Maria Monk, helped the state succumb to the tune of 'Sam,' the Know-Nothing pied piper.

In March 1855 the most serious manifestation of Know-Nothingism in Rhode Island occurred. It was aimed at the 'female Jesuits,' the Sisters of Mercy, who, because of their 'mysterious' community life, became a target for extremists. The sisters had for the most part been welcomed by open-minded citizens of Providence in 1851, but during the ensuing years their convent windows had been broken on several occasions, taunts shouted at them, and in early 1855 two sisters had their bonnets and shawls pulled off by a 'rowdy gang.' The child abduction slander ignited a general public distrust of the sisters that flared into a near riot at the Mercy Convent in March 1855.

On March 20, the Know-Nothing tabloid, the *Providence Tribune*, printed a lurid story concerning the 'captivity' of Rebecca Newell within the convent walls. Miss Newell became an immediate martyr, and the nuns were adjudged guilty by a gullible public. The story was repudiated by the *Providence Journal* the following day after a visit to the 'captive' in the convent by the mayor and the paper's editor, but even this authoritative statement, accompanied by Miss Newell's own response, did not allay the fears and doubts of the citizenry. On the same day a handbill appeared urging 'Native American born' citizens to appear at the convent at 8 p.m. on March 22, where 'Proceedings of the most solemn and unquestionable nature will be transacted. One and all to the rescue.' The *Journal,* trying to remain a Whig organ, but still courting Know-Nothing support, graciously reprinted the handbill with directions to the convent in its March 22 edition.

Bishop O'Reilly reacted vigorously to the threat. He asked for and received promises of protection from the authorities. He also called upon his flock, and they responded before the mob arrived. Historian Austin Dowling stated that 'Every foot of ground behind the hedge of the convent yard was alive with an Irishman.' Fearing the worst, the bishop sent his will and other valuable church records to Hartford; then he proceeded to the convent where over 2,000 people had gathered. Courageously addressing them he said, 'The Sisters are in their home; they shall not leave it even for an hour. I shall protect them while I have life, and if need be register their safety with my blood.'

Fortunately, the crowd was leaderless and the bishop was able to walk among them. The would-be rioters dispersed after scattered name calling and rock throwing. The high water mark of Know-Nothingism had been reached in the state and violence did not prevail.

In restrospect, the attitude of native Rhode Islanders to the Irish Catholic immigrant community was understandable if not justifiable. The Yankees of 1855 saw the Irish as a threat to traditional American institutions and values. When the newcomers — impoverished and often illiterate — tried to improve themselves, they became bitter economic rivals in the

> **AMERICANS!**
>
> TO WHOM THESE PRESENTS MAY COME.
>
> GREETING:
>
> WHEREAS, certain rumors are afloat, of a certain transaction, of a certain ANTI–SAM party in the vicinity of the corner of Claverick and Broad streets, every true Native American Born Citizen, is requested, one and all, to assemble there, Thursday Evening, March 22nd, 1855, at 8 o'clock, precisely. There with true regard to Law, and consulting the feelings and sympathies of SAM, proceedings of the most solemn and unquestionable nature will be transacted.
>
> One and All to the Rescue!! The Password is "SHOW YOURSELF."

The *Providence Journal* obligingly reprinted this Know-Nothing handbill on the eve of the convent demonstration. "Sam" was the mythical leader of the American party.

eyes of the unskilled native workers. Their life-style and socio-economic condition produced a disproportionate rate of crime, violence, intemperance, and pauperism when compared with the native population. Their authoritarian and dogmatic religion branded these Irish arrivals as a threat to American democracy, yet their numbers portended future political power.

The Pontiff of the age, Pius IX — after an early career as a liberal churchman — became a symbol of the old order and the Old World because of his opposition to the secular interests of Italian nationalism and his general defense of hereditary and 'legitimate' regimes. Thus the rise of liberalism and nationalism in Europe had strong anti-Catholic and anti-clerical overtones, while the forces of continental conservatism were strongly attached to the Church as a bulwark against change. All of these factors, when added to the traditional New England religious antipathy to the Church of Rome, make it easier to understand the native mind and the dangers Americans of all classes saw in the Irish immigrant and the 'foreign' Church he so strongly supported. Given the human condition, the native reaction was as predictable as it was unfortunate.

In Rhode Island these fears were slow to subside in the nineteenth century due to the rapid influx of immigrants from French Canada, Italy, Portugal, Poland and other Catholic nations. The most tangible reminder of native distrust was the extremely restrictive suffrage qualification imposed on the state's foreign born. Indeed, during the post-Civil War period, United States Senator Henry Bowen Anthony could only retreat to an obstinate and nativistic rebuttal when challenged by southern congressmen who asserted that he adhered to a double standard — support of the 14th and 15th amendments guaranteeing suffrage for freed blacks contrasted with opposition to the removal of the real property qualification for the foreign born in his own state. This hypocrisy must have presented a disturbing paradox to the immigrant since Rhode Island's political leaders were advocates of other social panaceas like abolition and temperance reform.

Despite these feelings, Rhode Island's flirtation with Know-Nothingism was moderate. No burnings, murders, or sacrilegious rioting occurred, as they did elsewhere in America. Even the visit in 1853 of the Papal Nuncio — Archbishop Cajetan Bedini — was peaceful, while his tour of the rest of the country raised havoc in most locales. Here bigotry was less violent but more subtle, less inflammatory but no less enduring, as future generations of Catholics would painfully come to realize.

By late 1856 the Know-Nothing or American party was evaporating as quickly and mysteriously as it came. But it left a legacy of bitterness in the hearts of its Irish Catholic opponents, and it helped to effect a realignment of political parties that influenced Rhode Island politics for generations to come. When the state's newly formed Republican party gradually absorbed both the Know-Nothing adherents and the intolerant spirit of that nativistic organization, Irish Catholic opposition to the Republicans became intense and nearly immutable.

Rhode Island's political culture in the late nineteenth and early twentieth centuries cannot be properly understood without reference to the religious antagonisms generated by Know-Nothingism in the decade of the 1850s and the partisan alignments that developed from the turbulent conflict between Yankee and Celt.

Growth Under Bishop O'Reilly

Throughout the O'Reilly episcopacy, the major problems of the diocese remained the same — the poverty of the faithful and the need for priests. The first approximate census count of Catholics in Rhode Island, undertaken by the bishop's successor in 1857, calculated some 30,000 residing in scattered parishes and missions from Woonsocket and Burrillville in the north to Newport, Wakefield, and Westerly in the south. The vast majority of these would today be labeled subsistence families who were most seriously affected by the fluctuations of the economic cycle and the ravages of disease. Thomas Hazard's report to the General Assembly in 1851 on the status of the poor and insane gives some insight into conditions. At the Dexter Asylum in Providence he found that of the 136 inmates (women and children included) sixty-one were born in Ireland, and the rest were native American or immigrants from England, France and Portugal. A survey in 1858 showed 163 inmates of whom 103 were native Irish.

While the government maintained a limited program for the poor, their numbers far outdistanced the facilities. The Providence overseer of the poor made many referrals to Bishop O'Reilly who, lacking funds,

A tattered Irishman contemplates a trip to "Amerikay" on the "Shamrock Line" in this painting by Scotsman Erskine Nicol.

"As my diocese reaches almost to the city of New York where the great part of the immigrants . . . arrive, the poor come continually . . . to look for employment in the factories in my area. . . ." This was Bishop O'Reilly's observation at the time these Irish immigrants landed at the Battery in 1855. The trunk in the lower right corner is labeled "Pat Murfy, for Ameriky."

could do little for them. This situation led to the formation of St. Vincent de Paul societies on the parish level beginning with the Cathedral unit in November 1853. This decentralized system of aid provided the necessities of life to those members of the parish family whose circumstance rendered them helpless. The societies, through the church poor box, lectures, and other events, raised funds for the sick and poor and gave them food and clothing. The Providence Vincentians also established a library-reading room, open evenings, and in 1857 founded the Brownson Lyceum, which quickly became the leading Catholic literary society in Rhode Island. Local units (of which there were five by 1872) remained the backbone of the diocese's social welfare program until the third decade of the twentieth century when the Catholic Charity Fund Appeal was instituted.

Since all of the parishes were poor in material resources, Bishop O'Reilly relied heavily upon the generosity of European missionary organizations. The universality of the Church made it possible for him to receive substantial aid from the Society for the Propagation of the Faith in Paris, the Ludwig Mission Association in Munich, and the Leopoldine Society in Vienna. An 1856 letter to the council for the Propagation of the Faith expressed his constant plea: 'The Catholics in these two states which comprise the diocese of Hartford have risen to between 55,000 and 65,000 souls. The two states are sustained principally by factories of different kinds; a great part of our Catholics are employed in these establishments. As my diocese reaches almost to the city of New York where the great part of the immigrants who come to the United States arrive, the poor come continually in such great numbers to look for employment in the factories of my area, so that the employers can hire the poor at a wage which they wish to offer. For this reason our Catholic population is utterly poor; I can even say that there is not a Catholic family in the diocese which can live without working.'

The money he received went to establish schools and parishes, educate seminarians, and relieve the

THE FORMATIVE ERA

plight of the poor. This support helped to create a number of new parishes and missions. In Providence, St. Joseph's in Fox Point (1851) and St. Mary's Broadway (1853) were established. The Hope Street parish commissioned noted architect Patrick Keely to design a suitable edifice and Keely's handiwork, St. Joseph's Church, was completed and blessed on December 19, 1853.

The Broadway parish was created primarily to serve the spiritual needs of Catholic workers in the Olneyville mills, but under its first pastor John Quinn, (1853–73), it initially serviced the Catholic population who lived in the area extending from the Auburn

St. Joseph's Parish on Hope Street, Providence was founded in 1851 to serve the Catholics of the Fox Point section. The church, designed by Patrick Keely, was completed and blessed on December 19, 1853.

section of Cranston to Georgiaville in the town of Smithfield — a parcel from which approximately two dozen parishes were eventually carved. The original wooden church, built in 1853, was in use by the parish until destroyed in the hurricane of 1938, but it was superseded as the primary place of worship in 1869 by a magnificent granite structure of Gothic design.

In the outlying areas, a parish was begun at St. Mary's in Warren (1851) under the direction of a Missouri native, the Reverend Hilary Tucker. The third pastor of this parish, the Reverend Michael McCallion, held that post from May 1854 until his death in August 1892 and was the dominant force in the Catholic life of Bristol County.

Mission churches were erected at various points throughout the state including Sts. Peter and Paul in Phenix (1853), Our Lady of Mercy (originally the Holy Name of Jesus) in East Greenwich (1853), St. Francis's in Wakefield (1854), St. Mary's in Bristol

Father James Gibson of St. Mary's ("Our Lady of Mount Carmel") in Crompton. He served the Catholics of the Pawtuxet Valley from 1851 until his death in 1892. He founded the mission of Sts. Peter and Paul, Phenix in 1853.

(1855), St. Philip's in Greenville (about 1856), and at St. Patrick's in Harrisville (1857) where a parish had been established three years earlier. The growing Irish Catholic community in Westerly attended St. Mary's Church (1851) in distant Stonington, Connecticut until Father Michael O'Reilly moved his pastoral residence to Westerly in 1861 when the construction of St. Michael's Church was completed in the adjacent Connecticut village of Pawcatuck.

In addition to his writing campaign to obtain priests and religious for these new parishes and missions, Bishop O'Reilly made two journeys to Europe to secure clergy and solicit funds. His first trip in 1852 resulted in a chance meeting at Maynooth seminary with a zealous Irish youth who intended to begin a career with the Jesuit missions in China or Japan. Hoping to win a priest for his diocese, the bishop described to the lad the challenge of New England life and the poverty of America's immigrant Church. So persuasive was O'Reilly that the young seminarian agreed to forget the Far East and decided to pursue his vocation in the Diocese of Hartford. In the following year this young missionary, Thomas F. Hendricken, was ordained to the priesthood, and in less than two decades he became the first bishop of Providence.

Late in 1855 the indefatigable O'Reilly journeyed again to Europe in search of a male teaching order to staff the Boys' Academy that he had opened on Lime Street in 1852. Hoping to obtain Christian Brothers for the faculty, the bishop traveled in France and Belgium with little success. Returning to Ireland to see his parents, he tried his persuasive powers on the Irish brothers. After a short stay and without a definite commitment from the Order, O'Reilly embarked on the steamship *Pacific* for the dangerous winter passage to Boston. The ship left Liverpool on January 23, 1856 and was never heard from again. After a period of waiting filled with unfounded rumors — one to the effect that O'Reilly was not aboard the ill-fated craft and another alleging he was being held prisoner in Germany — the bishops of the New York province met and declared the see vacant. A

St. Mary's, Broadway outgrew the original wooden church (at right) and completed its beautiful granite Gothic church in 1869. This inspiring Christmas scene was done by Providence artist Charles H. Springer in 1891.

requiem Mass was celebrated on June 17, 1856 in the Cathedral at which Archbishop John Hughes delivered the eulogy for his friend and protégé.

In five short years Bernard O'Reilly had left his unmistakable imprint upon the diocese. A man of discipline, courage, and Christian zeal, he increased the number of parishes in the two-state diocese to forty-six with thirty-seven mission stations. Inheriting thirteen priests, he left forty-two, with twenty-two students supported in various seminaries. His dedication to Catholic education brought the Sisters of Mercy to the diocese and the establishment of the first Catholic high school in Rhode Island. He attempted to found a seminary, held the first diocesan synod in October 1854 and contributed to the establishment of three orphan asylums in his diocese including St. Aloysius Home (then known as St. Mary's). His unflinching defense of Catholicism against the Know-Nothing threat distinguished him as a leader of his people and a champion of religious toleration. As an immigrant, Bishop O'Reilly left a truly impressive record while laboring for his immigrant flock.

Bishop Francis P. McFarland —
Compassionate Scholar

The see of Hartford remained vacant for almost two years while the bishops of the New York province awaited information confirming Bishop O'Reilly's death. In the interim the Reverend William O'Reilly, the bishop's brother, served as administrator. After eighteen months, with all hope gone, they proceeded to elect Francis Patrick McFarland third bishop of Hartford.

A first-generation American of Irish parents who had settled in Waynesboro, Pennsylvania early in the nineteenth century, McFarland was born in 1819 at the family farm in Franklin. A child of superior ability, he attended local schools and went on to a teaching career at age eighteen in the academy at Chambersburg, Pennsylvania. His decision to study for the priesthood was made in 1839 when he entered Mt. St. Mary's Seminary in Maryland where he was immediately recognized as a sound scholar. After six years of study, he was ordained by John Hughes in New York.

Following a brief tenure teaching philosophy and theology at Fordham, he became pastor of a church in Watertown, New York, on the Canadian border. His parish included Brownsville, Sackett's Harbor and Carthage, which with Watertown, had been the scene of armed conflict between Americans and British

The Reverend John Quinn, D.D., First Pastor, Church of Saint Mary, Broadway, Providence, Rhode Island. Father Quinn took charge of the parish upon the dedication of the original church, May 29, 1853. He died June 8, 1873. The monument in front of the present church marks the place of his burial.

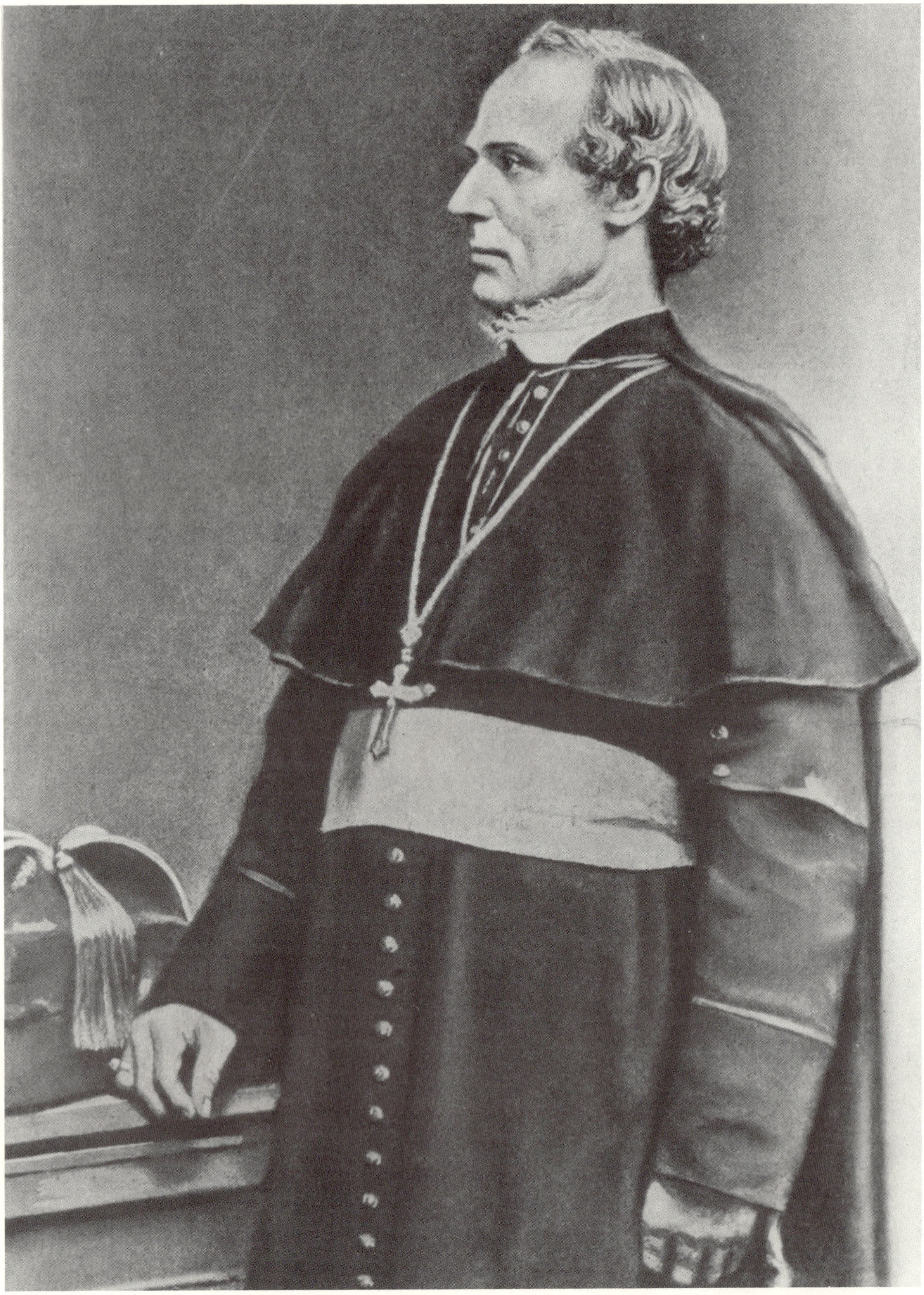

THE FORMATIVE ERA

Canadians during the prior decade. Inhabited mostly by Irish who had emigrated to the area after building the Erie Canal, these rugged towns offered a challenge to any young pastor. Traveling through his 'parish' on horseback the earnest priest labored four years in these missions. His work was rewarded in 1851 with an appointment as pastor of St. John's Church in Utica.

During his New York ministry McFarland gained a reputation for personal kindness, self-denial, patience, and hard toil. Recognizing his ability, Pius IX named him vicar-apostolic of Florida in 1857 but, desiring to stay with his congregation in the Diocese of Albany, he declined the prestigious post. A year later the bishops of New York province chose him to fill the vacancy at Hartford. Accepting the papal commission, he journeyed to Providence to be consecrated by Archbishop Hughes on March 14, 1858. Delivering the sermon on that day was Bishop John McCloskey of Albany, McFarland's former superior, who later became archbishop of New York and the first American cardinal.

Tall, erect, and austere-looking, the new bishop was a marked contrast to his predecessor. While O'Reilly was a hard-driving man whose relentless energy, courage, and powerful oratory were the badges of leadership, McFarland — more methodical and scholarly — won the respect of his people and the entire Rhode Island community in a different way. A man of great kindness and understanding, the bishop was a firm leader and a fine orator but one whose gentle and humble ways made him most approachable.

During the mid-nineteenth century there were two dissimilar traditions prevalent among Rhode Island Catholic clergymen. One was Irish-Catholic — zealous, militant, defensive, insular and antagonistic to the native Protestant community. Its archetype was Bishop Bernard O'Reilly. The other, a minority tradition, may be called Yankee-Catholic. It consisted of native American converts to the faith like Bishop William Tyler and conciliatory clerics who attempted to build bridges to the local Protestant community. Bishop McFarland belonged to this more tolerant tradition. His diary speaks of preaching in a local Protestant church and subscribing $500 to the establishment of Rhode Island Hospital on whose corporation he later served. As the emotionalism of the Know-Nothing movement subsided, the bishop was able to raise the level of religious dialogue to a more rational plane. During his fourteen years in Providence, he defended the Church's teachings and persuasively explained the most difficult doctrines of the day — the Immaculate Conception and, after the first Vatican Council, papal infallibility. His forte was Catholic apologetics. Through his learned approach he helped to alleviate tensions between the immigrant and native communities.

The plight of the less fortunate disturbed this sensitive man. At a forum of local clergymen on the American Indian in 1860, he said that a plan would have to be devised to protect the Indian from the 'lawless aggressions' of 'wicked men.' He urged that efforts to aid them should be based upon 'influences of the heart' rather than upon 'any attempt to indoctrinate them into a system of ideas!' On another occasion he petitioned William Sprague, Rhode Island's governor, to pardon a long-imprisoned criminal whose family had pledged to care for the disturbed offender. Other special concerns were the plight of the orphan and the education of Catholic youth. Sincere interest in his fellow man was a hallmark of McFarland's episcopacy. He was as gentle and compassionate as O'Reilly was militant and assertive.

Rhode Island Catholics and the Civil War

Our nation's greatest internal upheaval, the Civil War, was a testing ground that helped to lessen native fears of Catholic immigrants, especially the Irish. Galvanized by a desire to 'preserve the Union,' Irish immigrants and their sons fought side by side with Yankee boys. Sharing the same hardships and spilling their blood in the most costly battles in our coun-

Francis Patrick McFarland, third Bishop of Hartford (1858–74).

Crowds lined Exchange Place, Providence to see a Rhode Island regiment off to war in 1861. Irish-Americans served in all units and the small Franco-American community furnished fifty-six men. Local Catholic support for the Union cause helped lessen the prejudice against them.

try's history, they forged a common bond that diminished but did not eliminate the bitterness and distrust of the preceding decade.

In the north, Catholic sentiment stood behind Abraham Lincoln and the Union. The president's 1861 appointment of Archbishop John Hughes as a special emissary charged with persuading France's emperor Napoleon III to remain neutral was a factor in stimulating the Catholic war effort. The generalship of the devout William Rosecrans, a builder of St. Mary's, Newport, and Philip Sheridan swelled the pride of the Catholic population, and the ministrations of the nuns to the wounded earned them the title 'angels of the battlefield.' In a sense Catholic immigrants were given a chance to show their loyalty and prove themselves as Americans in an ordeal by battle.

An interesting aspect of this period was the Catholic attitude toward slavery. The official teachings of the Church did not condemn slavery since theoretically the institution was not opposed to the divine or natural law. In 1839 Pope Gregory XVI had reiterated the statements of earlier pontiffs by specifically denouncing the slave trade in his apostolic letter to the bishops of the world. In the United States, most Church leaders failed to question openly the 'peculiar institution.' Decidedly against abolitionism, the bishops adopted a stance that urged compliance with the established laws of the land. Their policy condemned the excesses of slavery, emphasized the protection of slave marriages, and urged improvement of the slave's condition.

In general, the Catholic laity was also adverse to abolitionism. Southern Catholics — most of them Irish and French — accepted the system and fought to preserve it. In the north and especially in the northeast, the Irish rejected any fusion with the abolitionists because leaders of this crusade were in many cases the same individuals who had spearheaded the Know-Nothing movement. With the coming of war, the Catholic hierarchy and laity with few exceptions followed the views of their section. The American Church for the most part did not enter the political arena or raise the question of the morality of slavery; rather its viewpoint reflected a strictly legalistic policy tempered by compassion for black men, women, and children.

In Rhode Island the reaction of the Catholic community followed the national trend. On the eve of the conflict, Bishop McFarland in a pastoral letter urged prayers for peace: 'If we turn to God with our whole hearts in humility and confidence, we may hope that He will turn from His fierce anger and deliver us from the evils that threaten us.' Later in 1861, preaching at the Cathedral, McFarland echoed the viewpoint of his fellow American bishops when he lectured on 'The Catholic Church and Slavery.' After reviewing the historical development of slavery throughout the world, the bishop rejected immediate emancipation as the answer and war as a tool to achieve it. 'Slavery, whether we consider it an evil or a sin is to be cured by removing the cause and eradicating the evil passions which have made slaves and slaveholders,' he said. This was to be done by a return of the community to the 'teachings of the Master,' for 'a slave cannot long be held by one who listens to these truths and believes.' Only then would emancipation be possible. Concluding his address, the bishop reiterated the Church's denunciation of the African slave trade and called for the necessary self-sacrifice to heal the nation's wound. There is little evidence regarding the attitude of the local Catholic community towards the question of slavery. It is reasonable to assume that it mirrored McFarland's position.

In the anxious weeks following the shelling of Fort Sumter, Rhode Island was prompt to answer Lincoln's call to arms. Governor William Sprague with the future Union general, Ambrose Burnside, led the First Rhode Island Regiment to Washington and the war's opening battle at Bull Run.

A chaplain of this regiment was the Reverend Thomas Quinn of the cathedral parish. Quinn had asked and received the bishop's consent to serve the spiritual needs of the Catholics in the unit. Commenting upon the unusual appointment, the thirty-two-year-old chaplain wrote to McFarland: 'I think that your permission that I should go on this duty has done a good deal towards annihilating the Protestant prejudice in Providence.' Father Quinn — a courageous but sometimes erratic cleric — saw action at Manassas and served briefly with the state's Third Regiment later in the war.

A more illustrious Civil War chaplain was the noted and prolific author, Monsignor Bernard O'Reilly, who served in the diocese for two years (1867–69) as pastor of St. Charles' Church in Woonsocket. O'Reilly distinguished himself by his heroic service with New York's famed Irish regiment, the 'Fighting 69th,' and later became the official biographer of Pope Pius IX.

Rhode Island provided a dozen regiments during the conflict. Early in the struggle the Irish citizens attempted to raise an exclusively immigrant unit, the Sarsfield Guards, but after eight companies enlisted the plan was abandoned and the Irish recruits were integrated with the formal state regiments. There are no exact figures regarding Catholic enlistments, but it is reasonable to assume that Catholics served in every Rhode Island unit, especially the Third Regiment. The Adjutant General's Report revealed that of the 23,457 soldiers that enlisted in Rhode Island regiments, 5,729 were of foreign birth or parentage, mostly Irish. This figure does not include those Rhode Islanders of foreign stock who enlisted in regiments of other states or enlistees in the Navy, and there was a considerable number in both these categories.

The *Providence Journal* described what was probably a typical send-off for Irish Catholic troops:

> About one hundred of the Roman Catholic soldiers assembled in the Cathedral Sunday morning, and after the celebration of mass, the Rev. Dr. Carmody addressed them in a very touching and interesting manner. In his address, the Doctor spoke to the men of the glorious cause for which they were to fight, and of the obligation they owed to this, their adopted country. Implicit obedience to their officers was most earnestly enjoined, and the men were exhorted to lead sober and pure lives, so that the examples of the Catholic soldiers might be as a shining light to the whole regiment.
>
> In accordance with a wish expressed by the pastor sufficient means were contributed to purchase prayer books and spiritual reading for the soldiers.

Father Hugh Carmody's advice to the troops emphasized the Catholic desire for acceptance without compromising their religious identity. His remarks illustrate the dilemma of Americanization that confronted the immigrant Catholic.

During four years of bloody strife, Rhode Island soldiers saw action at all of the major battles on the Virginia front — Antietam, Fredericksburg, Chancellorsville, Gettysburg, and the final campaign of Appomattox. Sixteen of the more than 23,000 Rhode Islanders who served received the Congressional Medal of Honor for acts of bravery, and among these heroic few, John Corcoran and James Welsh appear to be members of the local Catholic immigrant community.

On Saturday, April 15, 1865, Bishop McFarland's diary notes that he awakened to hear the news of

Father Bernard O'Reilly was a chaplain in New York's famed Irish regiment, "The Fighting Sixty-Ninth," attached to a company commanded by Thomas Francis Meagher. After the Civil War O'Reilly came to Woonsocket where he served briefly as pastor of St. Charles's parish from 1867 until January 1869, when he returned to New York. Later in his career the scholarly O'Reilly wrote numerous books including biographies of Pius IX and Leo XIII. He is shown here as he appeared in his mid-seventies, some thirty years after he left St. Charles.

The martial spirit was strong among the American Irish. This Irish militia company, depicted in Handlin's *Boston Immigrants*, had several Rhode Island counterparts in the post-Civil War era. The Boston *Pilot* in 1871 listed six such units — The Rhode Island Guards Battalion; the Kearney Cadets and the Wolfe Tone Guards of Providence; the Lonsdale Light Infantry; the Aquidneck Rifles of Newport; and the Light Infantry of Bristol.

Abraham Lincoln's assassination. The tragedy of the president's death ushered in the era of Reconstruction, and while the Rhode Island community enjoyed an initial period of material prosperity, the conditions of poverty wrought by the war in the South prompted the visit to Rhode Island of William Henry Elder, Bishop of Natchez, Mississippi. Elder, who had done pioneer work converting and educating slaves in the pre-war years, wrote to Bishop McFarland in November 1866, requesting permission to preach in the diocese with the hope of raising funds to rebuild Mississippi's war-torn churches. McFarland consented and the southerner raised $1,000 in Providence as he began his tour of the Rhode Island-Connecticut area. Elder returned again in 1868 and met with another warm reception.

Bishop Augustin Verot of Savannah, Georgia — once a strong secessionist — also preached in the state in an effort to raise money to care for the freed blacks of his diocese. These incidents reveal that the American Catholic Church, one of the few institutions that had remained united before and during the Civil War, was ready to play a significant role in effecting a peaceful reconciliation between the North and the South.

The Fenian Frenzy

In 1848 a revolutionary republican movement known as 'Young Ireland' was suppressed by the British government and its leaders were exiled. The spirit of rebellion persisted, however, and surfaced a decade later in the guise of the Irish Revolutionary Brotherhood founded in Dublin on March 17, 1858 by Young Irelander James Stephens. By April 1859 the society had spread to the United States. One of its American organizers, John O'Mahony, an exile of '48, reached into his store of Irish folklore and called the new revolutionary society the 'Fenians' after the heroic band of warriors, *Fianna Eireann*. The Fenian brotherhood was to be a modern replica of that ancient fighting force that would accomplish the design initiated by

National Fenian leader John O'Mahony addressed a large crowd of Fenian sympathizers at Rocky Point in 1865.

Wolfe Tone and carried forward by the '48 rebels — an Irish republic established by forceful revolt.

Based in New York and strongly imbued with the romantic idealism of the European liberals, the international society dreamt of freeing Ireland from centuries of English oppression. The Civil War gave impetus to the movement since Fenian leaders encouraged Irish soldiers to enlist their new-found military skill in the cause of Irish freedom once the American conflict had ended. Basically the American Fenian Brotherhood planned to supply money, arms, and, it was hoped, men to assist their Irish counterparts. To achieve these goals, O'Mahony called a national convention of interested Irishmen in 1863 and formed a secret society that became a quasi-Irish government in exile.

After the 1865 Fenian national convention in Philadelphia, the movement split over aims. One faction led by O'Mahony desired only to foment a revolution in Ireland, while the more popular group led by wealthy New Yorker, William Randall Roberts, hoped to use the large number of trained Irish soldiers just discharged by the Union and Confederate armies to launch an invasion of British Canada. By unleashing his Irish 'legions' Roberts wanted to instigate a war between the United States and England. If successful, this proposed conflict would divert the British and enable the movement in Ireland to secure its goal of independence.

As far-fetched as these schemes appear, the Fenian factions were in earnest. They were numerically strong — they boasted 45,000 members — and they had the moral support of a large segment of the Irish immigrant community. But their plans did not match their dreams and their efforts failed after a series of comic fiascoes. Attacks on Canada did take place — the first in 1866 when Civil War veteran John O'Neill led 800 followers from Buffalo, New York into a quixotic bout with Canadian militia — and the second in 1870 when Fenians made a foray across the border from St. Albans, Vermont, where they were driven back by one volley of rifle fire. The planned revolt in Ireland in 1867 also occurred but was easily suppressed. After the St. Albans raid the Fenian movement lost its vitality and its numbers. It lingered on for the next two decades with hopes unextinguished. But its peculiar, romantic appeal was gone.

The Fenian crusade had a direct bearing on Rhode Island. With its sizable Irish population and its proximity to New York, the state became a natural recruiting center for Fenianism. Early in 1865, New York organizers William J. Haynes and William Delaney brought the campaign for Irish independence to Providence and received a very enthusiastic reception. By August, support was so widespread that a state outing was held at Rocky Point in Warwick. Preceding the picnic, a parade was held in Providence with 1,500 marchers representing Fenian units from Pawtucket, Central Falls, Woonsocket, Cranston, Bristol, Harrisville, Newport, and the capital city. Arriving at Rocky Point by ferry and horse, over 5,000 supporters listened to national 'president' O'Mahony exhort the crowd to support the cause.

Under the leadership of state president Patrick McGreevey and able lieutenants Patrick O'Malley and John P. Cooney, most Rhode Island Fenians backed the O'Mahony faction when the movement split in 1866. A period of confusion over national allegiance ensued that was not settled until 1868 when the would-be conqueror of Canada, John O'Neill, appeared in Providence to heal the breach, and both factions united once again.

In 1868 Fenianism made a comeback in Rhode Island and cries for Irish independence were heard once more throughout the state. By 1870, however, the national movement began to wane, and its counterpart in Rhode Island also lost its vitality. The futile St. Albans raid, reaction to the violent Orange Riots in New York City, and the opposition of Bishop McFarland helped to discredit Fenianism locally.

During the five-year heyday of the brotherhood, the American Catholic Church looked with fear upon the movement, for it seemed analogous to the 'radical' republicanism that had engulfed Italy and other European countries. As early as 1865 Archbishop John McCloskey of New York had condemned the Fenians

THE FORMATIVE ERA

ENGLAND'S DIFFICULTY, IRELAND'S OPPORTUNITY.

The Fenian invasions of Canada were intended mainly as a diversionary tactic to preoccupy England in the New World while Ireland battled for her independence. This *Judge* cartoon, labeled "England's Difficulty, Ireland's Opportunity," shows a tattered Irish-American Fenian firing across the Canadian border ("Neutrality Fence") in an effort to distract and annoy England.

for their secretiveness and violence, but most American bishops, not wishing to alienate the Irish immigrant community, drew back from open condemnation. Bishop McFarland was in this difficult position. At least one of his clergy, Reverend Bernard O'Reilly of Woonsocket, was very sympathetic to the movement and a Fenian priest, Father Vaughn, visited the state on a lecture tour. Also, the state's Irish population vigorously supported the cause. While confiding in his diary distaste for the movement, the bishop waited until 1870 to oppose it openly. Reacting to the New York riots, he condemned the violence of that encounter and reiterated the Church's opposition to secret societies. His message was clear. It was followed by papal denunciation later the same year, and the movement disappeared from Rhode Island as quickly as it had come.

In 1870, however, the Ancient Order of Hibernians formed its first Rhode Island unit. This Irish fraternal organization also had a reputation for violence at this stage of its development. But the A.O.H. gradually shed its militancy and grew in numbers and respectability to become one of the most important Irish societies in the state.

The Politics of Prejudice

In the years before division of the diocese, Rhode Island Catholics became involved in major political and social questions of the day. The *Adopted Citizens' Association,* established in 1861 under the leadership of Peter A. Sinnot and Michael Brennan, worked strenuously during the Civil War years to secure the same voting rights for naturalized citizens as enjoyed by the native-born. The group — a forerunner of the Equal Rights party of the 1880s — was Catholic-led and quite vocal.

Another very dedicated group of reformers were the Catholic temperance advocates. These zealots, supported by the bishop, carried the message of abstinence to every parish in the state. Their campaign against the evils of 'John Barleycorn,' so ardently conducted in the 1850s, was submerged by the crises and dislocations of the Civil War but revived during the final years of McFarland's episcopacy.

The temperance movement was never embraced by a majority of the state's Catholic population, due primarily to the belief that alcohol was not evil in itself but only sinful when used in excess. Catholic temperance advocates stressed individual abstinence pledges as the most desirable way to achieve sobriety — a means that varied fundamentally from the position of Protestant churchmen who recommended state prohibition of the manufacture and sale of intoxicating liquor as the cure for overindulgence. Despite this difference in approach, Catholics had overcome some of their earlier apprehensions and were willing 'to stand together, shoulder to shoulder, battling for the cause of temperance' with their Protestant counterparts who dominated the new state movement.

The post-war Catholic temperance revival began in 1869. It took its inspiration from the memory of Father Mathew and its immediate impetus from visiting Passionist priests who preached temperance missions throughout the state in 1870. The movement's early history is traced in the pages of the *Boston Pilot,* which gave it detailed news coverage. The crusade spread rapidly throughout Rhode Island, and by October 1870 a Catholic State Temperance Union of Rhode Island was formed. Twelve parish units participated at the first state convention. The largest component in the new union was the Cathedral Total Abstinence Society with 523 members, while the combined statewide enrollment was estimated at 3,000 members. The aim of this 'Cold Water Army,' led by President James Cosgrove, was to win over those wage earners who were constantly tempted by the saloon. At the suggestion of Bishop McFarland, attention was also given to the children employed in the mills, who were recruited into 'cadet companies' that became auxiliaries to the adult units.

With the encouragement of both Bishop McFarland and his successor Bishop Hendricken, the temperance movement continued on a modest scale for the remainder of the century. Its adherents conducted their campaign against drink and its evil effects by holding mass meetings, parades, 'dry' picnics and non-alcoholic celebrations on St. Patrick's Day and other holidays. Both the temperance and the suffrage movements gradually gained momentum and were destined to reach a peak of intensity in the decade of the 1880s. They were important examples of the increasing Catholic presence in state affairs.

Despite the efforts of the *Adopted Citizens' Association,* no headway was made in the area of suffrage reform prior to 1872. Even such a limited concession as granting the franchise to foreign-born soldiers and sailors who served the Union cause during the Civil War was rejected by the electorate.

A constitutional amendment giving equal voting rights to naturalized servicemen honorably discharged from Rhode Island units was proposed by State Senator Elisha R. Potter, Jr. in August 1861. The South Kingstown legislator, who had drafted an enlightened statement on Bible reading in the public schools while commissioner of education in 1854, observed that the time had probably not arrived when the people of the state would repeal the property qualification completely, but he thought that the electorate would look with favor on those naturalized citizens who risked their lives for the preservation of the Union. Potter was wrong. His proposed amendment passed two successive sessions of the General Assembly, but it was soundly rejected at a popular referendum in October 1863 by a vote of 1,346 in favor and 2,594 against. Just before the balloting the *Providence Journal* published a series of editorials that raised doubts as to whether or not the proposed amendment would allow a naturalized citizen to vote who had simply enlisted in the state militia. These negative editorials, according to one knowledgeable observer, 'had a perceptible influence upon the vote.'

In 1864 the Legislature rephrased the amendment to grant the vote without a real property qualification to naturalized citizens who had been in the service of the United States and honorably discharged. This proposition fared better than the first. It received 2,174 votes in favor and 1,578 votes against, but it failed to pass by a margin of seventy-eight because a proposed amendment under Rhode Island's basic law needed the approval of three-fifths of those electors voting thereon.

In the period immediately following the Civil War the movement for general suffrage reform intensified. State statistician Edwin M. Snow noted in his 1865 state census that 'only one in twelve or thirteen of the foreign-born of adult age was a voter.' Leaders in the drive for liberalization of the franchise included Governor Ambrose Burnside, the former Civil War general, who supported the vote for naturalized veterans; former Democratic Congressman Thomas Davis, a Dublin-born Protestant who had been ousted from the United States House of Representatives by the Know-Nothing landslide of 1854; Providence Republican Mayor Thomas Doyle, a Protestant also of Irish descent; and State Senators Sidney Dean of Warren and Charles C. VanZandt of Newport.

The most fervent and outspoken advocate of suffrage reform in the post-war era, however, was young, energetic and articulate Charles E. Gorman from the Wanskuck area of North Providence, a section that was annexed by the city of Providence in 1873–74 and fell within the boundaries of St. Edward's parish.

Charles E. Gorman (1844–1917), leader in the campaign for equal rights and suffrage reform.

In 1844 Gorman was born in Boston, the son of Charles and Sarah J. (Woodbury) Gorman. His father was a native of Ireland but his mother was descended from one of the original settlers of the Massachusetts Bay colony.

Gorman, who was admitted to the bar in 1865, elected to the Rhode Island General Assembly in 1870, and elected to the Providence Common Council in 1875, is reputed to have been the first Irish Catholic to achieve each of these distinctions. During the last third of the nineteenth century he devoted most of his legal talent and his political energy to the cause of constitutional reform, or 'equal rights' as the movement was then called.

This cartoon, drawn after the suppression of the New York Orange Day riots of 1871 shows the Catholic Irishman as an ape-like, knife-wielding, shillelagh-swinging thug. This incident (and perhaps Nast's depiction of it) adversely affected the 1871 effort in Rhode Island to extend the vote to naturalized Irishmen.

In 1870, as a freshman representative, Gorman and Senator Dean sponsored bills calling for an unlimited state constitutional convention but both measures failed to pass. As a concession, however, the Assembly approved a resolution proposing three constitutional amendments, one of which called for the repeal of the real estate property qualification for naturalized citizens. This proposal met defeat in October 1871 by a wide margin — 3,236 votes were cast in its favor but 6,960 of the electors rejected it. The vote came less than three months after New York City's infamous 'Orange Riots' between Catholic and Protestant Irishmen, and this bloody civil strife prompted Henry B. Anthony's *Providence Journal* to equate suffrage extension with 'mob government.' The *Journal*'s views prevailed over the exhortations of three small newspapers (the *Rhode Island Lantern*, the *Weekly Review*, and the *Weekly Democrat*) founded by Irish Catholics in 1870 to publicize the need for political reform.

In November 1876 another futile effort was made to allow foreign-born soldiers and sailors to vote on the same terms as native citizens (11,038 for to 10,956 against), but this measure did not succeed until April 1886 when, under Gorman's lead, it became Article of Amendment VI to the Rhode Island constitution.

Meanwhile Gorman had sought protection for Irish-American and other naturalized citizens under the provisions of the newly-ratified Fourteenth (1868) and Fifteenth (1870) Amendments. As early as 1870 he had circulated a petition signed by nearly 3,000 citizens, which he presented to Congress asking it to decide whether or not the constitution of Rhode Island conflicted with the recent federal amendments. When Congress disclaimed jurisdiction, preliminary steps were taken by Gorman in 1872 to test Rhode Island's real estate qualification for voting in the United States Circuit Court. Before his case was reached for argument, the Supreme Court in three related decisions undercut his position.

While Gorman pressed for suffrage reform, United States Senator Henry B. Anthony worked in an equally zealous manner for restriction. In fact, Senator Anthony had helped to minimize Gorman's chance for a favorable court decision when Anthony fought to limit the Fifteenth Amendment to blacks alone. In 1869, during debate on the voting rights amendment, Senator Henry Wilson of Massachusetts submitted a plan to broaden the measure by abolishing all qualifications for voting or holding office based on 'race, color, na-

In this rendition of "The Ignorant Vote" Thomas Nast shows how the black Republican vote from the South cancelled out the Irish Catholic Democratic vote in the Northern cities. Republican Senator Henry Bowen Anthony tried to maximize the Negro vote and minimize the local Irish vote by supporting a restrictive version of the Fifteenth Amendment that covered only blacks.

tivity, property, education, or religious belief.' In effect, Wilson posed the controversial question of whether the amendment should confine itself to Negro suffrage or undertake sweeping reform of voting and office-holding qualifications.

Henry Anthony took sharp issue with Wilson on the floor of the Senate, chiding him for interference in Rhode Island's affairs. His state's voting laws, warned Anthony, 'were not made for the people of Massachusetts; they were made for us, and whether right or wrong, they suit us, and we intend to hold them; and we shall not ratify any amendment to the Constitution of the United States that contravenes them, and we have the satisfaction of knowing that, without our State, the necessary number of twenty-eight states cannot be obtained for the ratification of any amendment whatever.'

The anti-Irish Anthony knew Rhode Island's support for the Fifteenth Amendment was critical because several Southern states seemed certain to reject it. This undoubtedly inspired his threatening remark. Anthony and a majority of his colleagues, who were animated by different motives, eventually prevailed. The Fifteenth Amendment in its final form was limited to blacks ('race, color, or previous condition of servitude') and left such oppressed ethnic minorities as the Irish of Rhode Island and the Chinese of California unprotected.

When the Fifteenth Amendment came to Rhode Island for ratification in 1869 the controversy centered on the Irish rather than the Negro vote. Rhode Island blacks had enjoyed the suffrage since 1843 so the amendment would not affect their status, but overly-cautious Republican conservatives led by Anthony and Congressman Nathan F. Dixon feared the word 'race' in the amendment could be interpreted to mean 'ethnicity' and thereby invalidate Rhode Island's real estate voting requirement for the foreign-born. One contemporary reporter wrote that 'many Republicans were afraid of the Amendment not because they liked the Negroes less but because they feared the Irish more.' Supporters of ratification included Republican Governor Seth Padelford and Congressman Thomas A. Jenckes. This left the dominant party divided on the issue. One resourceful advocate of ratification said that if the amendment were interpreted to allow naturalized citizens equal voting rights, a literacy test could then be imposed to disfranchise many of them. Finally, in January 1870, the amendment prevailed despite factional feuding, constitutional confusion and ethnic tension, but it had been so emasculated by Anthony and his congressional colleagues and would be so narrowly interpreted by the courts that it afforded Charles Gorman and his Irish Catholic followers no comfort or relief.

Eventually, in response to the demands of Gorman and others, a committee of the United States Senate, chaired by Pennsylvania Democrat William A. Wallace, conducted an investigation of Rhode Island's governmental system. The committee's report of 1880 concluded that 'the rights of suffrage to *foreign-born* citizens of the United States is abridged by the constitution and laws of Rhode Island' to a greater extent

FRIEND (to newly-arrived Irishman). "Ah, Mike, me boy, you're just in time to Vote. Come away with me and get Naturalized. Yer may be an Alderman soon yerself, if yer like."

The potential political power of the Irish immigrant, as sketched by cartoonist Thomas Worth, was feared by the native American. The influx of Irishmen threatened to overturn native control of those cities where Irish settled. Rhode Island, more than any other state, minimized this threat by its real estate voting and officeholding requirement for the foreign-born.

EXTRACTS FROM REPORTS 572 AND 427 MADE TO THE UNITED STATES SENATE IN APRIL AND MAY, 1880, BY A SELECT COMMITTEE OF WHICH SENATOR WILLIAM WALLACE OF PENNSYLVANIA WAS CHAIRMAN

Restricted suffrage, registry taxes upon poor men alone, statutory closing of the polls at sunset, instead of eight o'clock, as formerly, by which the operatives in the mill are prevented from voting, and the compulsory payment of the registry tax ten months prior to the general election in a Presidential year, cause great complaints upon the part of the poor men and foreign-born citizens in Rhode Island; and to these features of her laws many intelligent witnesses ascribe the small percentage of voters among her people and the large amount of corrupt practices in the elections of the State.

. . . .

Your committee believes that there are good grounds for the complaints made that the government of Rhode Island, under its present constitution, is nearer an oligarchy than a democracy. The disfranchisement of so large a percentage of her people, by systematic effort and rigidly-enforced statutes, the small vote cast for President at a hotly-contested election, the small number of votes cast for members of Congress in four successive elections, when contrasted with the number cast in other States in the same elections, the choice of members of Congress, governors, and Presidents by the votes of one out of every ten of the people, whilst other States cast one vote for every five of theirs, the maintenance of the rule of three-fifths for the amendment of her constitution, by which the will of the majority has been twice defeated, all compel us to recognize Rhode Island as different in her government, her institutions, and her policy from all of her sister commonwealths in the Union, and lead us to grasp at any provision of the Federal Constitution which, fairly construed, will grant us power to enforce, for her people, 'a republican form of government,' by which we mean a government by the whole people, for the whole people of the State.

Rhode Island is the only State in the Union in which native and foreign-born citizens stand upon different grounds as to State qualifications for the right of suffrage.

. . . .

Your committee reports that the rights of suffrage to *foreign-born* citizens of the United States is abridged by the constitution and laws of Rhode Island.

KILLING THE GOOSE THAT LAID THE GOLDEN EGG.

"A certain man had the good fortune to possess a Goose that laid him a Golden Egg every day. But dissatisfied with so slow an income, and thinking to seize the whole treasure at once, he killed the Goose; and cutting her open, found her — just what any other goose would be." — Æsop.

The connection between the Catholic Church and Irish politicians in New York, whereby state funds were made available for Catholic purposes, is satirized by Thomas Nast. Yankee Republicans in Rhode Island were horrified by the New York situation, and they believed that an "ounce of prevention" — the disfranchisement of the naturalized Irishman — was "worth a pound of cure."

than anywhere in the nation. The committee report also disclosed a widespread practice of political intimidation by mill owners of their employees who could vote. Because of the absence of a secret ballot, the senators observed, 'at almost every election for years these men voted under the eye of their employers' agents who were Republicans, and in very many cases under circumstances showing intimidation and fear of loss of work.'

Eventually in 1887, when Gorman himself was speaker of the Rhode Island House of Representatives (the first controlled by Democrats since 1854), the Bourn Amendment was passed by the General Assembly. One year later it was ratified by a narrow margin to become Amendment VII to the state constitution. It removed the real estate requirement for voting that had discriminated against the foreign born, but it did so at a time when native-born citizens of Irish descent greatly outnumbered naturalized Irish.

In effect, the Bourn Amendment allowed newly arrived British, Franco-American and Italian immigrants to vote in *state* elections immediately upon naturalization. Republican leaders hoped these groups would align themselves with the G.O.P. and consequently check the rising political power of the native-born Democratic Irish from whom the newer ethnics were culturally estranged. Their hopes were realized. This political effect may explain how Republican boss Charles R. Brayton, Anthony's protégé and successor, could give his indispensable support to this pseudo-reform. But the Bourn Amendment is another complex story — one which shows that the political rivalry of Yankee and Celt, spawned in the 1840s, was still alive and virulent.

Church Growth under Bishop McFarland

During the McFarland episcopacy, the Church in Rhode Island continued its impressive expansion and gradually shed its image as a mission church. By 1870 the state had approximately 60,000 Catholic inhabitants. To serve this swelling flock the bishop continued to rely on Irish seminaries for priests, and he also utilized the new seminary of Louvain (established in 1857) from which he secured the services of eight Dutch or Belgian priests who had some facility in the German and French languages.

By the end of his administration, however, a significant number of diocesan vocations could be noted. In 1867 McFarland ordained ten men to the priesthood, fifteen in 1868, nine in 1869, and ten in 1871. This dramatic rise in native clergy (in 1862 only six of fifty-seven diocesan priests were American-born) was the beginning of a long-standing tradition of priestly vocations in the Rhode Island Catholic community. Even with these new sources, McFarland never had enough clergy for the Church's needs. The attrition rate was high, for illness and overwork caused many early deaths as the obituaries of priests in those years indicate. In 1871 there was only one priest for every 1,800 Catholics in the two-state area. When the Providence diocese was created in 1872 the ratio in Rhode Island rose to one for every 2,000 faithful, but the continuing increase in local recruits soon remedied this deficiency.

The Church became more self-reliant not only in the area of clerical vocations but also in the realm of finance. From 1845, when Bishop Tyler received a sizeable donation from the Leopoldine Mission Society of Vienna, until McFarland's final grant from the Society for the Propagation of the Faith in 1866, the diocese was very reliant on funds furnished by the foreign mission societies of Austria, Germany and France. The 'Propaganda' alone contributed $51,000 during this twenty-year period to maintain those priests who conducted roving ministries, to educate seminarians and to support orphans. By the late 1860s, however, the diocese was able to pay its own way and even furnished monies to Southern bishops who preached here to gain revenues for the reconstruction of their war-torn dioceses.

The number of Catholic institutions in the state continued to increase under McFarland's leadership. The further influx of immigrants led to the establishment of such important parishes as St. Michael's in

South Providence, a newly developed area that was part of the town of Cranston until 1868. Initially called St. Bernard's but renamed by Father Michael Wallace in 1868, St. Michael's was created in 1857 as a mission of Sts. Peter and Paul and elevated in 1859 to parish status. It was destined to become the most populous parish in the diocese and the socio-religious center of the predominantly Irish-Catholic South Providence neighborhood until the decline of that inner-city area in the decade of the 1960s.

Other parish establishments during the episcopacy of McFarland included Immaculate Conception (1857) in the North End of Providence. The Reverend Edward Cooney, its first pastor, enjoyed a twenty-one year tenure during which he supervised the building of a church (1858) followed by a school (1860) and a rectory. Through the generosity of the family of industrialist George Corliss, Cooney also acquired a mansion that was converted to a convent for the Sisters of Mercy, who ran the parish education program from 1860 to 1867, and for the Sisters of Charity who replaced them and served Immaculate Conception from 1867 to 1905, when the Mercy order returned. The Immaculate Conception convent was the only Rhode Island foundation of the Sisters of Charity, who were based at Mt. St. Vincent, New York. Immaculate Conception parish, like St. Michael's, was dramatically affected by mid-twentieth century changes in the population and physical landscape of the capital city. Its buildings were demolished and it was dismembered in the mid-1950s to make way for the West River Industrial Park, an urban renewal project.

St. Ann's, Cranston, near Sprague's Print Works, was created in 1858 as a mission of St. Mary's Broadway and received parish status in 1860. In 1859, through the initiative of Father Delany of 'Old St. Mary's,' Pawtucket, St. Patrick's of Valley Falls was established to serve the spiritual needs of Catholic mill workers in the Blackstone Valley. The cornerstone of St. Patrick's was laid in September 1860 and the completed church was dedicated by Bishop McFarland on July 21, 1861.

The last of the pioneer parishes created prior to the establishment of the Diocese of Providence were St. John's on Atwells Avenue, Providence (1870) and the Assumption in West Elmwood (1871). The parishioners of St. John's, under the long-time direction of Father John J. McCabe (1870–1907), commissioned the famous architect James Murphy to design an impressive church building that was dedicated in Sep-

The first church of St. Ann, Cranston, near the Sprague mill complex. It was completed and dedicated on July 18, 1858 as a mission chapel of St. Mary's parish, Broadway. St. Ann's became an independent parish in 1860.

First Church of St. Michael's parish in South Providence (originally St. Bernard's) was this former Baptist meeting house.

tember 1875. The formation of Assumption parish was largely the work of Father Michael Clune who served as first pastor from 1871 until his death in January 1888.

Several missions were also created during McFarland's episcopacy, most notably St. Joseph's of Geneva (1867), which served the Catholic mill workers of the populous Wanskuck area — a section that was transferred from North Providence to Providence in 1874, the same year the mission was accorded parish status and renamed St. Edward's.

In the years just prior to the creation of the new diocese, five other important parishes were well-advanced in their process of formation. In the early fall of 1867, the A. & W. Sprague Company donated a piece of land for a Catholic church on a hill overlooking the village of Natick. The gift was intended to

Immaculate Conception Church in Providence's North End. Founded in 1857, this noted parish was dissolved and the century-old church demolished to make way for the West River Industrial Park in the mid-1950s.

benefit the Irish mill hands of Natick and Pontiac and the newly arriving Franco-Americans. Construction of a church was begun on Thanksgiving Day, 1870, but work proceeded slowly. On Christmas 1872, Mass was celebrated for the first time in the basement of the church and the parish was formally constituted under the patronage of St. Joseph although it did not receive its first resident pastor, the Reverend Napoleon Riviere, until 1875.

In the other major river valley, the Blackstone, the Catholic population of the Ashton mission had increased sufficiently to separate that outpost from St. Patrick's of Valley Falls and make it an independent parish. The Reverend James A. Fitzsimmons was appointed first pastor of St. Joseph's of Ashton in November 1872, and he assumed permanent residence in the village two years later. In Pawtucket another parcel was carved from St. Mary's in August 1872, constituted as the parish of the Sacred Heart, and placed under the spiritual direction of Father James L. Smith. In 1873, St. Mary's was further subdivided when Catholics on the east side of the Blackstone River were formed into the parish of St. Joseph and placed under the spiritual care of Father Henry F. Kinnerney. In the northern mill village of Slatersville, on the Branch River, a church begun in the fall of 1871 was dedicated to St. John on May 24, 1872, and received its first resident pastor, Father James Berkins in 1873. This flurry of parish-building, coinciding with the arrival of Bishop Hendricken, was an auspicious beginning for the new diocese.

Fulfilling his predecessor's dream, Bishop McFarland was able to give the Mercy orphanage a new home in a large brick building on Prairie Avenue in St. Michael's parish. St. Aloysius Asylum, as this facility was renamed, opened in April 1862 to accommodate both boys and girls. The traditional Orphan's Fair continued with great success to support this social agency. In 1871 the yearly event yielded a grand total of $12,940.

The Church also increased its educational role in the Civil War decade. Since Catholics lacked funds and religious to establish a systematic parish school system, an elaborate Sunday school operation began — most successfully in the Cathedral parish where by 1870 some 1,600 students were taught by 100 members of the *Christian Doctrine Society*. The laity usually handled the teaching, while the Sisters of Mercy rendered whatever aid they could. The success of the Cathedral effort was due to James Gibson, superintendent during the 1860s. Upon his retirement in 1871, he was honored by the entire school with a gold watch for his 'untiring exertions.' Nearly all parishes had schools of this type, and until the latter part of the century they were the backbone of Catholic religious instruction because only one in three Catholic children were enrolled in parish schools.

The question of Catholic day-school education continued to be an important concern although the parochial school movement was still in its infancy. In Rhode Island, by the mid-1860s, about 3,000 students attended schools at the Cathedral, St. Patrick's, and Immaculate Conception parishes in Providence, as well as St. Mary's in Newport, St. Mary's in Pawtucket, and St. Charles in Woonsocket. The largest parish school, the Cathedral facility on Pine Street run by Sisters of Mercy, could no longer meet the demand by 1865, and Bishop McFarland decided to expand it. In 1868 he purchased a lot on Fountain Street and endeavored to bring the Christian Brothers to the city, but his hopes were not realized in that year because the Brothers were unable to provide the necessary faculty.

An industrial school was begun by the Mercy order in January 1867 at St. Aloysius Home and the first evening school in the diocese was opened in 1870 by the sisters at St. Xavier's. Little is known about these short-lived efforts, but they added other dimensions to Catholic education and further enhanced the preeminent role of the Mercy order in the development of the Catholic school system in Rhode Island.

Catholic elementary education in Rhode Island did not grow rapidly under Bishop McFarland. No new parish elementary schools were founded during his episcopacy subsequent to the establishment of the Immaculate Conception school in 1860, but notable advances were made on the secondary level under the able direction of the Mercy nuns. At St. Mary's Church in Newport — where these sisters had conducted the elementary school since 1854 — the Academy of St. Mary's of the Isle opened in October 1867 in Mercy convent with twenty-eight girls enrolled. This third earliest Catholic high school (operated on an informal basis since 1854) eventually expanded to include boys and endured for fifty-seven years before closing in 1924.

In 1868, the Mercy nuns, who had come to staff St. Mary's parochial school in Pawtucket seven years earlier, opened an academy and a boarding school for girls in the sisters' convent. The boarding school was discontinued after two years because the rooms were needed for the new sisters who were imported to staff the rapidly-growing elementary school. But the academy, named St. Patrick's, survived for twenty-three years before closing in 1891.

A third parish high school was founded by the Mercy sisters in Woonsocket. In 1869, they replaced the lay teachers at St. Michael's school (sponsored by St. Charles parish). During the following year they began St. Bernard's Academy in their Woonsocket convent with departments for boys and girls conducted separately. In the 1870s this high school enrolled well over 100 students yearly, most of whom were French Canadian. When the Franco-American community began to direct their children to Precious Blood parish (established in 1872) for instruction by the Religious of Jesus and Mary, enrollment dwindled and St. Bernard's Academy closed in 1884.

The final, most successful and enduring high school educational project launched during McFarland's tenure at Providence was the establishment of LaSalle Academy under the Christian Brothers (F.S.C.) of St. John Baptist de la Salle, a group of French origin that had first come to the United States in 1845. O'Reilly had vainly sought this noted order in 1855 to staff his Lime Street Academy for boys, but McFarland was more fortunate. Using as his emissary the Reverend Michael Tierney, rector of the Cathedral, the Bishop opened negotiations with the distinguished Provincial of the Order's American establishments, Brother Patrick (Murphy), F.S.C.

The discussions were most successful. The Brothers of the Christian Schools agreed to come to Providence.

St. Aloysius Orphanage, the oldest continuous social welfare agency in the diocese, transferred from the Mercy convent to these modern quarters on Prairie Avenue in 1862. At the time of the move the adjacent parish church was called St. Bernard's and the site was located in Cranston. In 1868 the parish was renamed St. Michael's and the area in which St. Aloysius was located was annexed by the city of Providence to become its South Providence section.

Their arrival, however, was delayed for one academic year. Thus the Fountain Street Academy for the instruction of the boys of Cathedral parish and its offspring St. John's, opened in September 1870 under local instructors. Finally in September 1871, at the start of the second school year, three Christian Brothers arrived and took up residence in a small two-and-a-half-story frame building at 125 Fountain Street next to the three-story brick academy. This established Rhode Island's first religious order of men.

Brother Ptolemy became the school's first director. He was assisted by Brothers Joachim of Sienna (John Sullivan, b. 1848) and Gedeon Francis (Michael Bracken, 1839–99), both born in Ireland. The initial instructional staff also included a layman (Mr. Goodwin) and Father Henry F. Kinnerney, then a young Cathedral curate. Kinnerney, who taught Latin and Greek, emerged as one of Rhode Island's leading Catholic intellectuals by the end of the nineteenth century.

Instruction for boys was initially conducted both on the grammar and high school levels, and the academy

LaSalle Academy initially called the Fountain Street Academy. An early photograph (*ca.* 1915) shows the school after it had expanded from its first building (immediately to the left) with the Christian Brothers' residence (extreme left). The school complex was located near the present LaSalle Square opposite the front of the Providence Civic Center.

was basically a parish institution. Gradually, however, the 'Brothers' School,' as it was popularly called, evolved into the present LaSalle Academy and stands as one of Bishop McFarland's most significant legacies to the Rhode Island Catholic community.

During this period, the Church in Rhode Island also adopted a legal identity. This change was necessary to clarify the vague legal status under which the diocese operated since its inception and to remedy the practice whereby the bishop held title to all church property in fee simple. The unresolved case of *Hannity* v. *O'Reilly,* which involved the diocese in a civil suit over an alleged loan of $3,000 from a Providence Catholic to Bishop O'Reilly, was the catalyst that prompted McFarland to seek a state law providing for the uniform incorporation of Church property.

The bishop lobbied successfully for the passage of the incorporation act, which passed the Rhode Island legislature in its January 1866 session and the Connecticut legislature in June of that same year. The legislation, designed to regularize and clarify parish ownership and responsibility, provided that the corporate body of each diocesan church would be composed of the bishop, his vicar general, the pastor, and two laymen of the parish. This group was empowered to expend up to $500 without the bishop's permission and to record the assets and liabilities of the parish. Three years later, in August 1869, the bishop filed incorporation papers for all the parishes of Rhode Island and conveyed the property he held in his own name to the new corporations. This system was a compromise with the lay trustee concept which subordinated clerical control to that of the congregation. It became the basis for parish organization in Rhode Island and has functioned reasonably well over the past century.

The level of Catholic intellectual life improved in the Civil War decade under the guidance of the schol-

THE FORMATIVE ERA

arly McFarland. In Providence the Brownson Lyceum sponsored appearances by leading Catholic lecturers to capacity audiences. The most popular speaker was the brilliant Isaac Hecker, a convert and the founder of the Paulist Fathers. Hecker, who is often referred to as the first American Catholic mystic, brought a simple but forceful message to his listeners — the compatibility of American democracy and Catholicism. The Lyceum's efforts were augmented by lectures from Bishop McFarland and diocesan priests. Church music also assumed importance as the Cathedral choir became noted for its renditions of the masters during Easter and Christmas services.

Catholic organizations flourished during McFarland's episcopacy and became an increasingly important part of parish life. In addition to the welfare-oriented St. Vincent de Paul societies, devotional and liturgical groups were formed including the Purgatorian Society (to pray for 'the souls of the faithful departed'), the Scapular and Rosary Society (to increase the use of these sacramentals), the Altar Society (to prepare the altar and sanctuary for services) and the Children of Mary, the Children of St. Aloysius, and the Children of the Guardian Angel (to provide spiritual exercises for the young). Quasi-religious Irish benevolent associations were also created such as the Immigrant Aid Society (1869). These organizations indicated and fostered a steady increase in the piety and the devotional level of Rhode Island Catholics.

In the late 1860s the non-Catholic community showed more interest in, and less suspicion of, its Catholic neighbors. While no precise figures are available, there was a rise in the number of conversions — owing largely to the persuasive witness of Bishop Mc-

Reverend Henry F. Kinnerney, first educational director of the Fountain Street Academy, first pastor of St. Joseph's Parish, Pawtucket, and one of the leading Catholic intellectuals in late nineteenth-century Rhode Island.

Father Isaac Hecker, founder of the Paulist Fathers in 1858, was the most popular Lyceum speaker. He instructed his audiences on the compatibility of Catholicism with Americanism.

> **ROMAN CATHOLICS DISGRACING THEMSELVES.**
>
> "Miss EDITH O'GORMAN, the well-known lecturer, suffered severe violence at the hands of a furious mob in Madison, N. J., on Friday evening, April 15. Madison is the seat of the Roman Catholic Convent in which Miss O'GORMAN first connected herself with the sisterhood as a nun. Miss O'GORMAN has renounced the faith, and now lectures on her experience while a nun. On Friday evening she delivered a lecture entitled 'The Romish Priesthood.' A great crowd gathered outside the hall, and though no disturbance was made during the lecture, at its conclusion, when Miss O'GORMAN was passing from the hall to the carriage in waiting, an assault was made upon her. The crowd yelled madly, and were about to tear the lecturer from her carriage and escort. Curses, disgraceful language, and all kinds of abuse found authors in the mob and an objective point in Miss O'GORMAN. A pistol was discharged as the carriage rolled off, but the shot passed over her head, leaving her unharmed. As the lecturer was borne to the Methodist parsonage the mob surrounded the house, and again would have assaulted her if a body-guard of Drew Seminary students had not prevented. The leaders of the mob are known."—*The N. Y. Sun.*

Edith O'Gorman, allegedly an "escaped nun," told her slanderous story in many states including Rhode Island. When Irish Catholics in Madison, New Jersey violently protested her falsehoods, Thomas Nast came quickly to her defense.

Farland. The appearance of anti-Catholic lecturers, such as the 'escaped nun' Gertrude Grey, was discouraged. Gertrude was greeted with hisses and snowballs when she appeared at the Providence Opera House. Miss Edith O'Gorman received an equally cold reception. Her colorful narrative of her experiences in a Sisters of Charity convent failed to arouse any sentiment other than laughter. The *Providence Journal* exposed Miss Grey as a professional 'flim-flam artist' who made a living with outrageous tales and the newspaper openly questioned the veracity of Miss O'Gorman's stories. Rhode Island's Protestant community had mellowed since the confrontation at the Mercy convent in 1855.

Pius IX's call in 1868 for a general council of the Church to gather in Rome was the major Catholic event of the nineteenth century. Vatican I, the first council since Trent, opened on December 8, 1869. The Church in America responded vigorously to the Pope's invitation by sending six archbishops, forty bishops and one mitered abbot. To Francis Patrick McFarland — member of the American delegation — diocesan priests made a gift of $5,000 to pay the expenses of his journey to Rome.

The definition of papal infallibility as a dogma of the Church produced the most heated discussion at the Council. The debates revealed three groups in opposition — those who denied the concept of *personal* papal infallibility by contending that a papal utterance required the consent of the bishops for such a guarantee; those who opposed the pronouncement because they thought papal infallibility was not so clearly revealed as to admit of dogmatic definition; and those who thought a statement unwise because it would create a further obstacle to the conversion of non-Catholics.

Hence, a small bloc in the Council was opposed to definition either because they were conciliarists, or they doubted the doctrine's definability, or they believed its definition would be inopportune. Among the last group stood McFarland with his metropolitan, Archbishop John McCloskey, and eighteen other American prelates. McFarland signed a petition addressed to the Pope in January 1870 that embodied the views of this contingent and reflected the effects of nativistic attacks on the Church in America. The twenty bishops did not question the doctrine, but they urged the Pope to consider the controversy that such a statement on infallibility would raise. The petitioners gave three reasons for their stand — discussion of the question would show a lack of unity in the Church; a definition would alienate non-Catholics and hamper conversion efforts; and a pronouncement on infallibility would produce harmful strife with the Church.

The Council, however, did proceed to discuss the volatile question and adopted the dogma after much theological and political debate. The American bishops accepted the decision on papal infallibility, but some did so reluctantly.

For Bishop McFarland, participation at the Council was short-lived. Not long after he signed the petition, he was forced to ask the Pope to dispense his obligation to attend for reasons of health. Most likely his physical constitution had been broken from the harsh frontier existence he had experienced earlier in New York, and his years in Providence had been marked by constant bouts with lung ailments and internal maladies. The former led to brief stays in sanatoriums and the latter caused chronic diarrhea. The recurrence of his illnesses in Rome prompted McFarland to take a momentous step — after weighing his fitness to continue in the Hartford diocese, he decided to ask the Holy Father to appoint a coadjutor for the see. His request was turned down but a decision to divide the diocese was made. The Pope desired that McFarland retain the leadership of the Church in Connecticut, while Rhode Island was to be designated a new diocese with its own spiritual head.

Official confirmation of the change was still a year away, and the Catholics of this state were unaware of the development when Bishop McFarland returned from Rome after convalescence in August 1870. His train was met by a huge contingent of Catholic societies and interested laity and, according to accounts in the *Providence Journal* and the *Weekly Review* (a new but short-lived Catholic newspaper), the bishop was greeted by a most sincere expression of love. A parade with bands, drum corps, and Catholic societies marched through downtown Providence to honor the returning shepherd who humbly thanked his well-wishers.

News of the impending division came in August 1871, but plans for McFarland's removal to Hartford were not completed until early 1872. Meanwhile, despite his fragile health, the bishop continued to confirm, lecture on the Council and its decisions, and administer his sizable diocese. Finally, in an emotional farewell to his Cathedral fold on Sunday, February 25, 1872, the bishop completed his stay in Providence. His remaining career in Hartford was brief. After a period of initial vigor, his health completely failed and he died on October 12, 1874 at the age of fifty-five.

The Irish Impact

On the eve of the creation of the Diocese of Providence, the Catholic Church in Rhode Island was *de facto* an Irish national church. This salient reality — essential to an understanding of local Catholicism — furnishes the basis for the tensions that developed within the Church as subsequent waves of immigrants encountered this Irish predominance.

The sources, extent, and nature of Irish-American Catholicism are best known through an examination of conditions in Ireland itself, for it was the Old World experience that shaped and conditioned the Irish religious outlook. Ever since the King of Leinster, Dermot MacMurrough, summoned King Henry II to Ireland in 1171, English presence had been a cardinal fact of Irish life. Perhaps the most tragic feature of that unhappy relationship from the time of the Reformation was the steady political, economic, social, and intellectual degradation of the Catholic Irish. James I's plantation of Ulster with Presbyterian Scots, Oliver Cromwell's massacres and land confiscations, the Irish defeat at the siege of Limerick (1691) by William of Orange with the subsequent flight of the old Catholic leadership, and the era of anti-Catholic penal legislation that followed (1695–1746), were only the low points in a relentless and sustained British effort aimed at depriving the Irish Catholic people of all wealth and ambition — to make them poor and keep them poor both in substance and in spirit.

With the suppression of Catholic power, control rested with a small minority of Anglo-Irish members of the established Church of Ireland (Anglican). These Anglo-Irish were the proprietors of the great estates composed of the Catholic lands confiscated in the wars of the sixteenth and seventeenth centuries. This Protestant aristocracy owned five-sixths of the land in Ireland. Like feudal lords, they completely ran the affairs of the country, dispensed justice, and collected exorbitant rents on the meager plots held by the dispossessed native Irish. 'If you want to know what can be done by the spirit of conquest and religious hatred combined with the abuses of aristocracy, but without any of its advantages, go to Ireland,' the perceptive Alexis de Tocqueville caustically stated after his visit there in 1835.

The small farmers comprised one group of Catholic Irish. They rented from the Ascendancy as mere tenants at will without security of tenure. Since expired leases went always to the highest bidder, and the tenant in possession received no preference, the farmers had to concentrate upon rent-paying products such as cereals and cattle. These they raised for market to get money for rents, while potatoes were grown for food. If a tenant improved his property the landlord raised the rent. With industry thus penalized, it was in the tenant's self-interest to be lax.

Far more numerous and destitute than farmers were the cottiers — the large, fixed substratum of the population. They were completely landless, neither owning nor having any rights to the soil. From some more fortunate farmer they rented the *use* of enough ground for a crude cabin and a potato patch, paying for it by their labor and by the sale of chickens and pigs. Cottiers subsisted on potatoes, to which they occasionally added a bit of milk — these two staples constituting the whole of their diet.

By the end of the seventeenth century the lowly cottier class comprised about eighty percent of the population, a proportion that gradually increased

An Irish peasant cottage with children, chickens and spinning wheel.

A late nineteenth-century Irish peasant village in County Donegal.

thereafter. The total population of Ireland also expanded dramatically — from slightly less than a million in 1660 to over eight million by 1840, a high percentage of whom were impoverished and almost totally dependent upon the ubiquitous potato, the staple that furnished the largest amount of food on the smallest surface of ground with the least sustained effort. As the cereal crop and livestock were exported to support the landlord system that oppressed them, the potato — and only that — kept millions of Catholic Irish alive. The visiting de Tocqueville was told by an Anglican that 'the Irishman cultivates beautiful crops and takes his harvest to the nearest port, and puts it on an English ship; then he goes home and eats potatoes. He rears cattle, sends them to London and never eats meat.'

The great masses of rural Irish eventually came to accept their situation as unavoidable. They became reconciled to — if not content with — their inferior status. Such resignation, frustration, and despair fostered drunkenness and improvidence among the peasantry, and from time to time begot a reckless desperation expressed in violent outbreaks that brought swift and merciless reprisals from the Ascendancy.

Despite these degrading conditions, Irish Catholic migration to America was not substantial during the colonial era except perhaps during the Cromwellian regime. At the turn of the nineteenth century the suppression of the Wexford rising of 1798 and the revolt of 1803 sent some political refugees to our shores. These refugees were accompanied by those skilled workmen who were adversely affected by the passage of the Act of Union in 1801 — a measure that crippled incipient Irish industrial development.

In the wake of the War of 1812, the first significant migration of Catholic Irish to North America began as Irish agriculture experienced a period of reorganization. Tenant farmers of all classes suffered from the post-war decline in agricultural prices. This condition led to expansion of the grazing industry with its concomitant consolidation of farm land and eviction of the peasant farmer. Failure of the potato crop in 1818 and 1822 and the disfranchisement of the small tenant farmers in 1829 provided further sources of discontent.

Loosening of restrictions on passenger travel in 1827 — immediately reflected in cheaper fares — brought a sharp upturn in emigration to America. This liberalization of the passenger acts coincided with the onset of chronic crop failures. The introduction of inferior quality potatoes, a succession of wet seasons, and the appearance of blight had rendered the staple food of the peasantry utterly unreliable. In thirteen of the seventeen years after 1828, there were partial failures of the vital potato crop. Departure from this stricken land seemed for many the only rational solution.

Prior to 1835 the typical Irish migrant came from the farming class, was usually poor but seldom destitute, and possessed the rudiments of education. During the late 1830s more low cottiers, impoverished and illiterate but not devoid of hope or ambition, undertook the voyage to the New World. This was especially true after the passage of the Irish Poor Law of 1838, which shifted the increasingly heavy burden of supporting Irish paupers from English taxpayers to Anglo-Irish landlords. Faced with this onerous levy, the landlords found it desirable to promote emigration of the impoverished, because it was no longer politically or economically profitable to keep the peasants on the land. This was facilitated by the act itself which integrated eviction and emigration into a new economic policy. Under its provisions the dispossessed could be lodged in workhouses. Since the measure also provided for assisted emigration, the logical succes-

"Irish emigrants leaving home, the priest's blessing" — a typical departure scene.

sion developed from eviction, to workhouse, to emigrant ship.

This change in 1838 increased the quantity of Irish immigration and lowered its socio-economic level, prompting a nativist reaction in America. It is more than coincidence that Henry B. Anthony launched his campaign against the 'foreign vagabond' in 1838 and set in motion the wave of anti-foreignism that engulfed Rhode Island in the 1840s and 1850s.

Such were the basic causes and nature of the pre-famine migration. During the three decades between 1815 and 1845 a million Irish — most of them Roman Catholics — came to North America. Perhaps 5,000 of these settled in Rhode Island, many after taking a circuitous route to the state. Those who could afford it went to Liverpool, England, sailed to New York or Boston, then came overland to Rhode Island's mill villages. Those more impoverished took the less expensive route from Ireland to Quebec or the Maritime Provinces either in packets or in the empty holds of returning timber ships. This traffic was not burdened by the American laws regulating passenger room and safety precautions. From Halifax and St. John's some boarded a steamer to Eastport, Maine, transshipment point for Boston, while others wandered down the New England coast, a few continuing as far as Rhode Island. The distribution of the Catholic Irish in New England extended from the port of Boston outward but, especially in the early period, from the New Brunswick-Maine immigrant route southward. In these years men often came first, such as those in the all-male Woonsocket congregation for whom Father Fitton celebrated Mass in 1828. Once established and employed they sent for their wives and children.

Then came the deluge with the advent of a serious potato blight late in 1845 and the crop's complete failure in the fall of 1846. For five terrible years Ireland went through a succession of miseries that left it in economic ruin. Deprived of their staff of life, tens of thousands of Irish starved to death and more than a million fled in abject destitution.

During the calamity the English repealed the Corn Laws (1846) — destroying Ireland's protected position in the English market — and passed an Encumbered Estates Act (1849). Both measures stimulated wholesale evictions and in the seven-year period from

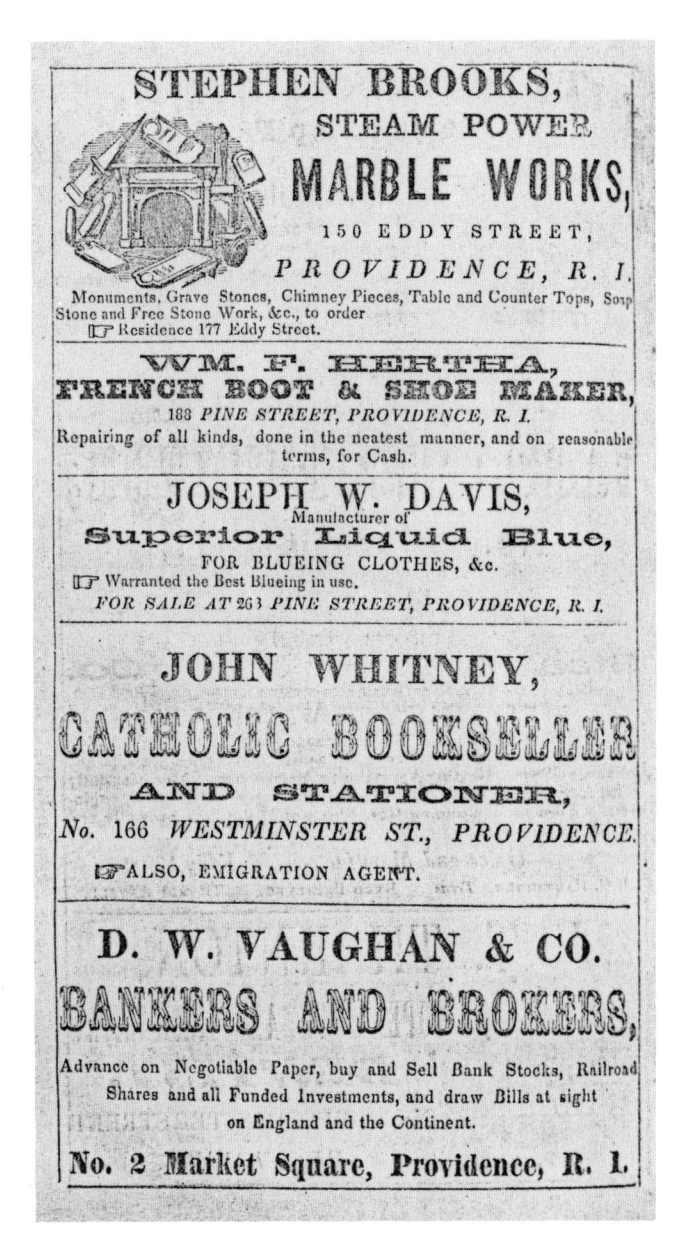

STEPHEN BROOKS,
STEAM POWER
MARBLE WORKS,
150 EDDY STREET,
PROVIDENCE, R. I.
Monuments, Grave Stones, Chimney Pieces, Table and Counter Tops, Soap Stone and Free Stone Work, &c., to order
☞ Residence 177 Eddy Street.

WM. F. HERTHA,
FRENCH BOOT & SHOE MAKER,
188 PINE STREET, PROVIDENCE, R. I.
Repairing of all kinds, done in the neatest manner, and on reasonable terms, for Cash.

JOSEPH W. DAVIS,
Manufacturer of
Superior Liquid Blue,
FOR BLUEING CLOTHES, &c.
☞ Warranted the Best Blueing in use.
FOR SALE AT 263 PINE STREET, PROVIDENCE, R. I.

JOHN WHITNEY,
CATHOLIC BOOKSELLER
AND STATIONER,
No. 166 WESTMINSTER ST., PROVIDENCE.
☞ ALSO, EMIGRATION AGENT.

D. W. VAUGHAN & CO.
BANKERS AND BROKERS,
Advance on Negotiable Paper, buy and Sell Bank Stocks, Railroad Shares and all Funded Investments, and draw Bills at sight on England and the Continent.
No. 2 Market Square, Providence, R. I.

Migration was subsidized by "remittances" through passenger agents like Providence bookseller John Whitney.

1849 to 1855, a total of 350,841 Irish were legally ejected from their lands. A political revolt of the Young Ireland party in 1848 was swiftly crushed and its leaders exiled, adding to the exodus. There seemed to be no hope, only panic and desperation.

According to the leading student of American immigration, Oscar Handlin, the famine migration was unique. 'The nature of its distinctiveness,' states Handlin, 'may be gathered from the circumstances that produced it. This exodus was not a carefully planned movement from a less desirable to a more desirable home. This was a flight, and precise destination mattered little. The *Cork Examiner* noted, "The emigrants of this year (1847) are not like those of former ones; they are now actually *running away* from fever and disease and hunger, with money scarcely sufficient to pay passage for and find food for the voyage." No other contemporaneous migration partook so fully of this poverty-sticken helplessness.' The Irish reached America a thoroughly downtrodden people, with searing memories of religious persecution and devastating economic hardship.

In each of the peak years 1847–54, over 100,000 Irish, mostly from the cottier class, came to America. Irish migration to the United States in the thirty-year period from 1840 through 1870 was unequaled by any other immigrant group up to that time. In 1841–50, a total of 780,719 Irish made their exodus and in the peak decade 1851–60 that figure rose to 914,119. In the period 1861–70 the volume declined to 435,778 but that number was second only to the German arrivals. Throughout the era, migration was subsidized by 'remittances' from Irish in America to their relatives in the homeland, though sometimes this passage money went astray. Father Charles O'Reilly, the pastor in Woonsocket, described in a public letter how his entire congregation had been swindled by an unscrupulous passenger agent.

The overwhelming majority of the Irish became urban dwellers despite their rural background. They entered this unfamiliar milieu because they needed immediate employment and lacked funds to continue onward to the more promising frontier areas. In addition, the Irish cottier was hardly an agriculturalist in the normal sense but a wretched subsistence farmer who clung to the soil for survival and for whom the land held bitter memories.

Rhode Island got its share of this outpouring from

RIGHT: An eviction. The *Illustrated London News* (December 16, 1848) said of this typical scene that "Tenants are dragged out with the help of troops and the tumbling of the houses begins."

Famine funeral at Skibbereen. This *Illustrated London News* sketch (January 30, 1847) is captioned "Coffins are unprocurable."

A contemporary engraving shows a starving crowd at the gate of a workhouse during the Great Famine.

BELOW: This sketch from the 1847 *Illustrated London News* depicts the ravages of the "Great Hunger."

117

SCHEDULE I. Free Inhabitants in the 5th Ward, Providence in the County of Providence State of Rhode Island enumerated by me, on the 20th day of July, 1850. Edwin M. Stone, Ass't Marshal.

1	2	3	4	5	6	7	8	9	10	11	12	13	
		John Degnan	8	M	W			Ireland		1			1
		Margaret Degnan	6	F	W			Ireland		1			2
109	197	Peter Creed	43	M	W	Laborer		Ireland			+		3
		Bridget Creed	30	F	W			Ireland			+		4
		Bridget Creed	13					Ireland					5
		Margaret Creed	11	F				Ireland		1			6
		Michael Creed	4	m				R.I.					7
		Peter Creed	4/12	m				R.I.					8
		Patrick McCauley	24	m		Laborer		Ireland			+		9
110	198	Barney Flinn	30	m		Laborer		Ireland			+		10
		Ann Flinn	27	f				Ireland			+		11
		Catherine Flinn	8	f				Ireland		1			12
		Elizabeth Flinn	6	f				Ireland		1			13
		Maria Flinn	2	f				R.I.					14
		Edward Flinn	23	m		Laborer		Ireland					15
		James Flinn	23	m		Laborer		Ireland					16
		Michael Flinn	22	m		Laborer		Ireland					17
111	199	Michael Cavanah	37	m		Laborer		Ireland					18
		Catherine Cavanah	35	f				Ireland					19
		Catherine Cavanah	10	f				Ireland		1			20
	200	Hugh Mitchell	50	m		Laborer		Ireland			+		21
		Bridget Mitchell	50	f				Ireland			+		22
		Hugh Mitchell	19	m		Laborer		Ireland					23
	201	John Degney	28	m		Laborer		Ireland			+		24
		Winefred Degney	24	f				Ireland			+		25
		Bridget Degney	4	f				Ireland					26
		Mary Ann Degney	3	f				N.Y.					27
		Rosanna Degney	1/12	f				R.I.					28
112	202	John Bohn	30	m		Laborer		Ireland					29
		Lucy Bohn	20	f				Ireland					30
		Patrick Bohn	1	m				R.I.					31
	203	Mary Bohn	60	f				Ireland			+		32
		Frank Creed	30	m		Laborer		Ireland			+		33
		Mary Creed	28	f				Ireland			+		34
		Michael Kenna	25	m		Laborer		Ireland			+		35
		Mary Kenna	25	f				Ireland			+		36
		Francis Kenna	2	f				R.I.					37
		Mary Kenna	2/12					R.I.					38
	204	John Galloher	40	m		Laborer		Ireland					39
		Mary Galloher	30	f				Ireland					40
		Patrick Galloher	7	m				Ireland		1			41
		Margaret Galloher	5	f				Ireland		1			42

118

Ireland. The federal census of 1850, the first national survey to record the nativity of the population, revealed that the state had 23,111 foreign-born in a population of 147,545. At this point the natives of Ireland totaled 15,944 or 68.99 percent of the immigrants from foreign lands. By the first state census in 1865 the foreign-born population had climbed to 39,703 in a total of 184,965. Of this figure the Irish-born accounted for 27,030 or 68.03 percent. In 1870, on the eve of the creation of the Diocese of Providence, there were 31,534 Irish natives, but the beginnings of large-scale French Canadian migration had cut Ireland's percentage of the total foreign-born to approximately fifty-five percent.

However impressive, these figures do not indicate the full Irish impact upon the state at this time. Many Irish émigrés went first to England, Scotland, or British America, established a domicile there, and had children before coming to the United States. Such wanderers would be listed as arrivals from their most recent country of residence and their children regarded as natives of that nation rather than Irish. The number of Irish who followed this pattern of migration was considerable. A census in 1841 showed that 419,256 persons born in Ireland were domiciled in England and Scotland. Many of this number later came to the United States with their English- and Scottish-born children as did the Irish who had resided for a period of years in Canada. It is more than mere coincidence that natives of England and 'British America' rank second and third behind Ireland in the censuses previously cited.

Another factor in assessing the physical impact of the Irish is parentage. Rhode Island's own superintendent of the census, Edwin M. Snow, was the pioneer among the nation's statisticians in recording not only foreign nativity but also the parentage of the native-born. As Snow stated in the 1865 state census, the first in the nation to record this demographic factor: 'It seems to me, then, to be of the utmost importance that in our censuses, and in all our statistical investigations, that we should be able to classify the population *Not only by nativity, but also by parentage,* that we should be able to show not only the facts related to those of foreign birth, but also those relating to their children, as distinguished from the children of American parents.' That 1865 enumeration indicated 21,106 native-born children of Irish parentage, a figure that pushed the Irish share of the total foreign stock in Rhode Island to 73.1 percent, and this figure did not include 3,558 persons of 'mixed' parentage, a high proportion of whom had either a mother or a

An Irish construction worker is depicted in a cartoon from the 1850s. Entitled "Paddy's Ladder to Wealth in a Free Country," it seemed that "Paddy's" physical ascent was much more rapid and assured than his movement up the socio-economic ladder during this decade of intolerance.

father of Irish extraction. By 1865, therefore, nearly three out of every eight Rhode Islanders were of Irish stock.

Of these thousands of Irish who flocked to the state in the three decades before the establishment of the diocese, many were depressed to the status of paupers by the conditions of their flight from Ireland, driven into debilitating slums or drab mill villages by their

LEFT: Rhode Island received its share of the famine exodus according to this 1850 census sheet of Providence's Fifth Ward (Cathedral parish). All the entrants on this page are of Irish birth or descent and all whose occupations are listed are classified as "laborer."

RIGHT: The "American River Ganges," one of Nast's most famous cartoons. Irish Catholic bishops (with ape-like faces and miters resembling voracious alligators) prepare to attack native school children defended by a man with the King James' Version of the Bible at his chest. This invasion has been preceded by the shelling of the "U.S. Public School" (center). While Boss Tweed and his Tammany lieutenants sacrifice the native school children, including blacks and Indians, by voting aid to Catholic education, Dame Columbia, symbol of the Republic, is led to the gallows by an Irish thug (top right). St. Peter's Basilica (top left) is shown as Tammany Hall with the Irish and the Papal flags flying atop the twin domes.

LOWER RIGHT: The Irish were often stereotyped as drunken, brawling disturbers of the peace as in this Thomas Nast rendition of "The Day We Celebrate: St. Patrick's Day, 1867."

BELOW: Frederick B. Opper's rendition for *Puck* magazine of Paddy and his wife in their native habitat, entitled "The King of A-Shantee," suggests a connection between Irish Celts and Black Africans (the Ashanti tribe), while Paddy's simian features, common in cartoons of this era, suggests that the Irish are the "missing link" between man and ape.

THE AMERICAN RIVER GANGES.

"THE DAY WE CELEBRATE." IRISH RIOT.
RUM. BRUTAL ATTACK ON THE POLICE. BLOOD.

LET US HAVE PEACE
EQUAL RIGHTS TO ALL.
FREEDOM OF THE
PRESS
FREEDOM OF
SPEECH
WITH MALICE TOWARDS NONE WITH CHARITY TO
THE CONSTITUTION OF THE UNITED STATES
76
RIOTS IN NEW YORK AND OLD CORK.
BRITISH GOLD
Th. Nast.

position as unskilled laborers, and isolated intellectually by their cultural background and physical segregation. These Irish saw distinct social, economic, and religious barriers between themselves and the natives. So long as these barriers persisted, they stimulated and perpetuated group consciousness in both Irish and Yankees and left the community divided.

The most pressing economic concern of the newcomers was to obtain employment, but most post-famine Irish had escaped into a way of life completely alien and unfavorable to them. These poverty-stricken peasants, rudely transposed to an urban industrial area were excluded by training and discrimination from most decent jobs. This exclusion forced the vast majority into the ranks of an unskilled proletariat, whose cheap labor and abundant numbers energized all aspects of the state's industrial development. In the economic sphere the Irish woman also played an important role as a factory hand, a home seamstress, or a domestic for the well-to-do Yankee merchants, industrialists and professional men.

Despite their willingness to work, the Irish found the value of their labor low, often too low to support them and their families adequately. Further, from the day they landed these immigrants competed for jobs that were fewer than the number of available men. Through all these years unemployment was chronic, and those at the bottom of the rung were particularly hard-hit in times of local or national depression, such as the difficult conditions associated with the panic of 1857.

This economic uncertainty was compounded in some areas by squalid living conditions. Immigrant rents were high beyond all reason, tenements were overcrowded, sewerage and sanitation facilities were primitive where they existed at all. These conditions took their toll in sickness and lives.

When a cholera epidemic ravaged Providence in 1854 Dr. Edwin M. Snow in a report to the city council noted that the highest percentage of fatal cases were in the neighborhoods of India Street and Fox Point Hill — both Irish ghettoes. Nine-tenths of all deaths occurred among foreigners and these, said Snow, were influenced by the wretched tenements in which they lived and by their habits of life.

In 1850 Thomas R. Hazard was authorized by the General Assembly to study the provisions made by the cities and towns of the state for the support of the poor and the insane. Hazard's report, submitted to the legislature in January 1851, did much to focus attention on the plight of the sick and the poor and led to some important reforms. However, public charity and even the emergency public works programs sponsored by Providence in the late 1850s, such as the filling of the old Cove, were far from sufficient to meet the needs of the Catholic immigrant. Church-related efforts such as the charitable fairs held by the Sisters of Mercy and the almsgiving of the six St. Vincent de Paul societies that were formed in various parishes played a major role in caring for the destitute. These efforts were augmented by certain fraternal agencies such as the *Shamrock Benevolent Aid Society* of Woonsocket established in 1858 during the depression.

The upward mobility of the American Irish varied from place to place. In Rhode Island it was slow and unspectacular with few Horatio Alger careers from 'rags to riches.' By 1870 there were some notable breakthroughs into the mercantile class and an increasing number of skilled workers, but these constituted a definite minority. The bulk of the Irish population was still lodged in the lowest socio-economic class.

Robert A. Wheeler's recent study 'Fifth Ward Irish: Immigrant Mobility in Providence, 1850–1870,' indicates that considerable geographic mobility occurred as many Irishmen went from one mill area to another in search of work, but it shows little movement up the ladder of success. Wheeler concludes that immigrants endured a very low level of occupational

The Irish-Catholic was viewed by nativists as rowdy, prone to violence and the cause of much of America's internal dissent. "Dame Columbia," symbol of the Republic (which was often depicted as a school), confers with her English counterpart "Dame Britannia," who informs the American lady that the unruly Irish boy has given her "so much trouble in my school." Items confiscated from the young ruffian include a gun, a knife and a bottle of rum. They have been placed atop the teacher's desk next to the "Holy Bible."

mobility. The typical Irish-born worker who came to Providence's Fifth Ward (along the west bank of the river from downtown to Rhode Island Hospital) 'did not stay; the typical immigrant who stayed remained unskilled or at best moved up one occupational level.'

Four decades after their large-scale arrival, the Irish still formed the substratum of Rhode Island society. Regarded as lower class menials, and victimized by economic discrimination ('No Irish Need Apply') they were caught in a web of poverty and social alienation from which they would not escape until new immigrants arrived to take their place. Even politics, the road of Irish in other states to power and prestige, was blocked by formidable constitutional obstacles that rendered Rhode Island's Irish politically impotent. By 1872 their most commanding achievement and their most notable success was the Church of Providence.

The Nature of Nineteenth-Century Irish Catholicism

The historian of Irish-American nationalism, Thomas N. Brown, has observed that the Irish 'had emerged into the modern world from a past in which Catholicism had played perhaps a stronger role than among any other people of Western Europe. By the end of the seventeenth century, the Irish were a conquered people, their leaders had either fled or been despoiled, and thereafter Gaelic cultural disintegration matched strides with the expansion of English authority. The peasant Irish, therefore, found their security in the Church and their leadership in the priesthood. Hatred and fear of English Protestantism were part of their cultural heritage.' Catholicism was their red badge of courage and by the mid-nineteenth century, through the efforts of Daniel O'Connell, it was also a symbol of their nationalism. One reinforced the other.

O'Connell in his crusades for Catholic emancipation and the repeal of the Act of Union forged a fundamental alliance between Church and nation in his attempt to create an Irish state. Historian Emmet Larkin explains the consequence of O'Connell's strat-

GETTING WARMED UP.

KERRIGAN *(a trifle full).*—T'roth, Rosie Deasey, youse is th' (hic-gl) foinest gurrul in th' War-r-d to be callin' on a could night!

egy: 'In joining Church to nation he not only made their future both more certain and secure, but more sane for he provided thereby for the containment of most of the violent aspects of the nation's personality as represented by the Young Ireland, Fenian, and republican Sinn Fein tradition. The price that he paid for that containment was the integration of the Church in an inextricable way into the pattern of constitutional politics. What O'Connell did not foresee ... was that the Church in the generation after his death [in 1847] was going to build itself socially and economically into the very vitals of the nation until it became virtually at one with the nation's identity and an essential part of its consciousness.'

The fusion of religion and nationality was so complete in Irish Catholic culture that it extended even to their linguistic view of the English. The Gaelic word *Sassenach* means both 'Protestant' and 'English-

THE LANDLORD WEAKENED.

THE WIDOW MURPHY.— And so yez would put me out for the rint, would yez? The minute yez lay a finger on that goat, Oi 'll have yez arrested by the S. P. C. A.

Nineteenth century cartoons, whether intended to be humorous or satirical, ridiculed the Irish. Favorite themes were violence, intemperance, and poverty. Typical were these cartoons from *Puck,* a magazine of political and social commentary.

man.' As one English Catholic remarked at the turn of the present century: 'The Irish are Catholic because they are Irish, and Irish because they are Catholic. They will not allow that I, as an Englishman, am a Catholic, for that is a privilege which belongs to them.'

But the situation in Ireland would be misunderstood if the word 'religion' is taken in a purely doctrinal sense. 'Religion' also marked social, economic, and political boundaries. One nineteenth-century commentator observed that 'the term Catholic is not a mark of religious distinction, but of every distinction whatever.' According to another student of Irish character: 'Religion in Ireland has indeed a close connection with the national life; the atmosphere of public opinion is charged with it; it intervenes in all social and political affairs.'

When the Catholic Irish arrived in the United States and were confronted by native intolerance (Protestantism and Americanism were also long synonymous) they transposed their antipathy for the English Protestant oppressor to their Yankee antagonists of English descent. This basic religious conflict was magnified in Rhode Island not only by the usual political, economic, and social rivalries but also by the unique constitutional discrimination against the naturalized Irishman that the Yankees stoutly defended through the agency of the Republican party. But much more than a nationalistic vendetta against English Protestantism or its American counterpart, Irish Catholicism was also an amalgam of clerical deference, ultramontanism, asceticism, missionary zeal, militancy, 'puritanism' and conservatism — reinforced by the Irish 'Devotional Revolution' of the mid-nineteenth century.

Some Catholic nations have a tradition of anticlericalism because their priests and prelates have aligned themselves with an entrenched upper-class establishment. The reverse was true in Ireland. Tocqueville in 1835 reported 'an unbelievable unity between the Irish clergy and the Catholic population.' Nearly three quarters of a century later another French observer, L. Paul-Dubois, reinforced this view. 'The power of the Irish clergy may be traced to two principal causes,' contended Paul-Dubois, 'the one psychological — the faith and the essentially religious character of the nation — the other historical, the fact that the priest has been for centuries the sole guide and sole protector of the Irish people.' He concluded that 'nothing could be more touching to see than this attachment which still exists, this respect, this confidence, this intimacy, between the priest and his parishioners.'

The priest came from much the same social and economic background as the peasantry to whom he ministered. He was often a farmer's son, so the wretched cottier's cabin held no shock for him. As one of the few educated Catholics, the priest was doctor, lawyer, and advisor to the poor and unlettered Irish people. He was not merely their spiritual shepherd but their guide and counsellor in temporal affairs. Yet despite this great influence, Sir Horace Plunkett, the noted Irish Protestant leader, could avow that 'the immense power of the Roman Catholic clergy has been singularly little abused.' In the eighteenth century there had been some clerical laxity, but after the founding of Maynooth seminary in 1795 there occurred a steady improvement.

Not merely a spiritual and social benefactor, the priest was a political leader as well. O'Connell's mass movement for Catholic emancipation rested on the shoulders of the parish priests, all of whom were *ex officio* members of O'Connell's political society, the *Catholic Organization.* Many of these priests were drawn into politics by the rarity of educated lay leaders and by their desire to control violence and popular excesses. Gustave Beaumont, traveling companion of Tocqueville, characterized the priesthood as the 'most national body in Ireland' belonging to 'the very heart of the country.' Small wonder that the people referred to their clerics by the Gaelic phrase, *soggarth aroon,* or 'priest dear.' This mutual affection between priest and people was carried by the Irish to America and contributed to an outpouring of religious vocations. As Father James Shannon observed: 'It has been remarked that the Irish religion is not a bond with the Church as an organization and still less with the Church as a place, but rather a personal bond between the Irish people and their priests. . . . And in the Irish homes, in the United States as in Ireland, there was created an admirable tradition of respect for the priesthood and the religious life.' The influential role of the priest, in conjunction with the force of the people's uniquely adverse religious experiences in Ireland and America, prompted the Irish — far more than any other European Roman Catholic group — to recruit for the Church.

The support and deference given to the parish priest extended to the hierarchy also, for in a sense the Irish considered their bishop as the parish priest writ large. This support did not end at the local episcopal see but went on to Rome itself. Most Irish during the nineteenth century were strong adherents of papal supremacy and earlier Gallican attitudes declined. This ultramontane position is ironic. For many Italians the Pope was an obstacle to national unification but for the Irish the Pontiff was a symbol of their nationalism. The epithet 'papist' was usually employed by the Protestant Irish to describe their adversaries; up to 1829 the formal political oath in Ireland calumniated the Catholic religion and the Holy Father and the Orangemen's offensive slogan — 'To hell with the Pope' — aroused intense resentment. When an Irishman sprang to the Pope's defense he was striking a triple blow — for the Papacy, for Catholicism, and for the nationalism which his religion had come to signify.

Occasionally the Papacy ran afoul of extreme Irish nationalism as when Pius IX condemned the Fenians, but this did not affect the pro-papal stance of Irish clerics. Ultramontanism was strengthened considerably during the 'Devotional Revolution' of the mid-nineteenth century because its leaders realized that Rome was the source of their power and influence within the Irish Church. Despite this deference to the Papacy in spiritual matters, politics was a domestic concern, hence the prevailing Irish dictum: 'Our religion from Rome, our politics from home.'

Asceticism and mysticism were other factors accounting for the high incidence of religious vocations among the Irish. Many Irish looked with aversion on the materialistic and secular goals of the earthly city and possessed an otherworldly concern for spiritual advancement. George Potter has observed that 'the Gaels had little feel for trade and commerce; they held the merchant in rather low estimate.' They exalted 'scholars, poets, priests and warriors,' while in contemptuous contrast Ulstermen were 'weavers, shopkeepers, and merchants.' A nineteenth-century observer said of the Catholic Irish that 'they rarely exhibit the combination of qualities that make for industrial success. They lack the keen interest in money-making, the sharp eye for a chance of profit ... which characterize the Englishman, Scotchman, and Ulsterman.'

Nathan Glazer and Daniel P. Moynihan in *Beyond the Melting Pot* acknowledge the role that Irish Catholics have played in the development of the American Church but, they observe, 'in secular terms it has cost them dearly in men and money. A good part of the surplus that might have gone into family property has gone to building the church. . . . The celibacy of the Catholic clergy has also deprived the Irish of the class of ministers' sons which has contributed notably to the prosperity and distinction of the Protestant world.' Glazer and Moynihan further contend that the withdrawal from the marketplace and into the religious life of so many of its able young men and women has also affected the upward economic mobility of the Irish-American community.

Edgar Litt in a recent socio-political study notes that the great emphasis the Irish placed upon 'security' has 'left its mark on the social mobility of the American Irish Catholic.' He observes the 'strong tendency for Irish Catholics to select as their employers those corporate and governmental bureaucracies in which career lines are predicated on gradual and orderly personal advancement' and he concludes that this factor has slowed their socio-economic advance.

Despite the existence of such achievement-inhibiting attitudes, which these commentators undoubtedly exaggerate and mistakenly universalize, Irish-American Catholics presently occupy a higher educational level and socio-economic status than any other ethnic group except Jewish-Americans, according to surveys conducted by priest-sociologist Andrew Greeley, director of the National Opinion Research Center. This incongruency can be explained in part by the advantages of earlier arrival, fluency in the English language, residence in the major urban centers and the inapplicability of the ascetic stereotype to such Irishmen as the pragmatic machine politician.

Although some priests and bishops were conciliatory to the Yankee community, most of the nineteenth-century Irish clerics who founded the Diocese of Providence were a very intense and aggressive lot. The Irish Church that influenced them was in every sense a church militant. As Kevin Sullivan has noted: 'Irish Catholicism in order to hold its own in a land dominated by an English Protestant culture, has developed many of the characteristics of English sectarianism: defensive, insular, parochial, puritanical.' In the United States many Irish prelates — such as Bishop O'Reilly and Archbishop Hughes — assumed that a good offense was the best defense for the faith. They boldly confronted Protestants, sought converts, entered into acrimonious religious debates, and demanded public aid for Catholic schools. They were a match for the equally strident natives who took the field against them.

They were also imbued with missionary zeal. 'To the Irish Catholic mind,' as Thomas Brown notes, 'the fabled troubles of Ireland were part of a great religious drama, a long martyrdom permitted by God, in order to spread His Word.' Aware that emigrating Irish were carrying Catholicism everywhere throughout the English-speaking world, many churchmen saw in their tattered figures an arm of the Lord and in the famines that sent them forth, the mysterious 'logic of God.' After World War I the Irish launched their famous large-scale evangelical effort towards the non-Christian world as well.

Some of the Irish militancy and much of its stern puritanical nature has been traced to the influence of Jansenism, but it appears that too much emphasis has been placed upon this factor. Jansenism was a doctrine, eventually declared heretical, which had strong adherents in France where many Irish priests were trained during the eighteenth century. When Maynooth seminary was established in 1795, it was allegedly staffed by Jansenist-oriented French clerics who had fled the ravages of the French Revolution. One of the principal Jansenist teachings posited that after Adam's fall man's nature was intrinsically depraved and corrupted and evil in itself. Mankind, therefore, was enslaved by sinful desire, and sin was possible even without interior freedom of choice. Jansenists subscribed to predestination, claiming that Christ died for the elect only and that the mass of men are damned. Consequently man was dependent for salvation not on his own works and striving for good, but on the mysterious flow of God's grace. This grace when it touched the human heart was irresistible, but it could not be summoned by human will.

This heretical system, akin to Calvinism, was definitely not accepted in substance by Irish clerics. It may have reinforced the spirit of moral austerity that characterized the Irish Church, but there is no positive evidence of a cause and effect relationship between Jansenism and Irish Catholicism. Desmond Fennell believes that the nineteenth-century Victorian ethic that permeated the British Isles had a far more important cultural impact on the Irish mind. Fennell correctly downgrades the Jansenist impact.

While the connection between Jansenism and Maynooth is exaggerated, there is little doubt that the French-educated professors at this influential seminary, which trained the great majority of Irish bishops and priests, inculcated in their students a very strict code of moral theology. The typical Maynooth graduate was well-educated, well-disciplined, pastorally attentive — 'he was at once a patriot in politics and a rigorist in moral theology.'

More significant in forming the Irish moral outlook than the alien imports of Jansenism and Victorianism was the indigenous factor of Irish family life. William Shannon tells us that the Irish people of the seventeenth and eighteenth centuries had developed both the habit of introspection and a system of moral checks and balances. They lived in a predominantly rural, secluded society in which property was not secure, administration of justice arbitrary, and opportunities for improvement legally circumscribed. They were strangers in their own land. Under these circumstances it was natural for them to center their world and their values within the microcosm of the family and to guard that retreat jealously against exterior influences and interior tendencies to defilement and impurity.

The entire family system depended upon the delicate balance of mutual interests and upon individual self-restraint. The authority of the father had to be respected, the role of the mother exalted, and absolute chastity outside the marriage relationship accepted and esteemed to preserve the integrity of the family unit. These were absolute values; promiscuity was antithetical to this abiding sense of family obligation.

It must be noted that the Irish did not harbor a neurotic aversion to sex in the Manichean or Jansenistic sense. In the pre-famine years they married very early and possessed one of the world's highest birth rates — factors that contributed to the overpopulation of the country by 1845. Discussing their 'good morals,' Tocqueville observed: 'In Ireland, where there are hardly any illegitimate children, and where, therefore, morals are very chaste, women take less trouble to hide themselves than in any other country in the world, and men seem to have no repugnance to showing themselves almost naked.' Any sexual aversion on their part, it seems, was for extra-marital sex alone, a fact that is well-documented by Professor K. H. Connell in his recent social analysis, *Irish Peasant Society*. Connell and Professor Robert E. Kennedy, Jr. also show that social and economic factors arising in the wake of the great famine, more than the inhibiting moral influences of Irish Catholicism, account for the high rate of postponed or late marriage and permanent celibacy among the Irish people in the last half of the nineteenth century.

Their tradition of sexual purity gave Irish Catholics their well-known and well-deserved reputation for chastity and intolerance for the obscene. As Bishop Kinsley told Tocqueville: 'Twenty years of confession have taught me that for a girl to fall is very rare, and for a married woman practically unknown.' The perceptive French visitor was perhaps more impressed by this virtue than any other. He recorded that even the occupying English soldiers attested to the strong conjugal fidelity of the Irish wife. This attitude helps to explain why Irish clerics in Ireland and America have vigorously supported censorship of obscene materials and opposed the permissiveness of the civil libertarians.

A final salient ingredient in nineteenth-century Irish Catholicism was its socio-political conservatism. Nineteenth-century liberalism fed by the doctrines of the French Revolution was vigorously opposed by the Irish Catholic community except for their fast-fleeting sympathy with the Young Ireland movement of 1848. Although they had no taste for monarchy *per se* as a system of government, the Irish hierarchy condemned revolutionary radicalism in Catholic Spain, Austria, and Italy and defended the 'legitimate' regimes.

Their stand on the Italian question was especially strong because 'unification' directly threatened the power of the Pope. Most Irish churchmen thought that the European upheavals of 1848 and thereafter represented a 'spirit of radical Protestantism' that had 'crept into every class of society, into every . . . political order,' and which threatened 'the true Catholic spirit.' Time after time the Irish Catholic press in

Irish-American support for the Papacy and opposition to the Italian republican seizure of the Papal States is satirized by Nast in 1871. Garabaldi, Mazzini, Cavour and their associates topple Pius IX from his temporal throne despite the excommunication of the new Italian government, while Irish Americans kiss the papal toe and submit a petition, signed by "Patrick O'Blarny" and others, affirming that "the Roman people have no rights."

America and its conservative ally, Orestes Brownson, attacked 'red' republicanism in Europe as part of a plot by Protestantism to undermine Catholic civilization. Instead they maintained 'the necessity of subordination and obedience to lawful rulers' and disdained republican leaders such as Garibaldi and Mazzini of Italy, the Hungarian Louis Kossuth, and the Yankee filibusterers in Latin America. The hierarchy even joined Pope Pius IX in condemning the radical Fenian brotherhoods.

This Irish respect for what they considered 'legitimate authority' and their staunch conservatism alienated them from both native New England reformers and some later immigrant arrivals, notably the Italians. The Irish, however, drew a distinction between democratic republicanism as it existed in the United States — which they warmly supported — and the anti-clerical, 'socialist-inspired,' 'red' republicanism of Europe — which they vigorously condemned.

Toward government's role in promoting social improvements the Irish Catholic community also looked with apprehension. Long oppressed by an 'illegitimate' and hostile government, they harbored an ingrained fear and suspicion of government-enforced reforms such as temperance or government-controlled compulsory education, for these, they believed, used the state as an instrument for strengthening secular against religious forces.

Professor Aaron I. Abell, the leading student of Catholic social action, has described this attitude best. In the opinion of Irish conservatives, states Abell, 'any serious attempt to change or reform the social order must terminate in revolution and anarchy. They could see no halting point between the stability of the status quo and the chaos of radical overturn.'

To some degree Catholic thought in this country mirrored the impasse in Europe between the Catholic Church and the liberal movement. But chiefly most Irish-American Catholic thinkers were apprehensive of reform in its American setting. They believed that the reforming impulse stemmed from the humanitarian and antislavery crusades of pre-Civil War days, that it was inherently and inexorably socialistic, and

Paul Cardinal Cullen, Archbishop of Dublin and Apostolic Delegate of Pius IX, led the Irish "Devotional Revolution" of the nineteenth century. This movement had a substantial impact on Irish-American Catholicism.

motivated by an anti-Catholic animus.

Most Irish Catholic leaders believed that education and charity prospered best under private and religious auspices, but they favored — and secured in Rhode Island and elsewhere — a limited government subsidy for their more important and expensive charities. They relied principally on moral suasion and the Church's efforts in the socio-religious field, and believed that only the Church itself, through the associated endeavors of its members, could minimize the dangers to the faith and morals of its poor immigrant flock posed by 'socialistic' reform efforts.

Most Catholic clerics and journalists who advanced economic and social opinions were more inclined to praise the virtues and redemptive role of Christian poverty, and to blame social problems on the decline of religion, than they were to attack the premises and practices of *laissez-faire* capitalism.

In the 1880s a more liberal brand of social Catholicism emerged to challenge this conservative approach. Its spokesmen defended labor unions, once thought too radical, and suggested state intervention to mitigate social disorder as an alternative to socialism. This minority movement was led by such Irish-American clerics as James Cardinal Gibbons, Archbishops John Ireland and John Keane, and Father Edward McGlynn. But these 'Americanists' did not prevail. Their efforts were successfully checked by a coalition of Irish and German prelates led by Archbishop Michael Corrigan and Bishop Bernard McQuaid.

The various attitudes and values that endowed Irish Catholicism with its unique outlook were stimulated and reinforced by a great religious revival that swept Ireland in the mid-nineteenth century — a spiritual upheaval, analogous to America's 'Great Awakenings,' known as the 'Devotional Revolution.' It had its origins during the pre-famine era in the moral crusade of Father Mathew and the nationalistic agitation of Daniel O'Connell, but it reached full flower in the wake of the great famine under Paul Cullen, Archbishop of Dublin and apostolic delegate of Pius IX.

Due to the trauma of the famine, the Irish who remained were psychologically and socially ready for a great evangelical revival, while economically and organizationally the Irish Church under Cullen became concurrently ready to meet the religious and emotional needs of its people. This movement, however, as its historian Emmet Larkin has shown, satisfied more than the negative factors of resentment and fear induced by the great catastrophe of the mid-forties. It strengthened not only Catholicism but national identity as well and made Irish and Catholic almost interchangeable terms. The Devotional Revolution and its causes 'are crucial to understanding the development of Irish nationalism and the cultural importance of Irish Catholicism in that development,' Larkin contends.

The movement was also effective because the decline in Ireland's post-famine population allowed the increasing number of clergy to exert a more direct and immediate influence on the Irish people. In 1840 there was only one priest for every 3,000 faithful, but by 1870 the ratio was one for every 1,250, and the quality of the clergy had improved.

In extending their increasing zeal and piety to the laity, priests centered their attention on the sacraments, especially Penance and the Eucharist, and conducted stimulating missions in nearly every parish in Ireland during the decade of the fifties. In addition, a whole series of devotional exercises were encouraged to instill piety through their ritual beauty and intrinsic mystery. Sponsored by various religious sodalities and bolstered by devotional aids, these services touched the whole range of senses and emotions, and became a mainstay of the Church in the era between Vatican I and Vatican II.

The ferver of Irish religious life was captured by Frenchman Paul-Dubois in his 1907 study *L'Irlande Contemporaine*:

> No one can visit Ireland without being impressed by the intensity of Catholic belief there, and by the fervour of its outward manifestations. Watch the enormous crowds of people who fill the churches in the towns, the men as numerous as the women; see them all kneeling on the flagstones, without a sound or gesture, as though petrified in prayer! Go to early Mass on Sundays in Dublin and watch three or four priests simultaneously giving the Sacrament to throngs of communicants too great for the size of the churches. Observe in the country, above all in the West, the regular recitation of the Rosary in the family, the frequent practice of fasting two days before Communion, the 'stations' held at Easter and Christmas in every hamlet, with general Confession and Communion, by the parish priest who goes to the houses of the people and celebrates in them the Holy Sacrifice, according to a touching custom which dates from the times of persecution. How can we fail to admire a piety so ardent and so simple? . . . let us at least recognize that of all European peoples Ireland is the most fundamentally religious.

These cultural and religious values were transported to America during the second half of the nineteenth century by a continuing stream of Irish priests and laity. These more zealous Catholics substantially elevated the devotional level of Irish-American Catholicism and infused it with greater fervor and assertiveness. The cumulative result, as several recent sociological studies have shown, is that Irish-Americans came to share with the Franco-Americans the distinction of possessing the highest level of *formal* religious association and involvement of any Catholic ethnic groups.

Such were the varied influences its Irish founders impressed upon the new Church of Providence. This church had advanced in only forty years from a scattered handful of communicants to a vibrant institution with a formal organization and special identity. In its short existence its primary influences had been those distinctive Irish traits that had given the local Catholic community a unity of religious outlook. The vast majority of clergy were either trained in Ireland or educated in American facsimiles of Irish seminaries. The laity of Rhode Island was also overwhelmingly Irish in origin and perspective. Irishness and Catholicism had fused and produced what was in reality an Irish national church. In time clear distinctions would develop between Irish-American Catholicism and its Old World model, especially in the areas of ecclesiastical authority and clerical influence on matters that were not strictly spiritual; but these differences were much less obvious in 1872 than in later years.

A basic problem besetting the diocese during much of its first century was to harmonize and reconcile the intense Irish brand of Catholicism with the needs and attitudes of successive groups of Catholic immigrants who found the Irish Church significantly if not fundamentally different from their own. When social, cultural, linguistic, economic, and even political conflicts were added to the religious factor, the task con-

A Corpus Christi procession passing through a town in County Limerick at the time when Frenchman Paul-Dubois wrote in his commentary on Ireland "that of all European peoples Ireland is the most fundamentally religious."

An artist's rendition of a nineteenth-century "Irish colleen" holding her rosary beads.

fronting the multi-ethnic Diocese of Providence assumed formidable and challenging dimensions as its subsequent history would amply reveal.

La langue, la foi, et la patrie —
The Arrival of the Franco-Americans

> Where is the thatch-roofed village, the home of Acadian farmers, —
> Men whose lives glided on like rivers that water the woodlands,
> Darkened by shadows of earth, but reflecting an image of heaven?
> Waste are those pleasant farms, and the farmers forever departed!
> Scattered like dust and leaves, when the mighty blasts of October
> Seize them, and whirl them aloft, and sprinkle them far o'er the ocean.
> Naught but tradition remains of the beautiful village of Grand-Pré.

Those poignant words of Longfellow describing the forced French Canadian evacuation of Acadia in the mid-eighteenth century were equally applicable to the nineteenth century province of Quebec. The emigration of French Canadians to the United States and particularly New England during the period from 1860 to 1924 caused a depletion of the Quebec countryside. By 1900 more than 700,000 French Canadians resided within the borders of the United States, and of this number approximately 500,000 had settled in New England. This large exodus served to enrich American culture and invigorate Catholicism in the northeastern regions of the United States.

Less than a year after the British came to Jamestown, Samuel Champlain chose Quebec in 1608 as the first settlement of New France. The French Jesuits who accompanied this intrepid explorer made Catholicism an integral part of the colony. This tiny settlement was slowly and sporadically nourished by immigrants from the mother country as the French presence in the New World took shape. The French government, in an effort to encourage settlement, offered to its lesser nobility grants of land in Canada called *seigneuries*. The landlords or *siegneurs* parceled out their holdings to colonists but their attempt to establish the feudal system in the New World met with only limited success.

Other efforts to stimulate settlement in New France were also unproductive. By 1673 the colonial population of Canada was still less than 10,000. It is perhaps this failure of the mother country to supply her American colony with an adequate number of immigrants that resulted in the Canadian predilection towards early marriages and large families.

The French also established a series of trading posts and commercial towns along the great interior waterways of North America. Starting with Quebec and Montreal on the St. Lawrence, the French influence eventually spread through the entire Great Lakes region, penetrated the Ohio River Valley at Fort Duquesne (Pittsburgh), and extended to the Mississippi Valley where the outpost of St. Louis anchored the northern settlements and Mobile and New Orleans became French windows on the Gulf of Mexico. This far-flung empire of the Bourbon monarchy not only supplied raw materials to the mother country but also served to check the territorial encroachments of Protestant England.

The friction between England and France over the European balance of power and colonial ascendancy resulted in a series of wars that continued sporadically during the three-quarters of a century following England's Glorious Revolution of 1688 — an event that marked the ouster of England's Catholic king, James II. The last conflict, popularly known as the French and Indian War (1754–63) resulted in a sound defeat for the forces of Louis XV. The Treaty of Paris (1763) that concluded this 'Great War for Empire' stripped France of her North American empire and placed the French colonists under English rule.

French Canadian culture certainly did not die with General Montcalm on the Plains of Abraham in 1759 but the collapse of the French empire caused many French officials to return to their homeland. This exodus of civil authorities created a leadership vacuum. Faced with the prospect of English rule and the attempted imposition of the Protestant religion upon them, the rural French *habitants* looked to the clergy to preserve their religion, language and culture. '*La foi et la langue*' became the twin pillars supporting French Canadian cultural persistence. The bond between language and faith became inseparable. To adopt the English tongue became synonymous with a surrender to Protestantism. Consequently, all those who learned English or assumed English surnames were not only considered defectors but lost souls as well.

In 1774, as a result of British fears that the brewing revolution in the American colonies might spread to her newly-acquired French subjects in Canada, Parliament passed the Quebec Act. This act granted religious toleration to the Catholics of that colony, extended the boundaries of Quebec province southward to the Ohio River, eliminated the anti-papal oath of allegiance to the British Crown, and permitted a small degree of self-government. While slightly mollifying anti-British feeling, this opportunistic legislation did not win the loyalty of the French. In religious spirit, language, and culture, the *habitants* refused to be assimilated.

The French of Canada are a proud people. Their history is filled with a strong allegiance to Catholicism that has its roots with Champlain and his initial settlement. Like the Irish, their national identity was forged by a severe test for survival in their British-dominated homeland. The comparison extends further for the *habitant* and the cottier shared a common socio-economic lifestyle. They both came from an agricultural background that sometimes bordered on the subsistence level; they raised large families; they migrated to escape economic deprivation; and they were clannish by nature. The Church of France had been the defender and tutor of Irish Catholicism after Henry VIII's separation from Rome. The same strains of mysticism, moral rigor, and authoritarianism flowed through both churches to varying degrees. For both ethnic groups, religion and nationalism became a single entity from which they received the spiritual subsistence needed to lighten the hardships of a subjugated life.

François ("Fanfan") Proulx, first member of that pioneer French Canadian family to be born in the United States (*ca.* 1815). At the time of his death in January, 1884, at the age of sixty-nine, he was a leader of Woonsocket's Franco-American community.

Ironically, these two groups failed to co-exist in harmony. The French-Irish friction was one of the most serious internal problems that the Diocese of Providence faced during the first sixty years of its existence. This strife can be best understood when viewed from an economic and cultural perspective.

Life among the *habitants* of Quebec became one of increasing hardship. The farmlands, exhausted by overuse, produced smaller crop yields. The problem of inheritance and land tenure accelerated the economic decline. Upon the death of the father his farmland was subdivided among his surviving children. Because of this fragmentation of agricultural land and the bare subsistence farming it produced, many began to look beyond the Canadian borders for relief.

The trickle of what would become a flood of French Canadian immigrants to Rhode Island began in 1815. During that year Francis Proulx and his family settled in Woonsocket. Six years later the families of Prudent and Joseph Mayer chose northern Rhode Island as their new home. By 1846, a 'statistical survey of Woonsocket' conducted by S. C. Newman, revealed that 250 inhabitants in the Woonsocket area were of French Canadian ancestry in a total population of 4,856.

Most of the new arrivals were responding to what some have called 'the lure of the loom.' As early as 1810 Woonsocket textile entrepreneurs had opened the Social Manufacturing Company. Within a short period the clatter of textile shuttles could be heard along the banks of the Blackstone River. The continued expansion of the textile industry in Rhode Island prompted the mill owners to recruit the eager *habitants* of French Canada who were already experienced in the domestic production of textiles. With the coming of the Civil War the need for manpower to replace those serving the Union cause became so acute that many New England manufacturers set up employment agencies in Quebec province.

For those seeking an escape from the privations of farm life, the promise of a steady job and good pay was too tempting to refuse. And for those with large families, children now became an asset as potential wage earners. Many left Quebec never to return. Possessions and land were often auctioned off to provide train fare. Some *habitants,* however, envisioned their stay in America as a temporary one that would provide the means of insuring financial security when they returned to their homeland.

The reception of Franco-Americans in a strange land was often less than cordial. Willing to work a fifteen-hour day, six days a week, for a meager wage, the French Canadians represented a clear threat to the economic security of both Yankee and Irish millhands. It is not difficult to understand the derisive epithet that the Irish appended to these rivals — 'the Chinese of the East.' These economic fears partially explain the failure of the Irish to welcome the newcomers from French Canada. And since cotton and woolen manufacturing dominated the state's economic scene well into the twentieth century, the basis for this ethnic tension was slow to be eliminated. In the late 1880s politics became another point of Franco-Irish friction when most *habitants* reacted to Irish antagonism by allying with their employers — the Yankee Republican industrialists. As Father Austin Dowling observed in his 1899 history of the diocese: 'the French Canadian . . . votes the Republican ticket. It is his vote that keeps Rhode Island, Republican.'

George C. Ballou began cotton manufacture in Woonsocket in 1835. His factory attracted and employed many of the first French Canadian immigrants to whom this benevolent entrepreneur became known as "Uncle George."

Textile mills in the Blackstone and Pawtuxet Valleys attracted thousands of willing French Canadian workers. Shown here is the Clinton Cotton Mill, Woonsocket (1867 sketch) and a Centreville (West Warwick) factory near the French church of St. John the Baptist (photo *ca.* 1875).

French Canadian immigrants to Rhode Island retained that strong adherence to their faith, language and customs that had sustained their cultural identity in English-dominated Canada, but even their mode of Catholicism clashed with that of their Irish co-religionists. In Quebec the parish church was the center of religious activity and the higher echelons of Catholic authority exerted little if any control over their *curés*. Virtually all power was vested in the parish council that usually consisted of three laymen with the parish *curé* or pastor serving as president. Canadian immigrants to America found a centralized Catholic church — a church whose power base lay not in the parish but rather with the bishop. In Rhode Island after 1866, legal authority to transact the business of the parish was vested in a parish corporation. But it was the bishop not the pastor who served as president. To a people accustomed to local control by French-speaking *curés* this centralized church organization, dominated as it was by Irish prelates, represented a threat to their religious traditions. The Franco-Americans not only belonged to a church, in a sense they felt that it also belonged to them.

There were other novelties that caused the French Canadians to be uncomfortable in their new religious surroundings. Seat money and other offerings were levies to which they were unaccustomed because of the well-endowed status of their church in Canada. English-language sermons and confessions hampered them in the practice of their faith. The demand by the Franco-Americans for the preservation of their native tongue did not strike a responsive chord with many

Irish priests who felt that rapid Americanization of foreign-born Catholics would dispel the Church's foreign or alien image. Finally, the *habitant* missed the colorful and elaborate religious rituals that Irish priests, sensitive to Yankee criticisms of 'popish pageantry,' often simplified or eliminated.

The anxieties that these differences created could best be relieved and the spiritual needs of the migrants from French Canada could best be served by the ministrations of French Canadian priests working within the framework of French Canadian national parishes. This became not only the desire but the demand of the transplanted *habitants*. '*Survivance*,' the maintenance of their culture, was threatened by *les églises irlandaises* (the Irish churches).

By 1865 there were 3,384 foreign-born Rhode Islanders from 'British America,' and a substantial majority of this number were people of French descent from Quebec. Five years later the federal census recorded 10,242 immigrants from this source. Woonsocket continued to be the population and cultural center for the state's Franco-Americans but the Blackstone Valley mill villages of Manville, Ashton, Albion, Slatersville, Central Falls, Pawtucket and Marieville also attracted large numbers of *habitants*. Further to the south, the Olneyville section of Providence, the town of Warren, and the Pawtuxet Valley textile centers of Arctic, Natick and Lippittsville were affected by the influx of Franco-American migrants. Clearly the time had arrived to recognize the special religious and cultural requirements of this rapidly growing Catholic community.

During the administration of Bishop Tyler the only recorded visit of a Canadian cleric to Rhode Island was made by Father Zéphyrin Levesque of Quebec. His 1847 missionary effort was abridged by an illness that forced him to retire to New Orleans. Tyler's successor, Bernard O'Reilly, made the first attempt to recruit a French Canadian priest when the bishop's diocesan survey of 1853 revealed a Franco-American population of approximately 400. In a letter to Ignatius Bourget, Bishop of Montreal, O'Reilly requested the services of a 'zealous priest' for his Franco-American flock. Irish priests who spoke French were

Precious Blood, established in 1872, was Rhode Island's first Franco-American parish. Its church, completed in 1881, became the religious and cultural center of Franco-American life in Woonsocket.

available in the diocese but the perceptive O'Reilly reasoned that 'one of their country [French Canada] will have more influence for good over them than any other.' This unsuccessful plea was later repeated by Bishop McFarland with a similar lack of success due to a shortage of priests in Canada who could be made available for missionary work.

In 1862 Bishop McFarland estimated that French Canadians comprised about one-tenth of the 100,000 Catholics in his two-state diocese, and he took new steps to meet their spiritual needs. Since French Canadian priests were still unavailable, McFarland used French-speaking Irish clerics or the multi-lingual Dutch and Belgian priests from the new mission seminary at Louvain to perform pastoral functions for the Franco-Americans under his care. Priests with names like James Quinn, Florimond De Bruyker, Eugene Vygen, James Berkins, James Arnold Princen, Henri Spruyt, and Lawrence Walsh served as McFarland's spiritual emissaries to the *habitant* during the decade of the 1860s. Although these devoted priests spoke French, their dialect was often that of Paris rather than Quebec and their cultural tastes and religious customs were not those of the Franco-American.

The French Canadians of Woonsocket, the oldest and largest Franco-American settlement, especially desired to obtain a priest and a national parish of their own. Father Francis Lenihan, interim pastor of St. Charles parish in that city, told Bishop McFarland of his inability to communicate successfully with his French-speaking parishioners. Consequently in February 1866, McFarland petitioned the General Assembly to incorporate the 'Roman Catholic Church of St. Joseph of the Village of Woonsocket.' This well-intentioned action caused immediate problems. Unable to obtain a priest of Canadian extraction, Bishop McFarland appointed Father Eugene Vygen, a Belgian from Louvain, as pastor and listed Vygen among the five parish incorporators. Many French Canadians refused to accept the spiritual leadership of Father Vygen because of his ethnic, linguistic and cultural background. They expressed their dissatisfaction by petitioning the legislature for a new act of incorporation that substituted the names of three lay incorporators for those of McFarland, Vygen and the vicar general, William O'Reilly. The petition died, but so did the first attempt to create a French national parish in Rhode Island, because McFarland decided to defer the controversial project. Instead he assigned a succession of French-speaking curates to the parish of St. Charles where all of Woonsocket's Catholics worshipped. During their ministry in 1868 the local French community founded a St. Jean Baptiste soci-

Charles Dauray as a young man. This pioneer French Canadian priest served the Franco-Americans of Rhode Island from 1872 until his death in 1931.

ety to serve its social and cultural needs.

Finally in 1872 before his departure for Connecticut, Bishop McFarland gave the French of Woonsocket their long-awaited national church. In a move ratified by his successor, Thomas Hendricken, the bishop formed the French parish of Precious Blood, and he selected the newly-ordained French Canadian curate at St. Charles, the Reverend Antoine D. Bernard, as first pastor. The young priest secured temporary quarters in a North Main Street hall owned by the Harris Woolen Company as a place of worship for his joyful parishioners. On August 27, 1873, when a building fund reached sufficient size, Bernard purchased a parcel of land, bounded by Carrington, Park and Hamlet Avenues, and excavation began. The cornerstone of *L'église du Precieux Sang* was laid on

October 25, 1874, but Bernard was transferred to a ministry in Manville and was replaced by Father James Berkins, a Belgian priest. When this new appointment proved objectionable to the Franco-Americans, Hendricken replaced Berkins with Father Charles Dauray on November 12, 1875. Dauray assumed direction of the church building program that was hampered by severe wind damage to the uncompleted structure and inadequate financing. Finally, on July 17, 1881, the Church of the Precious Blood was dedicated.

The Rhode Island ministry of Charles Dauray is a story worth recounting. This young priest from Marieville in the diocese of St. Hyacinthe, Quebec, had come to Rhode Island on a vacation necessitated by ill health and overwork. Residing at his brother's home in Pawtucket, he attended daily Mass at St. Mary's. It was not long before the restless Dauray asked the pastor of the Pawtucket church, Reverend Patrick Delany, for permission to say Mass. Father Delany not only consented, he also suggested that Dauray conduct services for the French Canadians of the parish. Attendance at these services swelled as word spread of the presence of a French Canadian priest. This impressive display of religious devotion convinced Delany of the need for a separate French parish in the Pawtucket-Central Falls area. Sometime during the winter of 1872, he impressed this view upon Bishop Hendricken.

Meanwhile Father Dauray, his health restored, was preparing for his return to Quebec and the resumption of his duties at the college of Ste. Marie de Monnoir. Two days before his departure, Dauray journeyed to Providence to thank Bishop Hendricken for making his stay among the Catholics of Rhode Island a pleasant one. His parting remarks were cut short by Bishop Hendricken's appeal:

> "Father Dauray, you have had occasion here to reunite your people; they are numerous; they believe they are able to form and support a parish. . . . I want them to be happy; and I ask you to remain here for a little while longer. . . ."

Father Dauray did stay 'a little while longer.' For another fifty-seven years he labored in the diocese and became its most prominent Franco-American priest.

In September 1873 the legislature incorporated the parish of Notre Dame du Sacre Coeur. As its first pastor, Father Dauray wasted no time in formulating plans to house his ever-increasing congregation. He purchased land on Fales Street, Central Falls and constructed Notre Dame Church. Upon its dedication, on October 2, 1875, it became Rhode Island's first Catholic church completed and occupied exclusively by French Canadians. Immediately after this success,

Father Patrick Delany, pastor of St. Mary's, Pawtucket (1853–1879), arranged for Father Dauray to begin his long ministry to the Franco-Americans of Rhode Island.

Dauray was reassigned to Precious Blood parish.

While these national church projects developed in Woonsocket and Central Falls, a third pioneer French parish was forming to the southward in the valley of the Pawtuxet. Early French Canadian immigrants to the Pawtuxet Valley mill villages of Phenix, Arctic and Natick attended religious services at St. Mary's Church, Crompton during the 1860s.

Faced with the problem of parishioners who could not understand English, Reverend James Gibson, the pastor of St. Mary's, petitioned Bishop McFarland for a French-speaking assistant. The cooperative prelate assigned Belgian James Berkins to this ministry.

By 1872, continuing French Canadian immigration into this region created a clear need for a national parish. The failure of the French-speaking curate at St. Mary's to appear at a Sunday service was the incentive that prompted leaders of the local French-Canadian community to petition Bishop Hendricken for a national church in 1872. Several months later the bishop responded favorably and appointed Reverend Henri Spruyt — a Dutch immigrant who spoke fluent French — pastor of the new parish named in honor of St. John the Baptist, patron saint of the founders of New France.

Despite the financial hardships resulting from the 1873 depression, thousands of dollars were pledged and countless items donated for the new Pawtuxet Valley church. Additional funds were raised through bazaars, raffles, picnics, and other social gatherings. The self-sacrifice and small contributions of the French mill workers financed an imposing $40,000 edifice that was 115 feet long and 60 feet wide.

Construction of St. John the Baptist began on January 8, 1873. In the following year the parish was incorporated as 'St. John the Baptist of Centreville,

The church that Father Dauray built — Notre Dame de Sacre Coeur of Central Falls. This original structure on Fales Street was Rhode Island's first Catholic church completed and occupied by French Canadians. It was dedicated on October 2, 1875.

The first Franco-American church in the Pawtuxet Valley, St. John the Baptist, was begun on January 8, 1873 and dedicated on June 20, 1880. It was demolished in 1938.

Rhode Island's French Canadians, like their Quebec ancestors, steadfastly maintained their religion, language and culture. Here a Woonsocket group (*ca.* 1890) awaits the traditional St. Jean Baptiste Day parade on June 24.

Rhode Island.' When the beautiful gothic church was completed and dedicated on June 20, 1880, Bishop Hendricken praised the generosity of the French Canadian community and told them with accuracy and sincerity that the new church was 'a tribute to your religious fervor and the goodness of your race.'

In less than two years from Hendricken's accession (with the establishment of St. James in Manville and the laying of its cornerstone on April 26, 1874 and the formal establishment on February 8, 1874 of the parish of St. Charles in Providence) the Franco-Americans could point with pride to five national parishes, and there were twelve more to come. Through the medium of the national church and its cultural ally, the French national society, the religious heritage of the *habitant* was now secure — he had reason indeed to 'rejoice in hope.' Unfortunately, during the following decades, conflicts between the Irish-dominated hierarchy and some Franco-American Catholics developed and simmered until the bitter *Sentinelle* movement of the 1920s rocked the Diocese of Providence.

Portuguese, Cape Verdean and German Catholics

During the formative era of Rhode Island Catholicism only a handful of the faithful were of other than Irish or French descent. Two ethnic groups with more than a scattering of Catholic adherents were the Portuguese and the Germans.

In 1850 there were forty-eight Rhode Islanders of Portuguese birth. According to the state census of 1865 the Portuguese population included seventy-five foreign-born and 140 natives of Portuguese parentage — a total of 215. Ten years later the figures for 'Portugal and Western Islands' had reached 561 and 865 respectively, or a total of 1,426. In 1872, therefore, the Portuguese of the Providence diocese were more notable for the exciting and unusual manner of their arrival than their numerical size. But they were no strangers to the region, for the Portuguese presence in southeastern New England had been felt from colonial times. Successive colonies of Sephardic Jews from Portugal and Spain had made Newport their home. The first arrived via Holland, Brazil, and New Amsterdam in 1658; a second colony developed during the 1740s, and it endured until 1822. Among its notable achievements was the establishment of Touro Synagogue (1763). This predominantly Sephardic settlement produced such business and civic leaders as Aaron Lopez, Isaac Touro, Naphtali Hart and James Lucena, a Newport merchant who was Portuguese in nationality, Jewish in ethnic background, and Roman Catholic in religion. It appears from the records that Joseph Antunes, another Portuguese merchant, naturalized in 1750, was also Catholic and undoubtedly there were others, but the eighteenth century Portuguese community in Rhode Island was distinctively and overwhelmingly Jewish in faith and culture.

Not until the decade of the 1840s did a significant number of Portuguese Catholics make their debut in the southern New England area. This contact was established during the expansion of the New England whaling industry as New Bedford replaced Nantucket as the whaling capital of America, and other regional ports such as Fall River, Newport, Bristol, Providence, Mystic and New London expanded their fishing operations. When the whaling fleet grew and voyages reached farther and farther from home, the promoters looked for ways to cut operating expenses. One method of economizing was to hire foreign crewmen who were experienced and skilled but who worked for lower wages. The Atlantic islands of Portugal — the Azores and the Cape Verdes — had just such willing and able personnel. These isles were located near whaling grounds where skill and experience in this dangerous trade could be gained. These Portuguese possessions were misgoverned, isolated and poor, especially the Cape Verdes that suffered from periodic drought and famine and a very low standard of living. Wages that native Americans regarded as meager were most attractive to the Portuguese islanders, many of whom were exploited by the large landlords, and the chance to settle in America at voyage's end was for some an irresistible inducement.

Because these Portuguese mariners were eager to supply the American whalemen's demands, vessels with partial crews sailed from New Bedford and other New England ports first to the Azores and then to the Cape Verdes to take on food, provisions, and seamen. The first trans-Atlantic stop on a typical whaling cruise, the Azores, was a 400-mile-long archipelago of nine inhabited islands and a group of rock formations located 700 to 800 miles west of Portugal. These volcanic and mountainous isles, of which St. Michael's (297 square miles) was the largest, were inhabited principally by white descendants of migrants from continental Portugal, the nation which had annexed them in the 1420s.

The Cape Verdes, two island clusters 300 miles west of Dakar, Africa, were inhabited by people of mixed blood — chiefly the descendants of exiles from mainland Portugal and blacks from nearby Africa. Including such islands as São Vincente, Brava, Fogo,

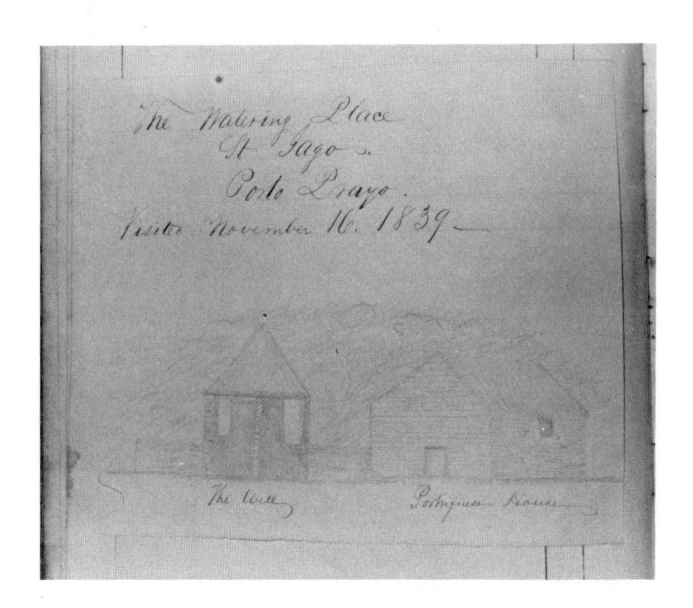

This drawing in a New Bedford whaleman's log was made during a stop at the Cape Verdean island of "St. Iago" (Santiago). Dated November 16, 1839, it shows a well and a "Portuguese house."

and Santiago (St. Iago), the Cape Verdes had been first colonized by Portugal in 1456.

Once recruited, the Portuguese whaleman usually sailed with his vessel into the South Atlantic, around Cape Horn, into the Pacific fishing grounds, and sometimes north to the Arctic Sea. This lengthy voyage could take three or more years. It gave the Portu-

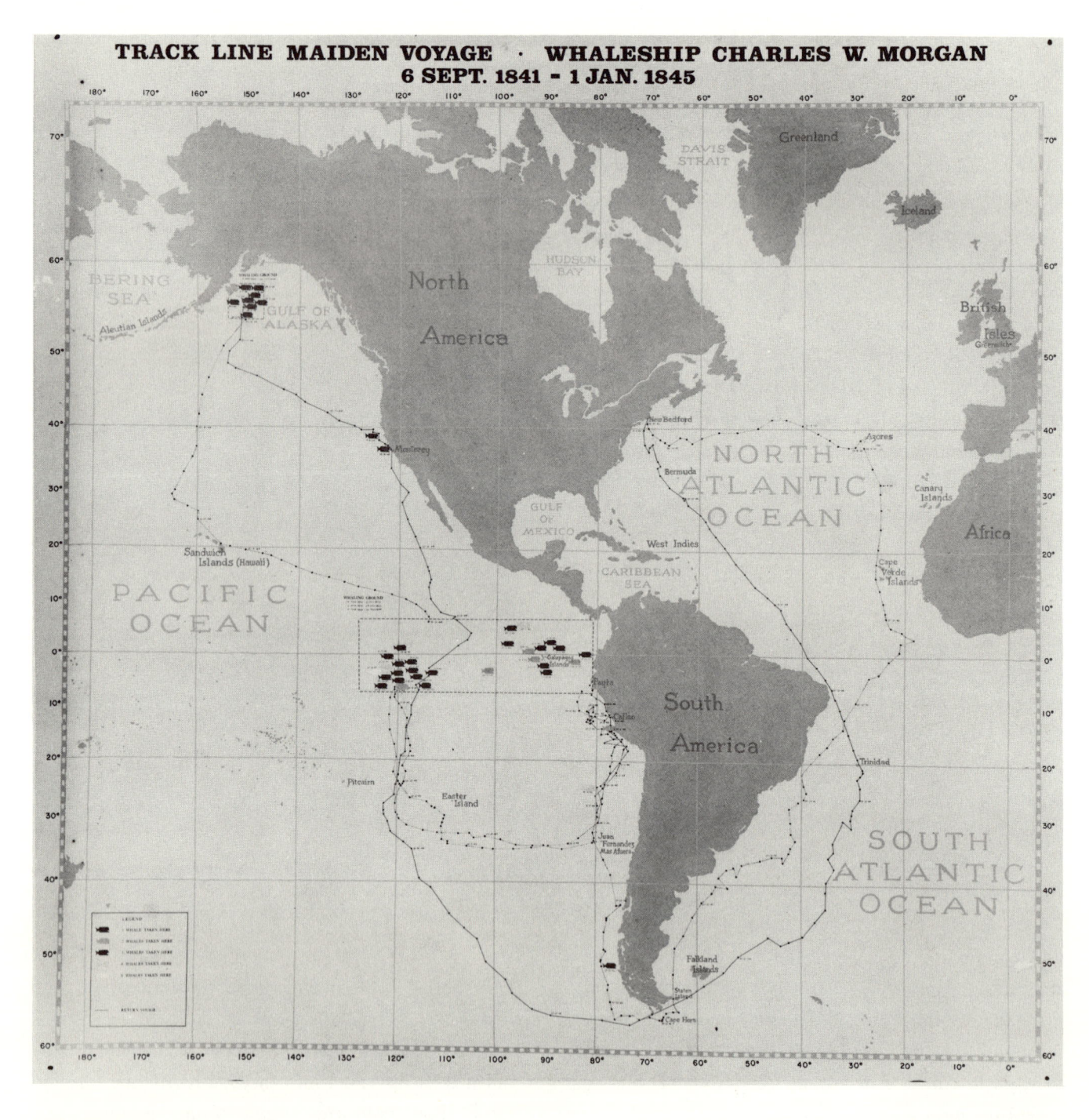

TRACK LINE MAIDEN VOYAGE · WHALESHIP CHARLES W. MORGAN
6 SEPT. 1841 - 1 JAN. 1845

The first voyage of the whaleship *Charles W. Morgan* (1841–1845) reveals a course which was typical for whalers of this era. Leaving New Bedford, it stopped at the Azores and Cape Verde Islands before sailing to fishing areas in the Pacific. It returned directly to New Bedford with its Portuguese crew. Today this restored ship is the principal attraction at Mystic Seaport.

guese contact with California and Hawaii, where some disembarked, but many others returned to their ship's homeport in New Bedford or another of the New England whaling towns. Here they stayed to become the pioneers and the beacons who inspired a more

Experienced Portuguese harpooners and boatmen, as well as green hands, were enlisted by whaleships on the outward voyage. This sketch by David Hunter Strother ("Porte Crayon") appeared in *Harper's New Monthly Magazine* in June, 1860.

massive Portuguese migration to southern New England during the dramatic expansion of the textile and related industries in the late nineteenth and early twentieth centuries when, as one historian has phrased it, 'the loom replaced the harpoon,' as the tool of the typical Portuguese immigrant.

This transformation in the purpose and character of the Portuguese immigration occurred in the 1870s, a decade during which 14,082 white Portuguese arrived in American ports as compared with the 2,658 who entered this country during the 1860s when whaling was the primary incentive for immigration.

Massachusetts, especially New Bedford, was the principal destination for both Azoreans and Cape Verdean Portuguese, but Rhode Island, especially the Fox Point section of Providence received a small but significant number before 1872. In fact, the census of 1870 showed 105 Portuguese natives in the population of Providence. Evidence of these early Portuguese settlers can be found on the baptismal register of St. Joseph's Church on Hope Street that served them spiritually until the establishment in 1885 of their own national parish, Holy Rosary, the third oldest Portuguese parish in the United States.

One of the principal benefactors of these newer immigrants was the Reverend Lawrence McMahon, founding pastor of St. Lawrence's parish, New Bedford, who began a ministry to the Portuguese residents of his city in 1865. Eventually McMahon secured for them Portuguese priests and a Portuguese national parish under the care of Reverend João Ignacio Azevedo da Encarnacão who came to New Bedford from the Azores in 1869. After the 'Whaling City' became part of the newly constituted Diocese of Providence in 1872, McMahon was named vicar general by Bishop Hendricken, and in 1879 this far-sighted friend of the Portuguese community was consecrated fifth bishop of Hartford.

The German-Americans were another element in the early history of Rhode Island Catholicism; but they were few in number, despite Germany's distinction of having sent more immigrants to the United States than any other country. Rhode Island was simply by-passed by the huge German migration, most of which went to the farms of the middle west and

This ferry transporting German immigrants from Castle Garden landing center to the Eire Railroad (*Erie Eisenbahn*) shows how German migrants by-passed Rhode Island. The railroad took most Germans to points west and to the cities listed on the ferry's walls—"Cleveland, Cincinnati, Louisville, San Francisco, Detroit, St. Louis, Chicago, St. Paul."

the cities of New York, Buffalo, Cleveland, Cincinnati, Chicago, Milwaukee, and St. Louis.

Since their arrival in the colony of Pennsylvania in the 1680s Germans have exerted an important influence on American life, but Rhode Island was relatively unaffected by German immigration until after the Revolution of 1848 — a liberal uprising that served as a catalyst for the exodus of thousands who objected to the repressive and authoritarian policies of those who ruled the divided German states. Economic factors were also very important inducements to German migration throughout the nineteenth century.

The federal census of 1850 enumerated 230 Rhode Islanders of German birth. By 1860 the number had grown to 815. The highly informative Rhode Island state census of 1865 listed 897 German-born residents and 1,626 more whose parents were German natives, while the 1875 state tally recorded 2,013 and 3,820 respectively, for a total of nearly 6,000 Rhode Islanders of German stock. About one-half of this community could be found in Providence where they worked at such skills as shoe manufacture, cabinetmaking, brewing, baking, and jewelry design.

Unlike the Portuguese, the Germans were of mixed religious affiliation. In addition to Roman Catholics, their group included sizable percentages of Lutherans, Episcopalians, Baptists and Jews. There is no statistical breakdown on the number of German Catholics in Rhode Island in 1875 but a state religious survey taken thirty years later revealed that Catholics were twenty-two percent of the total German population. If this ratio prevailed throughout the era, the state's German Catholic community in the early 1870s numbered approximately 1,200 souls. Curiously, the Rhode Island ratio is well below the national figure of thirty-five percent for the period computed by Father Colman J. Barry, a leading student of German-American Catholicism.

To serve the spiritual needs of this ethnic group Bishop McFarland appointed a young German priest, Father Joseph A. Schale. Under Schale's direction the religious Society of St. Boniface was formed, tak-

William Stang from Langbruken, Germany became the spiritual minister to Rhode Island's German Catholics in 1878. After holding many important diocesan posts, he was named first bishop of Fall River in 1904 when that diocese was formed from the Massachusetts sector of the Diocese of Providence.

THE FORMATIVE ERA

The first Church of St. Mary's parish, Broadway. It was in constant use from 1853 until its destruction by the hurricane of 1938. During the 1870s the St. Boniface Society, composed of German-American Catholics, held meetings here.

ing its name from Germany's patron saint. Because the Providence Germans settled mainly in the Olneyville and Manton sections, Father Schale said a Mass from them regularly in St. Mary's Church on Barton Street. When the diocese was divided in 1872, Bishop McFarland invited Schale to Connecticut where the pair collaborated in the establishment of a German national parish (St. Boniface) in New Haven.

The void caused by Father Schale's departure existed until 1878 when it was most adequately filled by twenty-four-year-old Father William Stang from Langbruken in the Grand Duchy of Baden, Germany. The scholarly Stang held regular services for the Germans at the Cathedral where he served as a curate, but he also ministered to German Catholics throughout the diocese. Eventually Stang became a pastor and then the first rector of the new Cathedral. He held many other important diocesan posts because of his great ability and also because of his cordial relations with the Irish hierarchy (one of his many publications was a pamphlet entitled 'Germany's Debt to Ireland'). In 1904 his brilliant career was capped by his appointment as first bishop of Fall River when this new see was carved from the Massachusetts sector of the Diocese of Providence.

Despite the presence of Stang, no German national parish was established in Rhode Island, for as late as 1886 a religious overview prepared for the 250th anniversary of the founding of 'Providence Plantations' asserted that the German Catholics 'were not yet wealthy or numerous enough to build a church.' Although their population continued to increase, the rapidity of their assimilation, the lack of conflict between them and the dominant Irish, and the relatively small size of the local German community combined to prevent a German parish from ever being formed within the state.

Those other Catholic ethnic groups who would come to play such an important role in the development of the diocese were virtually unrepresented during the formative era. The census of 1870 listed only twenty-seven Italians in Providence and ten residents of Polish birth. No mention of any ministry towards the Italian population is made until November 1874 when Father A. P. Petrarra, an assistant at St. John's on Atwells Avenue, gave a retreat for the Italian-speaking people of the city. Lebanese, Lithuanians and Ukrainians were unknown in the Rhode Island of 1872 when the Diocese of Providence was created.

There were a handful of 'colored' Catholics, however, in a black population of Providence which reached 3,557 in the city census of 1874. In 1878 a *Sodality of the Immaculate Conception* under the patronage of St. Augustine was formed by Cathedral curate, Reverend Peter Carlin, for the spiritual fellowship of this community. Forty to fifty blacks regularly attended the early meetings of this 'St. Augustine's Society.'

The New Fold and Its First Shepherd

On the last day of January 1872, with the promulgation of Pius IX's bull, *Quod Catholico nomine bene prospere,* a new diocese was created and the Church of Providence came of age. The formative era was

147

over; Catholicism in Rhode Island was firmly established and growing at a rapid rate. The labors of Tyler, O'Reilly, and McFarland for religious survival were to give way to a more planned and orderly growth, but other challenges were imminent as the Church stood on the threshold of the new immigration.

The Providence diocese encompassed all of Rhode Island and also extended into southeastern Massachusetts. Included in the latter was Bristol County with its urban centers of Taunton, Fall River and New Bedford, sparsely inhabited Barnstable County (the 'Cape' region), Martha's Vineyard, Nantucket, and three Plymouth County towns on Buzzards Bay — Wareham, Marion and Mattapoisett. This new diocese contained approximately 125,000 Catholics, forty-three churches with five under construction, fifty-three priests, six academies (five for girls and one for boys), nine parish schools with a combined enrollment of 4,225 and one orphan asylum (St. Aloysius) with 200 children. Of the total diocesan figures, as recorded in *Sadlier's Catholic Directory* for 1873, the Massachusetts portion of this new jurisdiction had a Catholic population of approximately 30,000 with fifteen churches and fifteen priests; the remainder belonged to Rhode Island.

The first choice to lead the Catholics of the new diocese was Thomas Francis Hendricken. His name headed a list of three submitted to the Holy Father by the ecclesiastical metropolitan for New England, Archbishop John McCloskey. Father Hendricken had been designated by the New York prelate after consultation with Bishop McFarland in August 1871. His selection was the culmination of a spiritual Horatio Alger story that had its beginning on a farm 3,000 miles from Providence.

Thomas Hendricken was born in Ireland just outside the town of Kilkenny, County Leinster, on May 5, 1827. His father John, descended from a German officer named Hendricken who fought at Boyne for the Catholic cause, was a cottier who scratched an existence from the unyielding soil for his wife and six children. His death left the eldest son James head of the household. James worked together with his mother and the younger children to maintain the farm. Their efforts were aided by the generosity of a Kilkenny merchant, James Fogarty, who had married Mrs. Hendricken's sister. Impressed by Thomas's studious nature, Fogarty and his wife took a special interest in him and promoted his formal education. Enrolling at St. Kiernan's College (Kilkenny) in 1844, Thomas excelled in his studies — particularly English literature, which became his lifelong interest. Three years later he entered the seminary at Maynooth to begin his journey to the priesthood. The future bishop was an idealist who dreamed of joining the Jesuits and laboring for God in the missions of China and Japan. A fateful encounter at Maynooth in 1852 with Bernard O'Reilly, bishop of Hartford, changed his goal. Hendricken's resultant decision to head west instead of east was the turning point of his life.

Father Hendricken may well have second-guessed the wisdom of his choice after his initial experiences on board the steamer *Columbia* bound for the United States early in 1854. One of the female passengers, dying of a contagious disease, desired the last rites of the Church. Wishing to bring her the consolation of religion, the young priest was confronted by the ship's officers and crew, who refused to allow him access to the woman. In spite of their warnings that contact with the unknown disease might endanger both passengers and crew, Hendricken insisted upon comforting the unfortunate woman. Fearing contagion and professing hatred for his religion and nationality, the crew became enraged at his tenacity and decided to teach him a lesson. After beating him senseless, they were about to cast him overboard when a fellow passenger to Rhode Island, Reverend Samuel Davies, a young Protestant clergyman from Germany, 'interposed and rallied a lot of the German emigrants on board to the priest's rescue . . . and nursed him back to life.'

This experience, coming at the height of Know-Nothing intolerance, was a cruel initiation into American life for the immigrant priest. It did, however,

Thomas F. Hendricken, first Bishop of Providence (1872–86).

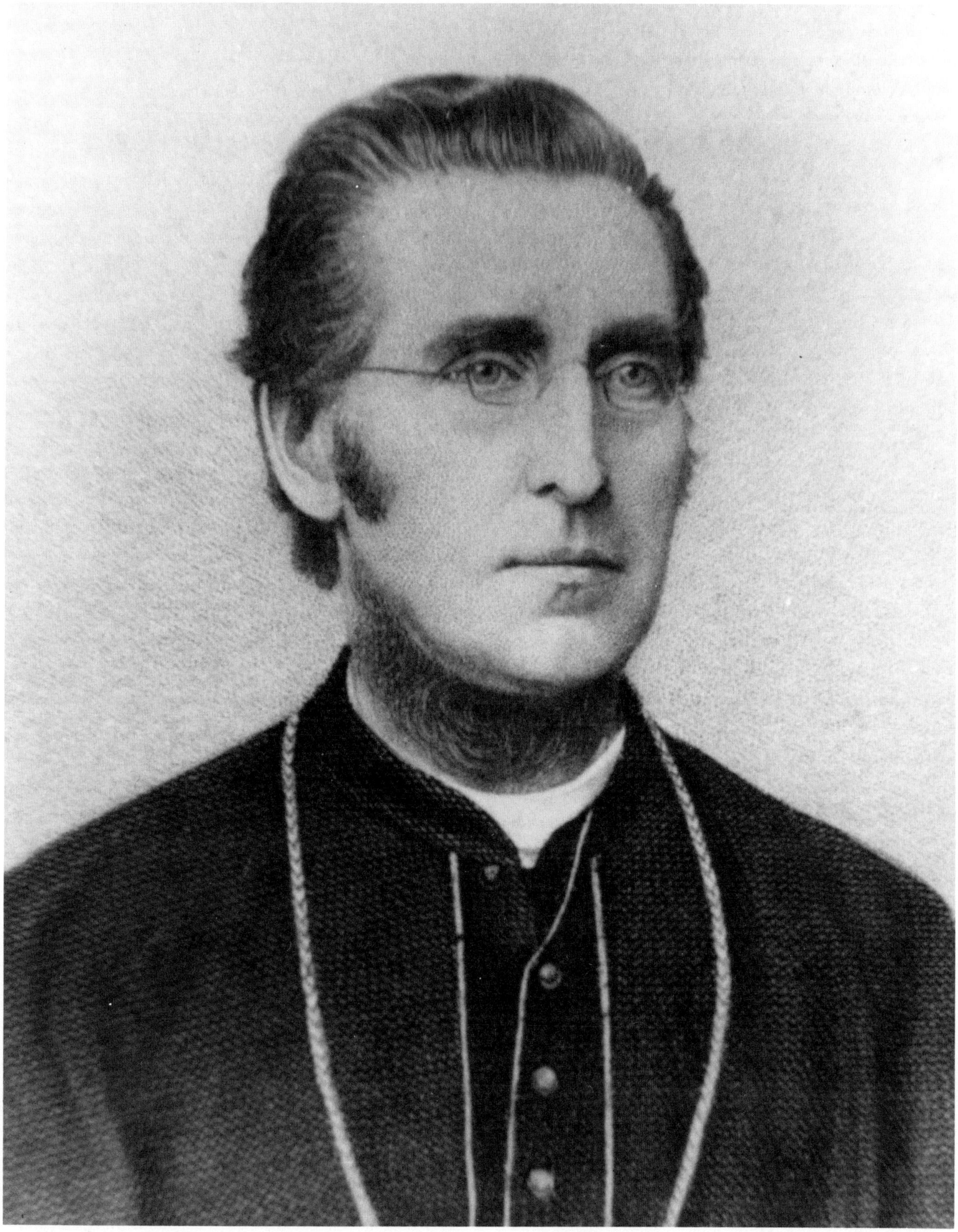

result in establishing a lifelong friendship between Hendricken and his benefactor. Reverend Davies eventually became superintendent of the Workingman's Home in Providence, and during the Hendricken episcopacy the bishop would substantially aid his friend's charitable endeavor.

The first few months of his ministry in Rhode Island were hectic. Bishop O'Reilly, a man who shifted his clergy frequently, appointed Hendricken first to the Cathedral, then to St. Joseph's in Providence, St. Mary's in Newport, and finally to St. Joseph's Church in Winsted, Connecticut, a rural parish covering a fifty-mile area. Once settled in this parish, Father Hendricken employed the exceptional administrative and organizational ability that was to mark his entire priestly life. In the sixteen months before being reassigned, he was able to pay the substantial debt on the church at Winsted and to secure eight additional church sites through the purchase of lots in the scattered villages of his parish.

In July 1855 Hendricken received an appointment that was to last seventeen years. Named as pastor of St. Patrick's in Waterbury, Connecticut, he built a religious complex that became the 'model parish' of its diocese. The youthful pastor, with characteristic zeal and administrative expertise, employed the foremost church architect of the day, Patrick Keely, to erect a new edifice for his growing congregation. Completed in three years, the Gothic structure was the most impressive church in the area. Dedicated by Bishop McFarland and renamed the Immaculate Conception in honor of the Blessed Virgin, it was the first church in the United States to bear that title following the papal pronouncement of 1854.

In rapid succession Hendricken followed up this initial success with a series of notable accomplishments. Turning first to education, he began teaching the children of the parish in an effort to develop a school. It was an impossible task in light of his many duties as the only priest in the community. Therefore, he invited the Montreal-based Sisters of the Congregation of Notre Dame to Immaculate Conception. Their acceptance resulted in the establishment of a day and boarding school for girls. Hendricken's interest in education also extended to the public schools through his service on Waterbury's board of education. In addition to these activities, he built a rectory, convent, and cemetery to complete the parish entity.

Father Hendricken's concern for his parishioners went beyond mere education and physical convenience. Basically, he wanted his people to be model Christians in all ways. It was natural, then, that temperance became an object of his enthusiasm. He fully supported the prohibition movement in the community — a cause he later espoused in Providence. It also appears that the future bishop was ahead of his time in his interpretation of the 1866 incorporation act. The by-laws he drew up called for the election of parishioners to his church's legal unit.

For his accomplishments Hendricken received several honors. In 1868 Pius IX named him a doctor of divinity. Earlier he had refused a promotion tendered by Bishop McFarland. He stated his feelings simply: 'I am now satisfied that I will best do the will of God by remaining quietly working and doing whatever good I can, where His will has placed me.'

When the bishops of the Province of New York deliberated upon whom to nominate as first bishop of Providence, they agreed that Hendricken 'was the most fitting candidate in every respect, health alone excepted.' Archbishop John McCloskey disregarded Hendricken's physical infirmity — a severe asthmatic condition — with the startling rationale that 'the labors of the new diocese would not be very onerous.'

Hendricken did not record his sentiments when he learned of his elevation to the episcopacy but, judging from the reaction of citizens of Waterbury, he must have been saddened to leave. The *Waterbury American* spoke for the community at-large by praising his 'urbanity and ability.' The parishioners at Immaculate Conception called a special meeting to pass a series of resolutions to wish him well and to honor his educational and temperance work.

On April 28, 1872, amidst all the religious splendor of the Church, Father Hendricken was ordained the first bishop of Providence by his sponsor, Archbishop

THE FORMATIVE ERA

Providence viewed from the hill on which the State House now stands as it appeared when the diocese was formed. The city's industries would soon attract new Catholic immigrant groups, especially the Italians and the Polish.

John McCloskey. The immigrant priest who had barely survived his voyage to the United States was now a bishop of his Church. Reverend Thomas M. Burke, O.P., a moving force in the 'devotional revolution' that had reinvigorated the Church in Ireland, preached at the ceremony. His presence in Providence that day symbolized in many ways the direction the new diocese would follow.

Under Bishop Hendricken, whose fourteen-year episcopacy would be marked by strong leadership, immigrant conflicts, and social involvement, the Diocese of Providence expanded physically and witnessed the growth of educational institutions and religious orders. In an indefinable way the eloquent Burke and the zealous Hendricken represented all that made late nineteenth-century Irish Catholicism so vibrant. Their joint appearance on that crisp April day in 1872 crowned nearly a half-century of steady progress against adversity and foreshadowed a much longer period of growth and vitality.

Bibliography

In writing this volume the authors have used both primary and secondary material including manuscript correspondence, diaries, newspapers, broadsides, public documents, state, local and parish histories, scholarly monographs and unpublished research papers. This select bibliographic essay is designed to acquaint the reader and those interested in more detailed research with the works we have found most useful in the preparation of this book. Broad studies of general utility are mentioned at the outset; then the essay moves in a chronological manner from the colonial origins to the establishment of the diocese in 1872. Occasionally second and third references to a source are necessary; such references list only the author's surname but a short title has been added if the person alluded to has written more than one work used in the preparation of the present volume.

General Works

The most useful general histories of American Catholicism are Thomas T. McAvoy, C.S.C., *A History of the Catholic Church in the United States* (1969) and John Tracy Ellis, *American Catholicism* (2nd ed., 1969). The standard study by John Gilmary Shea, *History of the Catholic Church in the United States,* 4 vols. (1886-92) is sparse in its treatment of New England. Theodore Maynard, *The Story of American Catholicism: The History of the Catholic Church in America* (1941), and Theodore Roemer, *The Catholic Church in the United States* (1950) also furnished good background information.

Biographical sketches of leading Catholics can be found in the *Dictionary of American Biography,* edited by Allen Johnson and Dumas Malone and in John J. Delaney and James Edward Tobin (comp.), *Dictionary of Catholic Biography* (1961). The cooperative study entitled *The Catholic Church in the United States of America,* 3 vols. (1912) contains valuable data on the various religious orders. Also useful in this respect is Elinor Tong Dehey, *Religious Orders of Women in the United States* (1930). On the bishops see Reverend Joseph Bernard Code, *Dictionary of the American Hierarchy* (1964); Maurice F. Egan, *The Hierarchy of the Roman Catholic Church in the United States,* 2 vols. (1888); Francis X. Reuss, *Biographical Cyclopedia of the Catholic Hierarchy of the United States, 1784-1898* (1898); Richard H. Clarke, *Lives of the Deceased Bishops of the Catholic Church in the United States,* 3 vols. (rev. ed., 1888); and Gerard Brassard, *The American Hierarchy in New England, 1808-1955,* volume III of *Amorial of the American Hierarchy* (1956).

Among the more specialized surveys the following have been frequently consulted: Reverend James MacCaffrey, *History of the Catholic Church in the Nineteenth Century (1789-1908),* 2 vols. (1910) for the European background; Gerald Shaughnessy, *Has the Immigrant Kept the Faith? A Study of Immigration and Catholic Growth in the United States, 1790-1920* (1925); Reverend Peter Guilday, *A History of the Councils of Baltimore, 1791-1884* (1932); Guilday (comp.), *The National Pastorals of the American Hierarchy, 1792-1919* (1923); John Tracy Ellis (comp.), *Documents of American Catholic History* (1956); and Ellis (ed.), *The Catholic Priest in the United States: Historical Investigations* (1971).

There are several important studies of the Catholic Church

in Rhode Island. Reverend James Fitton, *Sketches of the Establishment of the Church in New England* (1872) is a firsthand account of the formative era by one of its most important priests; Annie E. Campbell, et. al., *The Consecration [of the Cathedral of Sts. Peter and Paul] with Historical Sketches of the Catholic Church in Rhode Island* ... (1887) is brief but informative; Very Reverend William Byrne, et. al., *History of the Catholic Church in the New England States,* 2 vols. (1899) contains an excellent survey of the Diocese of Providence and its prehistory by the Reverend Austin Dowling, a rector of the Cathedral of Sts. Peter and Paul who later became Archbishop of St. Paul. However, Dowling's study (I, 351-464) and that of Reverend Thomas F. Cullen, *The Catholic Church in Rhode Island* (1936), are episodic and institutional in nature with a narrow focus. Neither work attempts to view local Catholicism against the broader backdrop of Rhode Island's political, economic and social development.

The most useful general history of the state is Charles Carroll, *Rhode Island: Three Centuries of Democracy,* 4 vols. (1932). Its value for this study is enhanced by the fact that Carroll, as a Catholic, emphasized many previously neglected topics that shed light upon the state's Catholic community. Carroll's, *Public Education in Rhode Island* (1918) and his *School Law of Rhode Island* (1914) were also of considerable utility. Other important general accounts are Edward Field, (ed.), *State of Rhode Island and Providence Plantations at the End of the Century: A History,* 3 vols. (1902) and Welcome Arnold Greene, *The Providence Plantations for Two Hundred and Fifty Years* (1886), a work that contains historical, statistical, and biographical material on all the towns and data on their religious establishments. Similar in format and value is the anonymously published work *1636: History of the State of Rhode Island* (Hoag, Wade & Co., 1878). Thomas Williams Bicknell, *The History of the State of Rhode Island and Providence Plantations,* 6 vols. (1920) is useful mainly for its three biographical volumes.

Informative local histories include Richard M. Bayles (comp.), *History of Providence County, Rhode Island,* 2 vols. (1891) containing a survey of the churches in each town; Bayles (comp.), *History of Newport County, Rhode Island* (1888), which contains a 'History of the Catholic Church in Newport' (pp. 469-474) by Reverend James Coyle; J. R. Cole (comp.), *History of Washington and Kent Counties, Rhode Island* (1889); John Williams Haley, *The Lower Blackstone River Valley: The Story of Pawtucket, Central Falls, Lincoln, and Cumberland, Rhode Island* (1937); John Hutchins Cady, *Rhode Island Boundaries, 1636-1936* (1936); and Cady, *The Civic and Architectural Development of Providence 1636-1950* (1957).

Economic and social developments are well treated in Peter J. Coleman, *The Transformation of Rhode Island, 1790-1860* (1963), and Brother Joseph Brennan, F.S.C., *Social Conditions in Industrial Rhode Island: 1820-1860* (1940). Basic legal and constitutional data are found in Patrick T. Conley, 'Rhode Island Constitutional Development, 1636-1841: Prologue to the Dorr Rebellion' (Unpublished doctoral dissertation, University of Notre Dame, 1970) and the *General Laws of Rhode Island* (the compilations of 1798, 1822, 1844, 1857 and 1872).

Sketches of prominent Rhode Islanders, both Catholics and those whose actions affected the Catholic community, can be found in the following works: *Biographical Cyclopedia of Representative Men of Rhode Island,* 2 vols. (1881); *Biographical Cyclopedia of Connecticut and Rhode Island of the Nineteenth Century* (1881); Richard Herndon (comp.), *Men of Progress: Biographical Sketches and Portraits of Leaders in Business and Professional Life in the State of Rhode Island* (1896); *Representative Men and Old Families of Rhode Island,* 3 vols. (1908); and Ralph S. Mohr, *Governors for Three Hundred Years, 1638-1954, Rhode Island and Providence Plantations* (1954).

Catholicism in Colonial and Revolutionary Rhode Island

John R. Bartlett (ed.), *Records of the Colony of Rhode Island and Providence Plantations, 1636-1792,* 10 vols. (1856-1865) is a good collection of published primary materials on colonial Rhode Island. It is selective, however, and should be supplemented by the original records in the Rhode Island State Archives. Howard M. Chapin (ed.), *Documentary History of Rhode Island,* 2 vols. (1916-19) publishes important primary materials relating to the origins of Rhode Island's earliest settlements. The best general survey of the colony is Sidney V. James, *Colonial Rhode Island: A History* (1975), but Charles McLean Andrews, *The Colonial Period of American History* (1934-38), II, 1-66 is still the best institutional account of the colony's early years, i.e., 1636-63 though it is rivaled by John E. Pomfret, *Founding the American Colonies, 1583-1660* (1970), pp. 210-31. Samuel G. Arnold, *History of the State of Rhode Island and Providence Plantations,* 2 vols. (1859-60) is an old but detailed and valuable treatment of the period from 1636 to 1790, while Irving B. Richman, *Rhode Island: A Study in Separatism* (1905) is a fine interpretative analysis of colonial Rhode Island. John Tracy Ellis, *Catholics in Colonial America* (1965); Charles H. Metzger, *Catholics and the American Revolution* (1962) and Arthur J. Riley *Catholicism in New England to 1788* (1936), provide excellent background material for this chapter.

The literature on Roger Williams is abundant. The so-called 'Progressive' historians writing during the second quarter of this century viewed Williams as primarily a political thinker and the first great hero of the American democratic tradition. They inordinately minimized Williams's religious thought and erroneously believed that his thirst for 'religious toleration was only a necessary deduction from the major principles of his political theory.' The chief among those historians viewing Williams in this romantic light were: Vernon L. Parrington, *Main Currents in American Thought* (1927), I, 62-75; James E. Ernst, *The Political Thought of Roger Williams* (1929); and Samuel H. Brockunier, *The Irrepressible Democrat: Roger Williams* (1940). Recent scholars, most notably Mauro Calamandrei, 'Neglected Aspects of Roger Williams' Thought,' *Church History,* XXI (Sept., 1952), 239-259; Perry Miller, *Roger Williams: His*

Contribution to the American Tradition (1953); Alan Simpson, 'How Democratic was Roger Williams?' *William and Mary Quarterly,* 3rd Ser., XIII (Jan., 1956), 53-67; Sacvan Bercovitch, 'Typology in Puritan New England: The Williams-Cotton Controversy Reassessed,' *American Quarterly,* XIX (Summer, 1967), 166-191; Richard M. Reinitz, 'Symbolism and Freedom: The Use of Biblical Typology as an Argument for Religious Freedom in Seventeenth Century England and America' (Unpublished doctoral dissertation, University of Rochester, 1967); and John Garrett, *Roger Williams: Witness Beyond Christendom* (1970) have properly offered a theological interpretation of his thought and writings. Ola Elizabeth Winslow, *Master Roger Williams* (1957) is the most balanced biography of the controversial Williams. The best study of Williams's ideology is the succinct and penerating Edmund S. Morgan, *Roger Williams: The Church and the State* (1967). Morgan suggests the principal reason for the erroneous identification of Williams as primarily a political theorist: 'Williams' every thought took its rise from religion. But in his writings . . . Williams was more often concerned with ecclesiastical and political institutions than with theology,' Morgan, *Williams* pp. 86-87. For a summary of the divergent views of Williams see LeRoy Moore, Jr., 'Roger Williams and the Historians,' *Church History,* XXXII (Dec., 1963), 432-451.

Much has been written on the early Catholic explorers, and their exploits have aroused some controversy. The authenticity of Miguel Corte Real's visit and his inscription on Dighton Rock is rejected by Samuel Eliot Morison, the foremost student of early American exploration, in his *The European Discovery of America: The Northern Voyages* (1971), pp. 244-247 and no specific mention is made of this incident in such basic works as Henry Harrisse, *Les Corte Real et leurs voyages au nouveau-monde* (1883) and Edgar Prestage, *The Portuguese Pioneers* (1933). However, several local historians have upheld Corte Real's 'discovery' including Edmund B. Delabarre, *Dighton Rock, A Study of the Written Rocks of New England* (1928); Manuel Da Silva, *Portuguese Pilgrims and Dighton Rock; the First Chapter in American History* (1971); and George F. W. Young, *Miguel Corte-Real and the Dighton Writing-Rock* (1970). Verrazzano's 'Letter' to Francis I is a detailed account of his explorations. It is translated with a superb account of Verrazzano's life by Lawrence Wroth, *The Voyages of Giovanni de Verrazzano, 1524-1528* (1970).

The Irish presence in colonial Rhode Island has been treated in antiquarian fashion by several researchers: Michael J. O'Brien, *Pioneer Irish in New England* (1937); Audrey Lockhart, 'Some Aspects of Emigration from Ireland to the North American Colonies Between 1660 and 1775' (Unpublished M. Litt. thesis, Trinity College, Dublin, 1971); Reverend Richard J. Purcell, 'Rhode Island's Early Schools and Irish Teachers,' *The Catholic Educational Review,* XXXII (Sept., 1934), 402-415; Thomas Z. Lee, 'The Irish of the Rhode Island Colony in Peace and War,' *American Irish Historical Society Journal,* XV (1916), 156-167; John J. Cosgrove, 'The Irish in Rhode Island, To and Including the Revolution,' *American Irish Historical Society Journal,* IX (1910), 365-385; and especially Thomas Hamilton Murray, 'The Irish Vanguard of Rhode Island,' *American Irish Historical Society Journal,* IV (1904), 109-133; 'Charles MacCarthy, A Rhode Island Pioneer,' *The Rosary Magazine,* XIX (Nov., 1901), 441-455; and 'Irish Rhode Islanders in the American Revolution,' *American Irish Historical Society Journal,* III (1903), 3-17.

The act of 1719 which deprived Catholics and Jews of their basic civil rights is found in the Digest of 1719 in the Rhode Island State Archives. This measure and the repeal statute of 1783 are reprinted in Bartlett's *Records* (II, 36-37 and IX, 674-675). A discussion of the origins of the 1719 law can be found in Sidney S. Rider, *Soul Liberty: Rhode Island's Gift to the Nation. An Inquiry Concerning the validity of the Claims made by Roman Catholics that Maryland was settled Upon that Basis Before Roger Williams Planted the Colony of Rhode Island,* No. 5 of the Rhode Island Historical Tracts, 2nd Series (1897); John Richard Meade, 'The Truth Concerning the Disfranchisement of Catholics in Rhode Island,' *American Catholic Quarterly Review,* XIX (1894), 169-177; and Conley, 'Constitutional Development,' pp. 21-25.

The French presence in Rhode Island during the colonial and Revolutionary eras has received the considerable attention it deserves. Elisha R. Potter, Jr. *Memoir Concerning the French Settlements in the Colony of Rhode Island,* Rhode Island Historical Tracts, 1st Series, No. 5 (1879), tells of the seventeenth century Frenchtown settlement in East Greenwich. Howard Mumford Jones, *America and French Culture, 1750-1848* (1927) and the excellent but somewhat neglected Mary Ellen Loughrey *France and Rhode Island, 1686–1800* (1944) deal with the broad aspects of Franco-American relations. The French alliance is ably treated by Samuel Flagg Bemis, *The Diplomacy of the American Revolution* (1935); Edward S. Corwin, *French Policy and the American Alliance of 1778* (1916); and William C. Stenchcombe, *The American Revolution and the French Alliance* (1969). The most detailed account of the French occupation of Rhode Island is still Edwin M. Stone, *Our French Allies in the Great War of the American Revolution, 1778-82* (1883), but it is poorly organized. Other informative works include Allan Forbes and Paul F. Cadman, *France and New England,* 3 vols. (1925-29); De B. Randolph Keim, *Rochambeau* (1907); Stephen Bonsal, *When the French Were Here* (1945); Preservation Society of Newport County, *Washington-Rochambeau Celebration, 1780-1955, Newport, Rhode Island* (1955); Henry J. Yeager, 'The French Fleet at Newport, 1780-1781,' *Rhode Island History,* XXX (Aug., 1971), 87-93; Arthur Tucherman, *When Rochambeau Stepped Ashore* (1955); and Howard Willis Preston, *Rochambeau and the French Troops in Providence in 1780-81-82* (1924). The French occupation of Rhode Island College (*i.e.,* Brown University) is discussed in Reuben Aldridge Guild, *Life, Times and Correspondence of James Manning and the Early History of Brown University* (1864); Walter C. Bronson, *The History of Brown University, 1764-1914* (1914); and Robert W. Kenny, *Town and Gown in Wartime: A Brief Account of the College of Rhode Island, Now Brown University, and the Providence Community During the American Revolution* (1976). The

Battle of Rhode Island as a critical testing-ground for the Franco-American Alliance is analyzed by Paul F. Dearden, 'The Rhode Island Campaign of 1778: Inauspicious Dawn of Alliance,' (Unpublished master's thesis, Providence College, 1971). William R. Staples, *Rhode Island in the Continental Congress with the Journal of the Convention that adopted the Constitution, 1765-1790* (1870) and Irwin H. Polishook, *1774-1795: Rhode Island and the Union* (1969) are the best accounts of Rhode Island during the Revolutionary War.

Rhode Island under the Bishops of Baltimore and Boston

The indispensable and basic source for this period is Robert H. Lord, John E. Sexton, and Edward T. Harrington, *History of the Archdiocese of Boston, 1604-1943*, 3 vols. (1944), an outstanding diocesan history. On Bishops Carroll, Cheverus and Fenwick the standard studies are Peter Guilday, *The Life and Times of John Carroll, Archbishop of Baltimore (1735-1815)* (1922); Annabelle M. Melville, *John Carroll of Baltimore* (1955); Melville, *Jean Lefebvre de Cheverus, 1768-1836* (1958); and Robert H. Lord, 'The Organizer of the Church in New England: Bishop Benedict Joseph Fenwick (1782-1846),' *Catholic Historical Review*, XXII (July, 1936), 172-184.

W. F. Adams, *Ireland and the Irish Emigration to the New World From 1815 to the Famine* (1932) is the classic study of early Irish Catholic migration. Rex Syndergaard, ' "Wild Irishmen" and the Alien and Sedition Acts,' *Eire-Ireland* (March, 1974), 14-24 discusses the influence of the Federalist-passed Alien Act on Irish allegiance to the parties of Jefferson and Jackson. Sister Mary Edward Walsh, R.S.M., 'The Irish in Rhode Island From 1800 to 1865,' (Unpublished master's thesis, The Catholic University of America, 1937) is poorly done. Zelotes W. Coombs, 'The Blackstone Canal,' Worcester Historical Society, *Publications*, n.s., (1935), 448-470; Edward C. Kirkland, *Men, Cities and Transportation: A Study in New England History, 1820-1900*, 2 vols. (1948); and George Rogers Taylor, *The Transportation Revolution 1815-1860* (1951) detail an important economic aspect of Irish immigration and settlement, while Caroline F. Ware, *The Early New England Cotton Manufacture: A Study in Industrial Beginnings* (1931); Paul F. McGouldrick, *New England Textiles in the Nineteenth Century* (1968); John B. McCann, "A Study of the Mill Worker in the Blackstone Valley, 1820-1830," (Unpublished master's thesis, Providence College, 1931); and Peter J. Coleman, 'Rhode Island Cotton Manufacturing,' *Rhode Island History*, XXIII (July, 1964), 65-80 discuss another.

The establishment of Rhode Island's earliest Catholic churches is outlined in the general histories by Fitton, Campbell, Dowling and Cullen. On the origins of Catholicism in Newport consult John H. Greene, Jr., 'The Story of Early Catholicism in Newport and History of St. Joseph's Parish,' in *The St. Joseph's Church Reference Book, Golden Jubilee, 1885-1935* (1935), 11-30; Greene, 'The Catholic Church in Newport, Rhode Island,' in *A Souvenir Book of the Consecration of St. Joseph's Church* (1922), 14-34; George Champlin Mason, *Reminiscences of Newport* (1884); and Reverend James Coyle's essay in Cole, pp. 469-474. On early church development in Pawtucket see Massena Goodrich, *Historical Sketch of the Town of Pawtucket* (1876); Robert Grieve, *An Illustrated History of Pawtucket, Central Falls, and Vicinity* (1897); Robert Grieve and J. B. Fernald, *The Cotton Centennial* (1891), which relates principally to the history of Pawtucket; Brendan Francis Gilbane, 'A Social History of Samuel Slater's Pawtucket, 1790-1830' (Unpublished doctoral dissertation, Boston University, 1969); and especially John H. McKenna, *The Centenary Story of Old St. Mary's Pawtucket, R.I., 1829-1929* (1929). William R. Staples, *Annals of the Town of Providence from its First Settlement to the Organization of the City Government in June, 1832* (1843) contains data on early Providence Catholicism. Material on other pioneer Catholic outposts is available in the following local studies: S. C. Newman, *A Numbering of the Inhabitants, with Statistical and Other Information, Relative to Woonsocket, Rhode Island* (1846); Erastus Richardson, *History of Woonsocket* (1876); James W. Smyth, *History of the Catholic Church in Woonsocket and Vicinity . . .* (1903); *St. Charles', Old and New, Being a Brief Record of the Origin and Development of Catholic Life in Woonsocket . . .* (1928); Oliver Payson Fuller, *The History of Warwick, R.I.* (1875); and Fuller, *Historical Sketches of the Churches of Warwick, Rhode Island* (1880). Sister Mary Christopher Loughran, 'The Development of the Church in the City of Fall River from the Beginning Until 1904' (Unpublished master's thesis, The Catholic University of America, 1932); Harold E. Clarkin, 'Pioneer Catholicism: The Life and Times of Father Edward Murphy, 1840-1887' (Unpublished research paper read before the Fall River Historical Society, Fall River, Massachusetts, May 16, 1949); and George E. Sullivan, *Centennial Observance of St. Mary's Cathedral, 1838-1938* (1938) contain material on the early history of Catholicism in what was once the Fall River section of Tiverton. St. Mary's was originally the parish of St. John the Baptist.

There is an abundance of material, both primary and secondary, relating to the Dorr Rebellion. The Sidney S. Rider Collection at Brown University's John Hay Library contains the Dorr Correspondence (14 vols.), the Dorr Manuscripts (46 vols.) and the Dorr Papers (*ca.* 100 folders). The Potter Collection, the John Brown Francis Collection, and the Carter-Danforth Collection at the Rhode Island Historical Society also contain many pertinent letters. Newspapers also shed much light on the controversy, especially the *Providence Journal* (the Law and Order voice), the *Republican Herald* (the Democratic party organ) and the *New Age and Constitutional Advocate* (a short-lived reform newspaper). The Henry Duff Petition is located in the Rhode Island State Archives. On Dorr himself and his philosophy [Thomas Wilson Dorr], *An Address to the People of Rhode Island . . .* (1834); [Thomas W. Dorr, et. al.], *The Nine Lawyers' Opinion [on the Right of the People of Rhode Island to form a Constitution]*, in Vol. XI, 1st Series of the Rhode Island Historical Tracts, Edited by Sidney S. Rider (1880); Dan King, *The Life and Times of Thomas Wilson Dorr* (1859); and Robert Wetmore Stoughton, 'The Philosophy of Dorrism'

(Unpublished master's thesis, Brown University, 1936) are revealing. Dorr's ecumenical letter to Father Thomas O'Flaherty is published by Sidney Rider in *Book Notes,* XXXII (March 13, 1915) 43-46. The best contemporary accounts of the rebellion from the Dorrite position are: Edmund Burke (comp.), *Interference of the Executive in the Affairs of Rhode Island,* 28 Cong., 1 Sess., House Report No. 546 [1844], a House investigation of Dorr Rebellion which censures Tyler and defends Dorr and [Frances H. Whipple], *Might and Right* (1844), the best of many pro-Dorr pamphlets. The most formidable anti-Dorr statements of a contemporary nature are John Causin (comp.), [*Minority Report of the Select Committee to Whom Were Referred the Memorial of the Democratic Members of the Rhode Island Legislature*], 28 Cong., 1 Sess., House Report No. 581 [1844], which upholds the Law and Order position; Elisha R. Potter, [Jr.], *Consideraions on the Questions of the Adoption of a Constitution and Extension of Suffrage in Rhode Island* (1842), a formidable criticism of the Dorr Rebellion by a learned Rhode Island Democrat; and Dexter Randall, *Democracy Vindicated and Dorrism Unveiled* (1846). For a convenient listing of the numerous Dorr War pamphlets see the bibliography in Arthur May Mowry, *The Dorr War or the Constitutional Struggle in Rhode Island* (1901).

Mowry's study was the only book-length treatment of the Dorr Rebellion for more than seventy years. As a spokesman for the conservative Rhode Island 'Establishment' he ignored or suppressed the ethno-religious aspects of the conflict. Two recent studies by Marvin E. Gettleman, *The Dorr Rebellion: A Study in American Radicalism: 1833-1849* (1973) and George M. Dennison, *The Dorr War: Republicanism on Trial, 1831-1861* (1976) also neglect this essential theme. Gettleman is a New Left historian preoccupied with placing the rebellion in the mainstream of American radicalism, while Dennison is concerned less with the episode itself than with its legal and constitutional ramifications. Some shorter treatments of the controversy such as Anne Mary Newton, 'Rebellion in Rhode Island: The Story of the Dorr War' (Unpublished master's thesis, Columbia University, 1947); J. Stanley Lemons and Michael A. McKenna, 'Re-enfranchisement of Rhode Island Negroes,' *Rhode Island History,* XXX (Feb., 1971), 2-13; William M. Wiecek, 'Popular Sovereignty in the Dorr War — Conservative Counterblast,' *Rhode Island History,* XXXII (May, 1973), 35-51; Chilton Williamson, "The Rhode Island Explosion,' Chap. 13 in *American Suffrage from Property to Democracy, 1760-1860* (1960), and Williamson, 'Rhode Island Suffrage Since the Dorr War,' *New England Quarterly,* XXVIII (March, 1955), 34-50, recognize political nativism as a primary factor in the Dorr Rebellion.

On the Gordon murder trial, its setting, and effect consult Edward C. Larned and William Knowles (eds.), *The Trial of John Gordon and William Gordon Charged with the Murder of Amasa Sprague* (1844) which is the published record of the trial; Benjamin Knight, *History of the Sprague Families of Rhode Island* (1881); J. Earl Clauson, *Cranston: A Historical Sketch* (1904); and Philip English Mackey, ' "The Result May be Glorious" — Anti-Gallows Movement in Rhode Island,' *Rhode Island History,* XXXIII (Feb. 1974), 19-30.

Rhode Island Under the Diocese of Hartford

The general references for the period 1844 to 1872 include some important primary material. Especially valuable are the papers and correspondence of Bishops Tyler, O'Reilly and McFarland located in the archives of the Archdiocese of Hartford. Many of the most important of these documents have been transcribed by Joseph Cichon and Reverend Robert Hayman and conveniently deposited in the archives of the Diocese of Providence together with informative transcribed manuscripts from several other repositories. The Providence diocesan archives contain material on Rhode Island's pioneer parishes and records of such social agencies as the Rhode Island Catholic Orphan Asylum (St. Aloysius Home). Of great value are the diary and letters of Bishop Hendricken.

The newspapers of the period are very informative, especially the *Providence Journal* (Whig-Republican), the Providence *Post* (Democratic) and the *Boston Pilot* (New England's first Catholic newspaper). Francis Robert Walsh, 'The *Boston Pilot:* A Newspaper for the Irish Immigrant, 1829-1908' (Unpublished doctoral dissertation, Boston University, 1968) is an excellent study of this paper's influence.

Sadlier's Catholic Directory and the *Metropolian Catholic Almanac* were annual statistical compilations which detailed Catholic growth in the several dioceses. They were invaluable reference works. The *Acts and Resolves of the Rhode Island General Assembly* (annual) contain statutes relating to various aspects of Catholic political, social and educational life.

On the early history of the Diocese of Hartford consult Reverend James H. O'Donnell, *History of the Diocese of Hartford* (1900), a separate edition of the material which originally appeared in Byrne's two volume history of the Catholic Church in New England; James A. Rooney, 'Early Times in the Diocese of Hartford, Connecticut 1829-1874,' *Catholic Historical Review,* I (July, 1915), 148-163; Thomas C. Duggan, *The Catholic Church in Connecticut* (1930); and the four histories of Rhode Island Catholicism cited *supra*.

Local histories not previously listed which deal with new areas of Catholic growth include: Noah J. Arnold, 'The Valley of the Pawtuxet: Its History and Development,' *The Narragansett Historical Register,* VI (1888), 222-259; Arnold, 'Further Reminiscences of the Valley of the Pawtuxet and Its Branches,' *The Narragansett Historical Register,* VII (1889), 233-280; Arnold, 'Biographical Reminiscences of the Pawtuxet Valley,' *The Narragansett Historical Register,* IX (1891), 153-194; William B. Spencer, 'A History of the North Branch of the Pawtuxet Valley,' *The Narragansett Historical Register,* VI (1888), 122-135; Mathias B. Harpin, *Patterns on the River* (1946), a study of the Pawtuxet River Valley; Harpin, *Trumpets in Jericho* (1961), an anecdotal history of West Warwick, especially Arctic and vicinity ('Jericho'); Martha R. McPartland, *The History of East Greenwich, Rhode Island, 1677-1960, with Related Geneology* (1960); Thomas Steere, *History of the Town of Smithfield . . . 1730-1871* (1881); Walter A. Nebiker, *The History of North Smithfield* (1976); Howard K. Stokes, *The Finances and Administration of Providence* (1903); Moses King, (ed.),

King's Pocketbook of Providence (1882); and *Providence Illustrated* (1886), a handsome volume which contains one hundred large plates of Providence in the 1880s (published by H. S. Inman). D. G. Beers, *Atlas of the State of Rhode Island and Providence Plantations* (1870) is a very useful tool which contains detailed maps of every city and town.

Histories of territorial parishes and missions founded during the period 1850-72 include: Joseph K. Streker, *et. al., Centennial Commemoration—St. Mary's Parish, Providence, RI 1853-1953* (1953), a very informative and well-illustrated volume; Reverend T. E. Ryan, *Burrillville, R. I. and the Catholic Church: A Historical Sketch* (n.d., ca. 1925), that deals with the origins of St. Patrick's in Harrisville; Paul Campbell, *et. al., St. Michael's Church, Georgiaville, Rhode Island, A Century of Faith and Sacrifice, 1875-1975* (1975) which contains material on the establishment of St. Philip's of Greenville; *Golden Jubilee . . . St. Michael's Church* (1909); Reverend Oscar Ferland, *et.al., One Hundred Years: St. Michael's Parish, 1859-1959* (1959); parish reunion booklet, Immaculate Conception Church, Providence [1971]; and Reverend Richard A. Walsh, *The Centennial History of St. Edward Church, Providence, Rhode Island 1874-1974* (1974), a scholarly, book-length survey.

The lives and episcopacies of Tyler, O'Reilly, McFarland and Hendricken are covered in their manuscripts, the general surveys of local Catholicism and the biographical directories of the American hierarchy cited *supra*. The only individual study of any of these prelates is Reverend Thomas F. Cullen, 'William Barber Tyler' *Catholic Historical Review*, XXIII (Apr., 1937), 17-30.

The origins of the Catholic educational system in Rhode Island, its purpose and early growth are explained in several important works. Reverend Americo D. Lapati, 'A History of Catholic Education in Rhode Island' (Unpublished doctoral dissertation, Boston College, 1958), is the indispensable treatment of the topic. On the broader aspects of this development consult Sister M. Carolyn Klinkhamer, O.P., 'Historical Reason for the Inception of the Parochial School System,' *Catholic Educational Review*, LII (Feb. 1954), 73-94; Sister M. Laurina Kaiser, *The Development of the Concept and Function of the Catholic Elementary School in the American Parish* (1955); Glen Gabert, Jr., *In Hoc Signo? A Brief History of Catholic Parochial Education in America* (1973); James A. Burns, C.S.C., *The Principles, Origin, and Establishment of the Catholic School System in the United States* (1908); Burns, *The Growth and Development of the Catholic School System in the United States* (1912); Burns and Bernard J. Kohlbrenner, *A History of Catholic Education in the United States* (1937); Edmund J. Goebel, *A Study of Catholic Secondary Education during the Colonial Period up to the First Plenary Council of Baltimore, 1852* (1937); Richard J. Gabel, *Public Funds for Church and Private Schools* (1937); and Vincent P. Lannie, *Public Money and Parochial Education: Bishop Hughes, Governor Seward, and the New York School Controversy* (1968), a very able treatment of recent vintage; Rush Welter, *Popular Education and Democratic Thought in America* (1962); Ruth Miller Elson, *Guardians of Tradition: American Schoolbooks of the Nineteenth Century* (1964); Sister M. Laurina Kaiser, 'Anti-Catholic Attitudes Reflected in Elementary History and Geography Textbooks from 1800 to 1850' (Unpublished master's thesis, The Catholic University of America, 1953); and Sister Marie Leonore Fell, *The Foundations of Nativism in American Textbooks, 1783-1860* (1941) show the white, Anglo-Saxon, Protestant bias of mid-nineteenth century public school education.

The significant educational (and social) role of the Sisters of Mercy receives detailed coverage in Sister Mary Catherine Morgan, R.S.M., *Mercy: A Little Sketch of the Sisters of Mercy in Providence, Rhode Island from 1851 to 1893* (1893); Anon., *An Historical Sketch of the Sisters of Mercy of St. Francis Xavier's Convent* (1901); Sister Mary Josephine Gately, R.S.M., *Seventy-Five Years in the Passing with the Sisters of Mercy, Providence, Rhode Island 1851-1926* (1926); Gately, *The Sisters of Mercy: Historical Sketches, 1831-1931* (1931); and Sister Mary Loretto O'Connor, R.S.M., *Mercy Marks the Century* (1951). These books draw on materials in the Archives of the Sisters of Mercy, Province of Providence, Provincial House, Cumberland, Rhode Island. Brother Angelus Gabriel, F.S.C., *The Christian Brothers in the United States, 1848-1948: A Century of Catholic Education* (1948); and Brother Albeus John Fitzgerald, F.S.C., 'A History of the Christian Brothers' Schools in Rhode Island' (Unpublished master's thesis, Manhattan College, 1954), tell of the founding of LaSalle Academy, Providence. Also useful are the *Report of the [Rhode Island] Commissioner of Public Schools,* Annual (1846-1922), especially Elisha R. Potter, Jr., *Report Upon Public Schools and Education in Rhode Island, October, 1854* (1855), which contains Potter's notable essay on 'The Bible and Prayer in Public Schools.' Charles Carroll, *Public Education in Rhode Island* (1918); Thomas B. Stockwell, *A History of Public Education in Rhode Island from 1636 to 1876* (1876); and Edward McEntee, (comp. and ed.), *Laws of Rhode Island Relating to Education* (1948) contain much essential information.

Catholics and the social questions of the nineteenth century are ably examined by Aaron I. Abell, *American Catholicism and Social Action: A Search for Social Justice, 1865-1950* (1960); Abell, *American Catholic Thought on Social Questions* (1968); James Edmund Roohan, 'American Catholics and the Social Question, 1865-1900,' (Unpublished doctoral dissertation, Yale University, 1952); John O'Grady, *Catholic Charities in the United States: History and Problems* (1930); and Robert D. Cross, *The Emergence of Liberal Catholicism in America* (1958). Local responses are described by Reverend Daniel T. McColgan, *A Century of Charity: The First One Hundred Years of the Society of St. Vincent De Paul in the United States,* 2 vols. (1951) that contains a chapter on Rhode Island.

The socio-economic dimensions of Catholic life are illuminated by Thomas R. Hazard, *Report on the Poor and Insane in Rhode Island* (1851) and Kurt B. Mayer, *Economic Development and Population Growth in Rhode Island* (1953), which serves as a useful continuation of the studies of Coleman and Brennan. In this area Samuel Green, *Rhode Island Mills and Mill Villages* (1940) and David Chase, *An Historical Survey of Rhode Island Textile Mills* (1969) are brief but valuable studies. For the temperance crusade consult Reverend Patrick Rogers, *Father Theobald Mathew: Apostle of Temperance* (1945); John A. Krout, *The Origins of Prohibition* (1925); and J. H. Stiness, *A Sketch of Rhode Island Legislation Against Strong Drink* (1892).

The two most illustrious Catholic intellectuals to visit Rhode Island and lecture to local audiences were Orestes Brownson and Father Isaac Hecker, both of whom made several appearances. On Brownson, his life and influence see Henry F. Brownson (ed.), *The Life of Orestes A. Brownson*, 3 vols. (1898-1900); Theodore Maynard, *Orestes Brownson: Yankee, Radical, Catholic* (1943); Arthur M. Schlesinger, Jr., *Orestes Brownson: A Pilgrim's Progress* (1939); and Americo D. Lapati, *Orestes A. Brownson* (1965). The best studies of Hecker are Vincent F. Holden, *The Yankee Paul: Isaac Thomas Hecker* (1958) and Reverend Joseph McSorley, *Father Hecker and His Friends* (1952). Ralph Henry Gabriel, *The Course of American Democratic Thought* (2nd ed., 1956) contains an excellent discussion of the efforts of Brownson and Hecker to harmonize Roman Catholicism with American ideals (pp. 57-69). For the general defense of Catholicism during this period see Robert Gorman, *Catholic Apologetical Literature in the United States, 1784-1858* (1939).

Valuable monographs of a miscellaneous nature are Reverend Benjamin J. Blied, *Austrian Aid to American Catholics 1830-1860* (1944); James F. Connelly, *The Visit of Archbishop Gaetano Bedini to the United States of America [June 1853-February, 1854]* (1960) that prints the highly informative Nuncio's report on the status of American Catholicism in the early 1850s; John R. Hassard, *Life of the Most Reverend John Hughes, D.D., First Archbishop of New York with Extracts from His Private Correspondence* (1886) that is still the best biography of the metropolitan of the Hartford see; Patrick J. Dignan, *A History of the Legal Incorporation of Church Property in the United States, 1784-1932* (1933); Robert F. McNamara, 'Trusteeism in the Atlantic States, 1785-1863,' *Catholic Historical Review*, XXX (July 1944), 135-154; and James Hennesey, S.J., *The First Council of the Vatican: The American Experience* (1963).

Information on Rhode Island Catholics and the Civil War is contained in Elisha Dyer (comp.), *Rhode Island Adjutant General's Report, 1861-1865*, 2 vols., a revised compilation published in 1893 of Rhode Island's Civil War volunteers, and Harold R. Barker, *History of the Rhode Island Combat Units in the Civil War* (1964). Barker's book contains a bibliography of Rhode Island units, the most important of which from the Catholic perspective is Frederick Denison, *The Third Rhode Island in the Rebellion* (1879). Robert Livingston Stanton, *The Church and the Rebellion* (1964) is a full discussion of the Civil War's impact on American religious denominations. See also Richard Roscoe Miller, *Slavery and Catholicism* (1957); Madeleine H. Rice, *American Catholic Opinion in the Slavery Controversy* (1944); Reverend Benjamin Blied, *Catholics and the Civil War* (1945); and Robert J. Murphy, 'The Catholic Church in the United States During the Civil War Period, 1852-1866,' *Records and Studies of the American Catholic Historical Society of Philadelphia*, XXXIX (1928), 271-346.

The post-war activities of the Fenians are described by Leon O'Broin, *Fenian Fever: An Anglo-American Dilemma* (1971); William D'Arcy, *The Fenian Movement in the United States, 1858-1886* (1947); Brian Jenkins, *Fenians and Anglo-American Relations during Reconstruction* (1969); and Maurice Harmon (ed.), *Fenians and Fenianism* (1968).

Immigration is a major theme of nineteenth-century Catholic history. Those general studies of this topic which were extremely valuable in the preparation of this volume include: George M. Stephenson, *History of American Immigration, 1820-1924* (1926); Daniel C. Brewer, *The Conquest of New England by the Immigrant* (1926); Carl Wittke, *We Who Built America: The Saga of the Immigrant* (1939); Marcus Lee Hansen, *The Atlantic Migration 1607-1860: A History of the Continuing Settlement of the United States* (1940); Maldwyn Allen Jones, *American Immigration* (1960); Oscar Handlin, *The Uprooted: The Epic Story of the Great Migrations that Made the American People* (1951); Handlin, *Race and Nationality in American Life* (1957); Handlin (ed.), *Immigration as a Factor in American History* (1959); Edward P. Hutchinson, *Immigrants and Their Children, 1850-1950* (1956); Michael Kraus, *Immigration, The American Mosaic: From Pilgrims to Modern Refugees* (1966); Philip Taylor, *The Distant Magnet: European Emigration to the U. S. A.* (1971); Terry Coleman, *Going to America* (1972); Peter C. Marzio (ed.), *A Nation of Nations* (1976), an excellent illustrated history of the immigrant experience; Helen I. Cowan, *British Emigration to British North America: The First Hundred Years* (rev. and enlarged ed., 1961); Edwin C. Guillet, *The Great Migration: The Atlantic Crossing by Sailing-Ship, 1770-1860* (2nd ed., 1963); David Ward, 'The Emergence of Central Immigrant Ghettos in American Cities, 1840-1920,' *Annals of the Association of American Geographers*, LVIII (Mar., 1968), 343-359; Barbara Miller Solomon, *Ancestors and Immigrants: A Changing New England Tradition* (1956), which stresses the Yankee-immigrant rivalry; and Marcus Lee Hansen, 'The Second Colonization of New England,' *New England Quarterly*, II (Oct., 1929), 539-560.

The effect of Catholic immigration upon Rhode Island is statistically detailed in several censuses and demographic studies: The decennial federal censuses of 1850, 1860, and 1870, especially those volumes dealing with population and embracing the tables of race, nationality and occupation; Edwin M. Snow (comp.), *Report Upon the Census of Rhode Island, 1865* (1867); Snow (comp.), *Report Upon the Census of Rhode Island 1875* (1877); C. W. Parsons, *Notice of the History of Population in the State of Rhode Island* [1859]; Rhode Island, Office of the Commissioner of Labor, *Church Statistics and Religious Preference* (1907); *Census of the Foreign-Born Population of Rhode Island* (Part I of the *Annual Report* of the Rhode Island Bureau of Industrial Statistics for 1907), an extract from the 1905 state census which contains tables on the earlier periods embraced by this book; Rhode Island Bureau of Industrial Statistics, *Some Nativity and Race Factors in Rhode Island* (1910); Snow (comp.), *Census of the City of Providence Taken in July 1855 . . . and an Appendix Giving an Account of Previous Enumerations of the*

Population of Providence (2nd ed., 1856); Snow (comp.), *Census of the City of Providence, May 1, 1874* (1874, City Document #91); and J. J. Spengler, 'Fertility in Providence, Rhode Island 1856-1929,' *American Journal of Sociology*, XXXVIII (1932-33), 377-397, which concludes that the fertility of foreign born women exceeds that of native-born; and the fertility of new immigrants exceeds that of old.

The influx of Catholic immigrants gave rise to the Know-Nothing Movement. The growth of this phenomenon is analyzed by Ray Allen Billington, *The Protestant Crusade 1800-1860: A Study of the Origins of American Nativism* (1938), the standard study; Colman J. Barry, 'Some Roots of American Nativism,' *Catholic Historical Review*, XLV (July, 1959), 161-185; William G. Bean, 'Puritan versus Celt, 1850-1860,' *New England Quarterly*, VII (1934), 70-89; Sister Loyola, S.N.D., 'Bishop Benedict J. Fenwick and Anti-Catholicism in New England, 1829-1845,' *Records and Studies, United States Catholic Historical Society*, XXVII (1937), 99-256; Reverend John J. Kane, *Catholic-Protestant Conflicts in America* (1955); Ira M. Leonard and Robert D. Parmet, *Amercian Nativism, 1830-1860* (1971); and Robert Francis Hueston, 'The Catholic Press and Nativism, 1840-1860,' (Unpublished doctoral dissertation, University of Notre Dame, 1972). Michael Fitzgibbon Holt, *Forging a Majority: The Formation of the Republican Party in Pittsburgh, 1848-1860* (1969); Holt, 'The Politics of Impatience: The Origins of Know Nothingism,' *The Journal of American History*, LX (Sept., 1973), 309-331; and John Mulkern, 'The Know-Nothing Victory in Massachusetts: A Triumph for *Vox Populi*' (Unpublished research paper delivered at a conference of the New England Historical Association held at Rhode Island College, May 1974) are recent path-breaking studies which stress the grass-roots appeal of this nativistic party.

There are several accounts of local nativism, namely, Charles Stickney, 'Know-Nothingism in Rhode Island,' No. 3 of the Papers from the Historical Seminary of Brown University, edited by J. Franklin Jameson (1894), reprinted in Rhode Island Historical Society, *Publications* (1894), 241-257; John Michael Ray, 'Anti-Catholicism and Know-Nothingism in Rhode Island,' *American Ecclesiastical Review*, CXLVIII (January, 1963), 27-36; and Larry Anthony Rand, 'The Know-Nothing Party in Rhode Island,' *Rhode Island History*, XXIII (October, 1964), 102-116. The political consequences of Know-Nothingism are discussed by Mario R. DiNunzio and Jan T. Galkowski, 'The Disruption of Rhode Island Politics: A Computer Study of Party Loyalty in the 1850s' (Unpublished research paper, Providence College, 1975); Laurence Bruce Raber, 'The Formation and Early Development of the Republican Party in Rhode Island, 1850-1865' (Unpublished master's thesis, University of Rhode Island, 1965); and Murray S. Stedman, Jr. and Susan W. Stedman, 'The Rise of the Democratic Party of Rhode Island,' *New England Quarterly*, XXIV (Sept., 1951), 329-341. The Know-Nothing line in unexpurgated form is found in the party's newspaper, the *Providence Daily Tribune* (1853-59).

Nativism persisted during the post-Civil War era in Rhode Island and elsewhere. Its continued vitality is described by Alvin Packer Stauffer, 'Anti-Catholicism in American Politics' (Unpublished doctoral dissertation, Harvard University, 1933) and John Higham, *Strangers in the Land: Patterns of American Nativism 1860-1925* (1955). William Gillette, *The Right to Vote: Politics and the Passage of the Fifteenth Amendment* (1965) contains an excellent analysis of the nativistic debate on the voting rights amendment, but it should be supplemented by the full transcript in the *Congressional Globe*, 40th Congress, Third Session. Charles E. Gorman, *An Historical Statement of the Elective Franchise in Rhode Island* (1879) is an extremely valuable first-hand survey of political nativism in Rhode Island during the 1860s and 1870s. Much information can also be found in the *Boston Pilot*, the *Providence Journal*, and two short-lived Providence reform newspapers, the *Weekly Democrat* and the *Weekly Review*. Useful secondary accounts on the politics of prejudice are Clifford Chesley Hubbard, 'Constitutional Development in Rhode Island' (Unpublished doctoral dissertation, Brown University, 1926); Mary Cobb Nelson, 'The Influence of Immigration on Rhode Island Politics, 1865-1910' (Unpublished doctoral dissertation, Harvard University, 1954); and Robert C. Power, 'Rhode Island Republican Politics in the Gilded Age,' (Unpublished honors thesis, Brown University, 1972). Arch-nativist Henry Bowen Anthony speaks for himself in 'Limited Suffrage in Rhode Island,' *North American Review*, CXXXVII (Nov., 1883), 413-421; *Defense of Rhode Island, her Institutions, and her Right to her Representatives in Congress* (1881); and the *Congressional Record*, 46 Cong., 3 Sess., pp. 1490-1499. On Anthony's political career consult William Barrie Thornton, 'Henry Bowen Anthony: Journalist, Governor, and Senator' (Unpublished master's thesis, University of Rhode Island, 1960) and Rhode Island General Assembly, *Henry Bowen Anthony, A Memorial* (1885). For a contrary view consult the reports of the United States Senate investigating committee chaired by Democrat William A. Wallace (46 Cong., 2nd Sess., Reports Nos. 427 and 572, Apr.-May, 1880).

The importance of ethnicity to an understanding of culturally pluralistic American Catholicism was a neglected factor until emphasized by several recent studies of a sociological nature: Will Herberg, *Protestant, Catholic, Jew: an Essay in American Religious Sociology* (rev. ed., 1955); Gerhard Lenski, *The Religious Factor: A Sociological Study of Religion's Impact on Politics, Economics, and Family Life* (1963); Milton M. Gordon, *Assimilation in American Life: The Role of Race, Religion and National Origins* (1964); Rudolph J. Vecoli. 'Ethnicity: Neglected Dimension of American History,' in Herbert J. Bass (ed.), *The State of American History* (1970), pp. 70-88; and Martin E. Marty, 'Ethnicity: The Skeleton of Religion in America,' *Church History*, XLI (March, 1972), 5-21. Harold J. Abramson, 'Ethnic Diversity Within Catholicism: A Comparative Analysis of Contemporary and Historical Religion,' *Journal of Social History*, IV (Summer, 1971), 359-388; and Abramson, 'The Ethnic Factor in American Catholicism: An Analysis of Inter-Ethnic Marriage and Religious Involvement' (Unpublished doctoral dissertation, University of Chicago, 1969) are stimulating and provocative studies devoted specifically to cultural diversity within American Catholicism. Reverend David F. Cunningham, 'The Historical Background of National Parishes' (Unpublished thesis for the Licentiate in Canon Law, Catholic University of America, 1930) also contains useful insights on the ethnic factor. Joshua A. Fishman, *et. al.*, *Language Loyalty: Maintenance of Non-English Mother Tongues* (1966) is an important analysis of a neglected topic that has particular relevance for an understanding of this Franco-American trait.

The causes and impact of the Irish migration are examined in the general histories of immigration cited *supra.* and in the following special studies: Cecil Woodham-Smith, *The Great Hunger: Ireland 1845-1849* (1962); R. Dudley Edwards, and T. Desmond Williams (eds.), *The Great Famine: Studies in Irish History, 1845-52* (1956); Thomas D'Arcy McGee, *A History of the Irish Settlement in North America* (1851); Edward J. Maguire (ed.), 'Reverend John O'Hanlon's *The Irish Emigrant's Guide for the United States:* A Critical Edition with Introduction and Commentary' (Unpublished doctoral dissertation, St. Louis University, 1951); Reverend Stephen Byrne, *Irish Emigration to the United States: What It Has Been, and What It Is* (1873); Frances Morehouse, 'The Irish Migration of the "Forties",' *American Historical Review,* XXXIII (Apr., 1928), 579-592; Arnold Schrier, *Ireland and the American Emigration, 1850-1900* (1958); Carl Wittke, *The Irish in America* (1956); William D. Griffin (ed.), *The Irish in America 550-1972* (1973); Lawrence J. McCaffrey, *The Irish Diaspora in America* (1976); Oscar Handlin, *Boston's Immigrants: A Study in Acculturation* (2nd ed., 1959), an excellent case study; H. M. Gitelman, 'No Irish Need Apply: Patterns of and Responses to Ethnic Discrimination in the Labor Market,' *Labor History,* XIV (Winter, 1973), 56-68; Robert A. Wheeler, 'Fifth Ward Irish-Immigrant Mobility in Providence, 1850-1870,' *Rhode Island History,* XXXII (May, 1973), 52-61; William Leonard Joyce, 'Editors and Ethnicity: A History of the Irish-American Press, 1848-1883' (Unpublished doctoral dissertation, University of Michigan, 1974); and James Martin Mahoney, 'The Influence of Irish-Americans Upon the Foreign Policy of the United States: 1865-1872' (Unpublished doctoral dissertation, Clark University, 1959).

The Irish were the subjects of cruel caricatures in several nineteenth-century popular graphic magazines, especially *Harper's Weekly, Puck, Judge,* and *Life.* Excellent studies of this pictorial prejudice are L. Perry Curtis, Jr., *Apes and Angels: The Irishman in Victorian Caricature* (1971); John J. Appel and Selma Appel, 'The Grand Old Sport of Hating Catholics: American Anti-Catholic Caricature Prints,' *The Critic,* XXX (Nov.-Dec., 1971), 50-58; and John J. Appel, 'From Shanties to Lace Curtains: The Irish Image in *Puck,* 1876-1910,' *Comparative Studies in Society and History,* XIII (1971), 365-375. The chief detractor of the Catholic Irish was Thomas Nast of *Harper's Weekly.* For his life and work consult Albert Bigelow Paine, *Thomas Nast: His Period and His Pictures* (1904) and Morton Keller, *The Art and Politics of Thomas Nast* (1968).

One of the most challenging and elusive tasks of the present study was to ascertain and describe the nature of nineteenth-century Irish Catholicism. The following writings were the most useful in shaping our analysis. Alexis de Tocqueville, *Journeys to England and Ireland,* edited by J. P. Mayer (1958) and L. Paul-Dubois, *Contemporary Ireland* (1908) are valuable commentaries by very perceptive Frenchmen. Emmet Larkin, 'Economic Growth, Capital Investment and the Roman Catholic Church in Nineteenth-Century Ireland,' *American Historical Review,* LXXII (Apr., 1967), 852-884; Larkin, 'The Devotional Revolution in Ireland, 1850-75,' *The American Historical Review,* LXXVII (June, 1972), 625-652; and Larkin, 'Church, State, and Nation in Modern Ireland,' *American Historical Review,* LXXX (Dec., 1975), 1244-1276 establish this scholar as the leading authority on mid-nineteenth-century Irish Catholicism. E. R. Norman, *The Catholic Church and Ireland in the Age of Rebellion 1859-1873* (1965) and Desmond Fennell, (ed.), *The Changing Face of Catholic Ireland* (1968) are also excellent analyses. K. H. Connell, *Irish Peasant Society: Four Historical Essays* (1968) and Robert E. Kennedy, Jr., *The Irish: Emigration, Marriage, and Fertility* (1973) are illuminating sociological studies of the Irish peasantry. Other useful works dealing with nineteenth-century Ireland are Máire and Conor Cruise O'Brien, *A Concise History of Ireland* (1972); Giovanni Costigan, *A History of Modern Ireland* (1970); William Harvey, *Irish Life and Humour: in Anecdote and Story* (n.d.); and Maurice Gorman, *Ireland Yesterday* (1971), a pictorial history covering the nineteenth and early twentieth centuries. Reverend M. O'Riordan, *Catholicity and Progress in Ireland* (1906) is an apologetic treatise.

The Irish-Americans are well-described in several interpretative studies: John Francis Maguire, *The Irish in America* (1868); George Potter, *To the Golden Door: The Story of the Irish in Ireland and America* (1960), an excellent account by a Pulitzer prize-winning *Providence Journal* writer; William V. Shannon, *The American Irish: A Political and Social Portrait* (rev. ed., 1966); Richard O'Connor, *The Irish: Portrait of a People* (1971); Andrew J. Greeley, *That Most Distressful Nation: The Taming of the American Irish* (1972); Arthur Mann, *Yankee Reformers in the Urban Age* (1954), which contains a chapter on 'Irish Catholic Liberalism' (pp. 24-51); Bruce Francis Biever, 'Religion, Culture, and Values: A Cross-Cultural Analysis of Motivational Factors in Native Irish and American Irish Catholicism' (Unpublished doctoral dissertation, University of Pennsylvania, 1965); and Donna Merwick, *Boston Priests, 1848-1910: A Study of Social and Intellectual Change* (1973). The political dimensions of Irish-American Catholicism are analyzed by Edward M. Levine, *The Irish and Irish Politicians* (1966); Nathan Glazer and Daniel Patrick Moynihan, *Beyond the Melting Pot: The Negroes, Puerto Ricans, Jews, Italians, and Irish of New York City* (2nd ed., 1970); Edgar Litt, *Beyond Pluralism: Ethnic Politics in America* (1970); Thomas N. Brown, *Irish-American Nationalism 1870-1890* (1966); Dorothy Dohen, *Nationalism and American Catholicism* (1967); and Charles C. Tansill, *America and the Fight for Irish Freedom: 1866-1922* (1957).

Information on Rhode Island's important Franco-American community is available in several excellent studies. Edward Hamon, *Les Canadiens Français de la Nouvelle-Angleterre*

(1891); Marie Louise Bonier, *Débuts de la Colonie Franco-Américaine de Woonsocket, Rhode Island* (1920); Bessie Bloom Wessel, *An Ethnic Survey of Woonsocket, Rhode Island* (1931) which contains an historical sketch by Henry W. Lawrence; Robert Cloutman Dexter, 'The *Habitant* Transplanted: A Study of the French-Canadian in New England' (Unpublished doctoral dissertation, Clark University, 1923); A. R. M. Lower, 'New France in New England,' *New England Quarterly*, II (April, 1929), 278-295; Marcus Lee Hansen, *The Mingling of the Canadian and American Peoples* (1940); Jacques Ducharme, *The Shadow of the Trees: The Story of the French-Canadians in New England* (1943); Iris S. Podea, 'Quebec to "Little Canada," The Coming of the French Canadians to New England,' *New England Quarterly*, XXIII (Sept., 1950), 365-380; Robert Rumilly, *Histoire des Franco Américains* (1958); and Joseph Gerald Doiron, 'The French Canadian Migration to Rhode Island' (Unpublished master's thesis, University of Rhode Island, 1959). Mason Wade, *The French-Canadians 1760-1967*, 2 vols. (1968) is the standard study. On Franco-American Catholicism Wade's 'The French Parish and *Survivance* in Nineteenth Century New England,' *Catholic Historical Review*, XXXVI (July, 1930), 163-189; Pierre Savard, 'Relations Between French-Canadian and American Catholics in the Last Third of the Nineteenth Century,' *Culture*, XXXI (Jan., 1970), 24-39; Sister Florence Marie Chevalier, 'The Role of French National Societies in the Sociocultural Evolution of the Franco-Americans of New England from 1860 to the Present . . .' (Unpublished doctoral dissertation, The Catholic University of America, 1972); and Ambrose Kennedy, *Quebec to New England: The Life of Monsignor Charles Dauray* (1948) are excellent. [Joseph Cichon], *St. John the Baptist Church, West Warwick, Rhode Island* (1974) and Anon., *Notre Dame Church, Central Falls, Rhode Island* (1974) are brief studies of two early French Canadian parishes. James S. Pula (ed.), *The French in America, 1488-1974* (1975) is a convenient collection of documents.

The Germans and German-American Catholicism are described in A. B. Faust, *The German Element in the United States*, 2 vols. (rev. ed., 1927); Henry A. Pochmann *et. al., German Culture in America, 1600-1900* (1957); Howard B. Furer, *The Germans in America, 1607-1970* (1973), a collection of documents; Colman J. Barry, *The Catholic Church and German Americans* (1953), the most valuable treatment of this topic; Emmet H. Rothan, *The German Catholic Immigrant in the United States, 1830-1860* (1946); Richard O'Connor, *The German-Americans* (1968); Robert Henry Billigmeier, *Americans from Germany: A Study in Cultural Diversity* (1974); and Jay P. Dolan, *The Immigrant Church: New York's Irish and German Catholics, 1815-1865* (1975). On William Stang and the local German community James E. Cassidy, D.D., *Right Reverend William Stang, D.D.: His First and Last Days as First Bishop of Fall River, Mass.* (1942); Francis J. Bradley, D.D., *A Brief History of the Diocese of Fall River, Massachusetts* (1931); and 'The Germans in Providence,' *Providence Board of Trade Journal*, October, 1910, pp. 432-435, are useful.

Published studies of the Portuguese and Cape Verdeans are few in number. Donald R. Taft, *Two Portuguese Communities in New England* (Portsmouth, R.I. and Fall River, Mass.) is a 1923 monograph tinged with the bias of Anglo-Saxon superiority. H. R. Lang, 'The Portuguese Element in New England,' *The Journal of American Folk-Lore*, V (1892), 9-17; Archibald Lyall, *Black and White Make Brown: An Account of a Journey to the Cape Verde Islands and Portuguese Guinea* (1938); Elisa Andrade, *Cape Verde Islands from Slavery To Modern Times* (1974); and Belmira E. Tavares, *Portuguese Pioneers in the United States* (1973) contain some useful data. Manuel da Silveira Cardozo (ed.), *The Portuguese in America* (1976) is a collection of annotated documents relating to the Portuguese experience. More helpful than these published works are several unpublished research papers: John Christian Bannick, 'Portuguese Immigration to the United States' (Unpublished master's thesis, University of California, 1917); Betty Ussach, 'The Portuguese in Rhode Island' (Unpublished master's seminar paper, Providence College, 1973); Philip Thomas Silvia, Jr., 'The Spindle City: Labor, Politics and Religion in Fall River, Massachusetts, 1870-1905' (Unpublished doctoral dissertation, Fordham University, 1973), a study that is also good on the Franco-Americans and deals with a city which was part of the Diocese of Providence from 1872 to 1904; David Bruce Tyack, 'Cape Verdean Immigration to the United States' (Unpublished honors thesis, Harvard University, 1952); Susan Sharf, 'Cape Verdeans in Providence' (Unpublished honors thesis, Brown University, 1965); and Manuel E. Costa, Sr., 'The Making of the Cape Verdean' (Unpublished research paper, Geneology Room, New Bedford Free Public Library, 1974). William Peter Gushue, 'Whaling in New Bedford, Massachusetts and its Decline During the Civil War' (Unpublished master's research paper, Providence College, 1976) contains an excellent chapter on 'Cape Verdeans and New Bedford Whaling,' pp. 88-108.

The early Italian arrivals during the formative era are identified by Ubaldo U. M. Pesaturo, *Italo-Americans of Rhode Island* (1936, 2nd ed., 1940).

Illustration Credits

page 2 Roger Williams, painting by Peter Frederick Rothermel, Rhode Island Historical Society

3 King Charles II, portrait from Charter of 1663, Rhode Island State House, photograph by Alec Tavares

4 Portuguese caravel, drawing by Robert Pailthorpe, Cranston, R. I.

5 Dighton Rock, photographs with preliminary chalking by Charles A. Hathaway, Jr., in 1907, Rhode Island Historical Society

Giovanni da Verrazzano, sketch from *Harper's Encyclopedia of United States History,* X, 44 (1907)

8 Act of 1719, from the *Digest of 1719,* Rhode Island State Archives

9 Colony House, Newport, sketch by G. Wall, Rhode Island Historical Society

10 Count de Rochambeau, painting by John Trumbull (detail from "Surrender of Lord Cornwallis at Yorktown"), Yale University Art Gallery

11 Marquis de Lafayette, portrait by Charles Willson Peale, from Washington-Custis-Lee Collection, Washington and Lee University

Gazette Françoise, November 17, 1780, Rhode Island Historical Society

12 French almanac, Newport 1781, Rhode Island Historical Society

British caricature of French troops, cartoon from the Library of Congress, Washington, D. C.

13 Act of 1783, Rhode Island State Archives

16 Bishop John Carroll, portrait by Gilbert Stuart, Georgetown University

17 Bishop Jean Louis Lefebre de Cheverus, portrait by Gilbert Stuart for Mrs. John Gore, Museum of Fine Arts, Boston

18 Father Francis A. Matignon, portrait from Robert H. Lord, et. al., *History of the Archdiocese of Boston,* I, opp. 480 (1945)

19 Notice of an address by Father John Thayer, *Newport Mercury,* July 1798, Rhode Island Historical Society

20 The Great Gale of 1815, from an engraving by J. Kidder, Rhode Island Historical Society

22 Bishop Benedict J. Fenwick, portrait from Thomas F. Cullen, *The Catholic Church in Rhode Island,* opp. p. 80 (1936)

23 Marker at Barney Street site of St. Joseph's Church, Newport, photograph by Leo P. Reardon, Rhode Island Historical Society

Fort Adams, Newport, photograph by the *Providence Journal-Bulletin*

25 Certificate of the Providence Association of Mechanics and Manufacturers, 1835, Rhode Island Historical Society

26 Old St. Mary's, Pawtucket, photograph from John H. McKenna, *The Centenary Story of Old St. Mary's,* opp. p. 12 (1929)

163

page 26 Mechanic's Hall, Market Square, Providence, from detail of Certificate of the Providence Association of Mechanics and Manufacturers, 1835, Rhode Island Historical Society

27 The Old Town House, Providence, *ca.* 1851, photograph courtesy of the Rhode Island Historical Society

28 Providence to Stonington railroad line at Stonington, Connecticut from a painting by Edward Lamson Henry, New York State Museum, Division of Historical Services

Railroad depot and steamship docks, India Street, Providence, sketch from Welcome Arnold Greene, *The Providence Plantations for 250 Years,* p. 141 (1886)

29 Map of Fox Point, Providence, 1849, by Cushing and Walling, Rhode Island Historical Society

30 Reverend John Corry, photograph courtesy of Reverend Thomas C. Brown, Pastor, St. John the Evangelist Church, Rensselaer, New York

31 Reverend James Fitton, photograph courtesy of St. Mary's Church, Newport

32 St. Patrick's Church, Providence, sketch from the *Official Souvenir, Sts. Peter and Paul Cathedral,* published by F. J. Flanagan (1889)

33 Tombstone from St. Patrick's Cemetery, Providence, photograph by Laurence E. Tilley

35 Map of Woonsocket Falls, 1838, from Marie Louise Bonier, *Débuts de la Colonie Franco-Américaine de Woonsocket, R. I.* (1920), original courtesy of the Woonsocket Historical Society

36 Michael Reddy, photograph from James W. Smyth, *History of the Catholic Church in Woonsocket,* opp. p. 57 (1903)

37 St. Mary's Church, Crompton, from cover photograph of the *Official Directory and Information Guide for the Diocese of Providence* [for 1973], Visitor Printing Company

38 Notice of skilled Irish worker, *Providence Gazette,* October 31, 1789, Rhode Island Historical Society

40 Thomas Wilson Dorr, from an early daguerrotype courtesy of Frank Mauran III, Providence

41 Henry Bowen Anthony, from a photograph courtesy of the Rhode Island Historical Society

43 Native American Citizens!, a March 1842 broadside, Rhode Island Historical Society

45 People's Party Ballot, April 1842, Rhode Island Historical Society

47 'The Paddy's Lament for Tom Dorr,' from *Ballads of The Dorr War,* published by Sidney S. Rider (1869), originally printed in the *Providence Journal,* March 30, 1843.

48 Big Mike Walsh, from an engraving courtesy of the New York Historical Society, New York City

49 The Duff Petition, Rhode Island State Archives

50 Governor Jackson and the Irish vote, 1846, Broadside file, Rhode Island Historical Society

52 The Sprague mill complex, from a textile label, Rhode Island Historical Society

53 Map of the Sprague Print Works, Cranston, 1844, by S. B. Cushing, Rhode Island Historical Society

General Thomas F. Carpenter, from a portrait by James Sullivan Lincoln, Rhode Island Historical Society

54 Court report of the Gordon murder trial, by Edward C. Larned and William Knowles, Providence, the Daily Transcript, March, 1844, at Rhode Island Historical Society

55 Rhode Island State Prison, 1845, from a sketch in the Samuel W. Brown scrapbook, Graphics Collection, Rhode Island Historical Society

58 William Barber Tyler, First Bishop of Hartford, from Very Reverend William Byrne (ed.), *History of the Catholic Church in the New England States,* II, opp. p. 122 (1899)

60 Map of Providence, 1844, drawn by N. B. Schubarth and published by B. F. Moore, collection of Patrick T. Conley

61 The First Cathedral of Sts. Peter and Paul, photograph, Rhode Island Historical Society

65 Archbishop John Hughes, from an engraving by George E. Perine in the *Dictionary of American Portraits,* edited by Hayward and Blanche Cirker, p. 318 (1967)

67 Total Abstinence Pledge, from the collection of Patrick T. Conley

68 Father Theobald Mathew (close-up), painting by Haverty from Patrick Rogers, *Father Theobald Mathew: Apostle of Temperance,* frontispiece (1945)

Father Mathew Preaching, from the *Illustrated London News,* 1843

69 Orestes A. Brownson, from an engraving by Alexander L. Dick in *Dictionary of American Portraits,* edited by Hayward and Blanche Cirker, p. 83 (1967)

71 Bernard O'Reilly, Second Bishop of Hartford, from Very Reverend William Byrne (ed.), *History of the Catholic Church in the New England States,* II, opp. p. 134 (1899)

72 Mother Mary Francis Xavier Warde, photograph from Anon. *An Historical Sketch of the Sisters of Mercy of St. Francis Xavier's Convent, Providence* (1901)

73 Mercy Convent, photograph from *Seventy-Five Years in the Passing with the Sisters of Mercy, Providence, Rhode Island 1851-1926,* opp. p. 73 (1926)

74 St. Xavier's Academy, Music lessons, photograph from Anon. *An Historical Sketch of the Sisters of Mercy of St. Francis Xavier's Convent, Providence* (1901)

THE FORMATIVE ERA

page 75 St. Xavier's Academy Assembly Room, photograph from Anon. *An Historical Sketch of the Sisters of Mercy of St. Francis Xavier's Convent, Providence* (1901)

76 Governor Philip Allen, from a portrait by James S. Lincoln, Rhode Island State House, photograph by Leo P. Reardon.

77 'Fort Sumter' (Nast), cartoon from *Harper's Weekly,* March 19, 1870

78 Elisha R. Potter, Jr., photograph of a bust, courtesy of the Rhode Island Historical Society

79 'Don't Believe in That' (Nast), cartoon from *Harper's Weekly* (undated), collection of Patrick T. Conley

80 The Convent Committee, courtesy of the American Antiquarian Society, Worcester, Massachusetts

82 American Handbill, from the *Providence Journal*, March 22, 1855. Original broadside in the John Hay Library, Brown University

83 'The Emigrant,' painting by Erskine Nicol in William Harvey, *Irish Life and Humour,* opp. p. 256 (n.d.)

84 Immigrants Landing at the Battery, 1855, a painting by Samuel B. Waugh, courtesy of the Museum of the City of New York

85 Reverend James Gibson, photograph from Mathias P. Harpin, *Trumpets in Jericho,* p. 133 (1961)

St. Joseph's, Fox Point, sketch from the *Official Souvenir, Sts. Peter and Paul Cathedral,* published by F. J. Flanagan (1889)

86 St. Mary's Broadway, an etching by Charles M. Springer (1891) from *Centennial Commemoration-St. Mary's Parish . . . ,* p. 72 (1953)

87 Reverend John Quinn, portrait from *Centennial Commemoration-St. Mary's Parish . . . ,* p. 20 (1953)

88 Francis Patrick McFarland, Third Bishop of Hartford, from Very Reverend William Byrne (ed.), *History of the Catholic Church in the New England States,* II, opp. p. 150 (1899)

90 Rhode Island Regiment Off to War, photograph courtesy of the Providence Public Library

92 Irish Militia, sketch from Oscar Handlin, *Boston's Immigrants,* p. 158 (2nd ed., 1959)

Father Bernard O'Reilly, from James W. Smyth, *History of the Catholic Church in Woonsocket . . . ,* opp. p. 84 (1903)

93 John O'Mahony, portrait sketch from *Harper's Weekly,* November 18, 1865

95 Fenian cartoon, from *The Judge,* March 21, 1885

97 Charles E. Gorman, photograph from Thomas Williams Bicknell, *The History of the State of Rhode Island and Providence Plantations,* biographical volume (Lister to Traver), opp. p. 201 (1920)

98 'Bravo' (Nast), cartoon from *Harper's Weekly,* July 29, 1871

99 'The Ignorant Vote' (Nast), cartoon from *Harper's Weekly,* December 9, 1876

100 The Naturalized Voter, cartoon by Thomas Worth from *Harper's Weekly* (undated), from the collection of Patrick T. Conley

102 'Killing the Goose' (Nast), cartoon from *Harper's Weekly,* November 18, 1871

104 The First Church of St. Michael's Parish, South Providence, photograph from *Golden Jubilee . . . St. Michael's Church* (1909)

The First Church of St. Ann's Parish, Cranston, photograph from *Centennial Commemoration-St. Mary's Parish . . . ,* p. 64 (1953)

105 Immaculate Conception Church, Providence, photograph from parish reunion booklet [1971]

107 St. Aloysius Home, photograph from *Providence Illustrated* published by Harris Smith Inman, plate 97 (1886)

108 The Original LaSalle Academy, photograph courtesy of the the Alumni Office, LaSalle Academy, Providence

109 Reverend Henry F. Kinnerny, from Anon., *History of the State of Rhode Island,* published by Hoag & Wade, opp. p. 238 (1878)

Father Isaac Hecker, from a portrait by G. P. A. Healy, courtesy of the Paulist Fathers Archives

110 Reaction to Edith O'Gorman, cartoon by Thomas Nast from *Harper's Weekly* (undated), collection of Patrick T. Conley

112 Irish cottage, photograph courtesy of the Ulster Museum

113 Irish village (*ca.* 1895), from a photograph courtesy of Belfast Central Library

114 The Priest's Blessing, sketch from the *Illustrated London News,* May 10, 1851

115 Emigration Agent, John Whitney, from *The Providence Directory for the Year 1858*, advertisement section

116 Boy and Girl at Cahera, sketch from the *Illustrated London News,* 1847

117 An Eviction, sketch from the *Illustrated London News,* December 16, 1848

Famine Funeral at Skibbereen, sketch from the *Illustrated London News,* January 30, 1847

Starving Crowd at the Workhouse Gate, from an engraving in the *Illustrated London News,* 1847, reproduced in Máire and Conor Cruise O'Brien, *A Concise History of Ireland,* p. 105 (1972)

page 118 The 1850 Census of Providence, from the manuscript schedules of the Seventh Federal Census (1850), Rhode Island Historical Society

119 'Paddy's Ladder,' cartoon from *Yankee Notions,* 1853, p. 254

120 'The King of A-Shantee,' a cartoon by Frederick B. Opper from *Puck,* February 15, 1882, reproduced with caption from L. Perry Curtis, Jr., *Apes and Angels: The Irishman in Victorian Caricature,* p. 63 (1971)

121 'American River Ganges' (Nast), carton from *Harper's Weekly,* September 30, 1871

'The Day We Celebrate' (Nast), cartoon from *Harper's Weekly,* April 6, 1867

122 'The Good-for-Nothing in Dame Columbia's Public School' (Nast), cartoon from *Harper's Weekly,* November 4, 1871

124–125 Irish Caricatures, typical late nineteenth-century cartoons from *Puck* (undated), collection of Patrick T. Conley

129 The American Irish and the Pope, cartoon by Thomas Nast from *Harper's Weekly,* January 21, 1871

130 Paul Cardinal Cullen, from the portrait at St. Patrick's College, Dublin

132 Irish Religious Procession, photograph in the possession of Kevin Danaher reproduced in Maurice Gorham (ed.), *Ireland Yesterday,* plate 69 (1971)

Colleen with Rosary, picture from the collection of Patrick T. Conley

134 François (Fanfan) Proulx, from Marie Louise Bonier, *Débuts de la Colonie Franco-Américaine de Woonsocket, Rhode Island* (1920)

135 George C. Ballou, portrait from Marie Louise Bonier, *Débuts de la Colonie Franco-Américaine de Woonsocket, Rhode Island* (1920)

136 Clinton Cotton Mill, Woonsocket, from a sketch in James Geldard, *Handbook on Cotton Manufacture* (1867)

137 A Pawtuxet Valley Mill (*ca.* 1875), photograph courtesy of the Rhode Island Historical Society

138 Precious Blood Church, Woonsocket, from James W. Smyth, *History of the Catholic Church in Woonsocket . . . ,* opp. p. 115 (1903)

139 Father Charles Dauray, photograph from Ambrose Kennedy, *Quebec to New England: The Life of Monsignor Charles Dauray,* frontispiece (1948)

140 Father Patrick Delany, from Reverend John H. McKenna, *The Centenary Story of Old St. Mary's,* opp. p. 22 (1929)

141 Notre Dame Church, Central Falls, photograph from *Notre Dame Church, Central Falls, Rhode Island,* p. 9 (1974)

St. John the Baptist Church, Arctic, from a photograph in *St. John the Baptist Church, West Warwick, Rhode Island,* p. 11 (1974)

142 St. John's Day Parade (*ca.* 1890), photograph courtesy of the Rhode Island Historical Society

143 Whaler's Log — Cape Verdean Entry, from 'Journal of a Whaling Voyage on Board Ship *Chili* of New Bedford During the Years, 1839, 40, 41, 42, & 43,' by E. G. Lindsey, courtesy of William Gushue and the Melville Whaling Room, New Bedford Free Public Library.

144 Chart of a Whaling Voyage, courtesy of Mystic Seaport, Mystic, Connecticut

145 Portuguese Whalemen, detail sketch by David Hunter Strother ('Porte Crayon'), *Harper's New Monthly Magazine,* June, 1860

German Ferry, sketch courtesy of the Smithsonian Institution, Washington, D. C.

146 Bishop William Stang, photograph from Francis J. Bradley, D.D., *A Brief History of the Diocese of Fall River, Mass.,* opp. p. 41 (1931)

147 The First Church of St. Mary's, Broadway, sketch from *Centennial Commemoration-St. Mary's Parish . . . ,* p. 64 (1953)

149 Thomas Francis Hendricken, First Bishop of Providence, photograph from Anon. *A Little Sketch of the Work of the Sisters of Mercy in Providence, Rhode Island from 1851 to 1893,* opp. p. 52 (1893)

151 Providence in the 1870s, sketch from Welcome Arnold Greene, *The Providence Plantations for 250 Years,* p. 215 (1886)

Index

Abell, Aaron I., 130
Abolitionism, 79, 83, 90-91
Academy of St. Mary's of the Isle (Newport), 106
Acadia, 133
Acote's Hill, 48
Act of Union (1801), 19, 33, 113
Adams, John Quincy, 51
Address to the People of Rhode Island, 44
Adopted Citizens' Association, 96
Albany, Diocese of, 69, 89
Albion (Rhode Island), 137
Algerine Law, 46, 48, 51
Alien Act (1798), 19-20
All Hallows Seminary (Dublin), 60-61, 70, 81
Allen, Charles B., 76
Allen, Governor Philip, 32, 33, 51, 55, 76-77, 79
Allen, Walter, 36
Allyn, Robert, 63
Altar Society, 109
American Citizens Association, 52
American Protective Association, 76
American Revolution, 4, 7, 9-10, 11, 13, 15
'Americanists,' 131
Ancient Order of Hibernians, 96
Anthony, Henry Bowen, 42, 46-47, 63-64, 82, 98-100, 103, 115
Antunes, Joseph, 6, 9
Aquidneck Island, 3, 6, 22
Aracambal, Louis, 19
Arctic (Rhode Island), 137, 141
Ascendancy (Irish), 112-113
Asceticism of the Irish, 125, 127

Ashton (Rhode Island), 105
Assumption Church (West Elmwood), 104-105
Atwell, Samuel Y., 54
Austria, 103
Azevedo da Encarnacão, Rev. João Ignacio, 145
Azores, 143-145

Baltimore (Maryland), 15, 16, 19
Bancroft, George, 51
Baptist, 6
Barbe-Marbois, François de, 4
Barber, Daniel and Virgil, 59
Bardstown (Kentucky), 16
Barry, Rev. Colman J., 146
Battle of Rhode Island, 10
Beaumont, Gustave, 126
Bedini, Archbishop Cajetan, 83
Belgian priests, 103, 138, 140
Bellomont, Earl of, 7
Berkins, Rev. James, 105, 138, 140, 141
Bernard, Rev. Antoine D., 139-140
Bible and public schools, 78
Blackstone Canal, 24, 29, 36
Blackstone River, 24, 35, 105, 135
Blackstone Valley, 104, 105, 137
Blake, Joseph M., 54
Block Island, 6
'Bloodless Revolution' of 1935, 51
(The) Bloody Tenent Yet More Bloody, 3
Boston (Massachusetts), 4, 12, 16, 17, 18, 19, 20, 21, 24
Boston, Diocese of, 16-17, 34, 57, 59, 69

167

INDEX

Boston and Providence Railroad and Transportation Company, 29
Boston Pilot, 59, 96
Bouchard, Rev. Claude Florent (Abbe de la Poterie), 18
Bourget, Bishop Ignatius, 138
Bourn Amendment, 103
Brady, Rev. John, 36, 55
Brayton, Charles R., 103
Brennan, Michael, 96
Bristol (Rhode Island), 11, 12, 18, 19, 85, 143
Brown, Thomas N., 42, 124, 127
Brown University, 11, 13
Brownson, Orestes A., 51, 68-69, 130
Brownson Lyceum, 84, 109
Buffalo, Diocese of, 69, 70
Burke, Rev. Thomas M., O.P., 151
Burnside, Ambrose, 91, 97
Byrne, Rev. Patrick, 22, 36
Byrne, Rev. Stephen, 67

Calhoun, John C., 51
Canada (British), 9, 15, 94, 115, 119, 133-134
Cape Verdeans, 142-145
Carey, Matthew, 42
Carlin, Hugh, 63
Carlin, Rev. Peter, 147
Carmody, Rev. Hugh, 72, 92
Carpenter, Thomas F., 53-54
Carroll, Charles, 23, 62
Carroll, Daniel, 15
Carroll, Bishop John, 4, 15, 16-17, 18, 19, 20, 63
Carroll, Michael, 37
Cathedral (see Sts. Peter and Paul Cathedral, Providence)
Cathedral Total Abstinence Society, 96
Catholic Charity Fund Appeal, 84
Catholic Layman (newspaper), 34
Catholic State Temperance Union, 96
Catholic Temperance Confraternity, 66-67
Catholic Temperance Society, 32-33, 66
Central Falls (Rhode Island), 137, 140
Champlain, Samuel, 133, 134
Charles I, King of England, 3
Charles II, King of England, 3
Charlestown (Massachusetts) Convent, 39, 79
Charter of 1663, 3-4, 7-9, 42, 44-46
Chastity of the Irish, 128-129
Chepachet (Rhode Island), 48, 51
Cheverus, Bishop Jean Louis Lefebvre de, 17, 20, 21, 36, 59
Children of the Guardian Angel, 109
Children of Mary, 109
Children of St. Aloysius, 109
Christian Brothers, 74, 76, 86, 106-107
Christian Doctrine Society, 105
Church of England, 7
Church of Ireland (Anglican), 112
Church organization and the French Canadian, 136
Civil War, 89-93, 94, 97
Clarke, John, 3

'Claudius Petrat,' 81
Clerical deference and the Irish laity, 125-127, 131
Clune, Rev. Michael, 105
Clyde (Rhode Island), 37
Coddington, William, 3
Confraternity of the Blessed Virgin Mary to Befriend Children, 66
Congregationalists, 19
Congressional Medal of Honor, 92
Connecticut, 7, 12, 19, 22, 147, 150
Connell, K. H., 128
Connolly, Rev. Peter, 27
Conservatism of the Irish Catholic, 129-131
Constitutional Party, 44-45
Cooney, Rev. Edward, 104
Corcoran, John, 92
'Corky Hill' (Providence), 29
Corliss, George, 104
Corn Laws, 115
Cornwallis, Lord, 11
Corrigan, Archbishop Michael, 131
Corry, Rev. John, 23, 24, 26, 29, 30-34, 37, 39, 66, 69
Corte-Real, Miguel, 5
Cosgrove, James, 96
Costello, Michael, 53
Coyle, John, 63, 65, 78
Cottiers, 112-114, 148
Cranston (Rhode Island), 24, 34, 37, 39, 52-53, 85
Crompton (Rhode Island), 37
Cromwell, Oliver, 6, 112
Cullen, Paul Cardinal, 64, 131
Cumberland (Rhode Island), 35

Dauray, Rev. Charles, 140-141
Davies, Rev. Samuel, 148, 150
Davis, Thomas, 97
Dean, Senator Sidney, 97-98
Deane, Joseph, 18
Death penalty, 55
De Bruyker, Rev. Florimond, 138
Delaney, William, 94
Delany, Rev. Patrick G., 26, 104, 140
Democratic-Republicans, 20
Democratic Party, 20, 42, 45, 46, 51, 76, 77, 78
Dennison, George, 48
'Devotional Revolution,' 125, 131-132, 151
Dexter Asylum, 83
Dighton Rock, 5
Dixon, Congressman Nathan F., 100
Doran, Mary, 37
Dorr, Thomas Wilson, 32, 39, 42-48, 51-55, 63, 76-77
Dorr Rebellion, 33, 42-52, 66, 76
Dowling, Rev. Austin, 81, 135
Doyle, Mayor Thomas, 97
Dubourg, Bishop Louis, 21
Duff, Henry J., 32, 33, 52
Durfee, Job, 54
Dutch priests, 103, 138, 141

INDEX

East Greenwich (Rhode Island), 6, 85
East Providence (Rhode Island), 35
Edict of Nantes, repeal of, 7
Elder, Bishop William Henry, 93
Elizer, Isaac, 7
Ellis, Rev. John Tracy, 5
Elmhurst (Providence), 24
Emmet, Robert, 19
Encumbered Estates Act, 115
England, 1-3, 6, 9-10, 93-94, 112, 119, 124-125, 133-134
Episcopalians, 20
Equal Rights Party, 96
Estaing, Count d', 10
Evening school, 106

Fall River (Massachusetts), 22, 24, 34-35, 143, 148
Family life of the Irish, 128-129
Famine (Great), 34, 37, 115-116, 128, 131
Father Mathew Benevolent Total Abstinence and Aid Society, 67
Federalists, 19, 20
Fenians, 93-96, 124
Fennell, Desmond, 128
Fennelly, Rev. William, 33
Fenner, Governor James, 51, 54
Fenwick, Bishop Benedict, 21, 22, 23, 25, 26, 30-31, 32, 33, 34, 39, 57, 59
Ferrari, Francis, 7
Fifteenth Amendment (United States), 98-100
'Fighting Sixty-Ninth,' 91
Fillmore, Millard, 76
Fitton, Rev. James, 23, 24, 34, 36, 37, 59, 62, 66, 69, 70, 115
Fitzpatrick, Bishop John B., 57, 59, 62, 70
Fitzsimmons, Rev. James A., 105
Fogarty, James, 148
Fordham University, 87
Fort Adams, 22, 23, 62
Fountain Street Academy, 76, 107
Fourteenth Amendment (United States), 98
Fox Point (Providence), 29, 123, 145
France, 7, 9, 16, 17, 18, 19, 21, 133-134
Francis I, King of France, 5
Franklin, Benjamin, 15
Freeman's Constitution, 46-48
French, 4, 5-6, 7, 9-10, 11, 12, 13, 16, 18, 19, 20, 39, 91
French and Indian War, 133
French Canadians, 36, 65, 105, 119, 133-142
French-Irish friction, 134, 135-137, 142
French Revolution, 17
Frenchtown (Rhode Island), 7

Gavazzi, Father, 81
Gedeon Francis, Brother, F.S.C., 107
General Assembly, 3, 6-7, 9, 19, 26, 44, 51-52, 54, 63, 78-79, 83, 97-98, 108
General Court (Massachusetts), 24
Georgetown University, 21, 23
Georgiaville (Rhode Island), 85

German-Americans (also Germany), 1, 61, 103, 145-147, 148
Gettleman, Marvin, 48
Gibbons, James Cardinal, 131
Gibson, Rev. James P., 37, 141
Gibson, James, 106
Glazer, Nathan, 127
Glorious Revolution (1688), 133
Goddard, William, 47, 64
Gordon, John, 53-55
Gordon, Nicholas, 53-55, 79
Gordon, William, 53-55
Gorman, Charles E., 97-100, 103
Gorton, Samuel, 3
Gravier, Charles (Comte de Vergennes), 9
Great Famine, 34, 37, 115-116, 128, 131
Greeley, Horace, 51
Greeley, Rev. Andrew, 127
Greenville (Rhode Island), 86
Grey, Gertrude, 110
Griswold, Bishop Alexander (Episcopal), 20

Hand, Rev. John, 60-61
Handlin, Oscar, 116
Hannity v. *O'Reilly,* 108
Harper, Mrs. Robert Goodloe, 23, 62
Harris Woolen Company, 139
Harrisville (Rhode Island), 86
Hart, Naphtali, 143
Hartford (Connecticut), 59
Hartford, Diocese of, 34, 37, 39, 57ff.
Hazard, Thomas, 83, 123
Haynes, William J., 94
Heath, General William, 10-11
Hecker, Rev. Isaac, 69, 109
Hendricken, Bishop Thomas F., 86, 96, 105, 139, 140-141, 145, 148-151
Hibernian Orphan Society, 24, 65-66
Hibernian Relief Society, 66
High schools, 74-76, 106
Holy Cross Cathedral (Boston), 18, 19, 36
Holy Cross College, 59, 62, 70
Holy Rosary Church (Providence), 145
Hoppin, Thomas C., 64
Hornsby, Thomas, 12
House of Representatives (United States), 52, 97
Hughes, Archbishop John, 33, 65, 69, 78, 80, 87, 89, 90, 127
Huguenots, 7
Hutchinson, Anne, 3
Hye, Francis, 26-27

Immaculate Conception Church (Providence), 104
Immaculate Conception School (Providence), 104, 106
Immigrant Aid Society, 109
Incorporation of church property, 108, 136, 150
India Point (Providence), 29
Indians, 4, 5-6, 12, 89
Infallibility, 111
Irish (also Ireland), 3, 4, 6, 15, 16, 18, 19, 20, 21, 22, 23, 24,

169

INDEX

27, 29, 36, 37, 39, 42, 44, 46-48, 51, 52-55, 61, 64-65, 70, 76-77, 81-83, 86, 89, 91-92, 93-96, 97-98, 100, 103, 104-105, 112-133, 147, 148
Irish-French friction, 134, 135-137, 142
Irish Catholicism, 124-133, 151
Irish Poor Law of 1838, 114
Italian Nationalism, 82
Italians, 5, 7, 82, 103, 130, 147
Ivers, Rev. William, 60, 69

Jackson, President Andrew, 20
Jackson, Governor Charles, 51
Jacobites, 9
James I, King of England, 112
James II, King of England, 7, 9, 133
Jansenism, 128
Jefferson, Thomas, 13
Jenckes, Congressman Thomas A., 100
Jesuit, 15, 21, 23, 133
Jews, 1-3, 6-7, 142-143, 146
Joachim of Sienna, Brother F.S.C., 107
Johnston (Rhode Island), 24

Kassedy family, 20
Keane, Archbishop John, 131
Keely, Patrick C., 62, 85, 150
Kelly, Rev. Daniel, 37, 70
Kendrick, Bishop Francis P., 70
Kennedy, Patrick and Helen, 34
Kennedy, Robert E. Jr., 128
King, Governor Samuel Ward, 48
King James Bible, 63, 78
King Philip's War, 6
Kinnerney, Rev. Henry F., 105, 107
Know-Nothings, 51, 64, 75-83, 148
Ku Klux Klan, 76

Lafayette, Marquis de, 10, 12, 67
Lambe, Rev. Patrick, 72
Landholders' Convention, 46
Language and the French Canadian, 134, 136
Lapati, Rev. Americo L., 74
Larkin, Emmet, 124, 131
La Salle Academy, 76, 106, 107-108
Law and Order Party, 46-48, 51-52, 54, 76-77
Lee, Rev. Constantine, 23, 27, 29, 30
Lenihan, Rev. Francis, 138
Leo, Father, 81
Leopoldine Mission Society (Vienna), 61, 84, 103
LeProphon, Dr. Edward P., 60, 70
Levesque, Rev. Zéphyrin, 138
Liberal Catholicism, 131
Lime Street Academy for Boys, 74, 76, 86, 106
Lippittsville (Rhode Island), 137
Litt, Edgar, 127
Longfellow, Henry Wadsworth, 133
Lopez, Aaron, 6-7, 143
Lord, Rev. Robert, 59

Lottery, 26
Loughrey, Mary Ellen, 7
Louis XIV, King of France, 7
Louis XV, King of France, 133
Louis XVI, King of France, 11
Louvain Seminary, 103
Lucena, James, 6-7, 9, 143
Ludwig Mission Association (Munich), 84
Lynch, Rev. Michael, 29

McAuley, Mother Catherine, 73
McAvoy, Rev. Thomas T., 39
McCabe, Rev. John J., 105
McCallion, Rev. Michael, 85
McCarthy, Charles, 6
McCarthy, John, 31, 32, 33, 34, 66
McClean family, 20
McCloskey, Bishop John, 89, 94, 111, 148, 150, 151
McFarland, Bishop Francis Patrick, 87-111, 138, 139, 141, 146-147, 148, 150
McGlynn, Rev. Edward, 131
McGreevey, Patrick, 94
MacHale, Archbishop John, 64-65
McMahon, Bishop Lawrence, 145
McMaster, James A., 68
McNamee, Rev. Joseph, 26
McNamee, Rev. Patrick, 29, 30
McQuaid, Bishop Bernard, 131
Maguire, John Francis, 65
Manning, Rev. James, 11, 13
Manville (Rhode Island), 137, 140, 142
Marieville (Rhode Island), 137
Maryland, 4, 15, 16, 21, 23
Massachusetts, 1-3, 24, 148
Mather, Cotton, 5
Mathew, Rev. Theobald, 67-68, 96, 131
Mathewson, Isaac, 27
Matignon, Rev. Francis Anthony, 16-17, 20, 21, 36, 59
Mayer, Prudent and Joseph, 135
Maynooth Seminary (Ireland), 72, 86, 126, 128, 148
Mechanics' Hall (Providence), 26
Metropolitan Catholic Almanac, 72
Middletown (Rhode Island), 6
Militancy of Irish Catholics, 89, 125, 127
Mills, Rev. Michael, 30
Missionary zeal of the Irish, 125, 127
Monk, Maria, 81
Mount Hope Bay, 5
Mowry, Arthur May, 42, 48
Moynihan, Daniel Patrick, 127
Murphy, Brother Patrick, F.S.C., 106
Murphy, Rev. Edward, 24, 34
Murphy, James, 105
Murray, Thomas Hamilton, 6
Mystic (Connecticut), 143

Narranganset Bay, 6
Natick (Rhode Island), 105, 137, 141

INDEX

National parish, 112, 132, 137-142, 145, 147
Nativism, 42-55, 76-83, 96-103, 115, 123, 135
Naturalization Act (1798), 19
Negroes, 18-19, 98, 100, 147
New Bedford (Massachusetts), 21, 143, 145, 148
New London (Connecticut), 62, 143
New York, 4, 5, 16, 19, 20, 21, 70, 84
New York, Archdiocese of, 69, 70
New York Freeman's Journal, 68
Newell, Rebecca, 81
Newman, S. C., 36-37, 135
Newport (Rhode Island), 3, 4-5, 10, 12, 13, 18, 19, 20, 22, 23, 24, 39, 62, 142-143
North Providence (Rhode Island), 11, 24, 33, 105
Norwich (Connecticut), 62
Notre Dame Church (Central Falls), 140
Nunnery Bill, 79

O'Brien, Rev. Matthew, 20
O'Connell, Daniel, 33, 67, 124, 126, 131
O'Connell, Patrick, 33
O'Connor, Bishop Michael, 73
O'Flaherty, Rev. Thomas J., 39
O'Gorman, Edith, 110
Olneyville (Rhode Island), 85, 137
O'Mahony, John, 93-94
O'Malley, Patrick, 94
O'Neill, John, 94
Orange Riots, 94, 98
Order of the Star-Spangled Banner, 76
O'Reilly, Bishop Bernard, 59, 69, 70-87, 108, 127, 138, 148, 150
O'Reilly, Rev. Bernard (Civil War chaplain), 91, 95
O'Reilly, Rev. Charles, 36, 116
O'Reilly, Rev. James, 23, 24
O'Reilly, Rev. Michael, 86
O'Reilly, Msgr. William, 87, 138
Orphan's Fair, 73, 105
O'Sullivan, John L., 51
Our Lady of Mercy Church (East Greenwich), 85
Our Lady of Mount Carmel Church (Crompton), 37
Otis, Harrison Gray, 21

Padelford, Governor Seth, 100
Panic of 1837, 30
Panic of 1857, 123
Parliament, 3
Parochial schools, 34, 62-65, 73-76, 78-79, 106
Paul-Dubois, L., 126, 131
Pawcatuck (Connecticut), 86
Pawtucket (Rhode Island), 18, 20, 21, 22, 24, 25, 31, 33, 35, 137
Pawtuxet Valley, 34, 37, 137, 141
Peoples' Constitution, 45-48
Peoples' Convention, 45
Petrarra, Rev. A. P., 147
Phenix (Rhode Island), 85, 141
Plunkett, Sir Horace, 126
Point Judith (Rhode Island), 6

Polish, 147
Pope Gregory XVI, 57, 90
Pope Pius VII, 16
Pope Pius IX, 70, 82, 89, 91, 110-111, 130, 131, 147, 150
Portsmouth (Rhode Island), 3, 18, 20, 22
Portuguese, 5, 6-7, 83, 142-145
Potter, Elisha R. Jr., 63, 78, 97
Potter, George, 127
Precious Blood Church, 106, 139-141
Presbyterian, 6
Princen, Rev. James Arnold, 138
Protestants, 1, 6, 7, 20, 21, 25, 42, 46, 63, 64, 66-67, 72-73, 80, 89, 109-110, 112, 124, 125, 126, 129, 134, 146
Proulx, Francis, 36, 135
Providence Daily Tribune, 78-79, 81
Providence Journal, 39, 42, 46-47, 77, 78, 79, 80-81, 92, 97-98, 110, 111
Providence Roman Catholic Orphans' Asylum and School Society, 66
Providence School Committee, 63-64
Provincial Councils at Baltimore, 57, 63
Ptolemy, Brother, F.S.C., 107
Purgatorian Society, 66, 109
'Puritanism' of the Irish Catholic, 125, 128
Puritans, 1
Putnam, Rev. Edward, 61

Quebec, 5, 6, 115, 133, 135, 136, 137, 138, 140
Quebec Act, 134
Quincy, Josiah, 21
Quinn, Rev. James, 138
Quinn, Rev. John, 85
Quinn, Rev. Thomas, 91
Quod Catholico nomine bene prospere, 147

Railroads, 27, 29
Reddy, Michael, 36
Religious of Jesus and Mary, 106
Remittances, 116
Repeal Movement, 33, 34, 66
Republican Party, 78, 83, 125, 135
Revolution of 1848, 146
Rhode Island Hospital, 89
Rhode Island Lantern, 98
Rhode Island Suffrage Association, 45
River Point (Rhode Island), 37
Riviere, Rev. Napoleon, 105
Roberts, William Randall, 94
Rochambeau, Count de, 10, 11-12
Rocky Point, Warwick (Rhode Island), 94
Rosary Society, 66
Rosati, Bishop Joseph, 25, 62
Rosecrans, William S., 62, 90
Ryan, Rev. Dennis, 33
Ryder, Rev. James, 62

Sacred Heart Church (Pawtucket), 105
Sadlier's Catholic Directory, 148

INDEX

St. Albans Raid, 94
St. Aloysius' Home, 66, 78-79, 87, 105
St. Ann's Church (Cranston), 104
St. Augustine's Society (Sodality of the Immaculate Conception), 147
St. Bernard's Academy (Woonsocket), 106
St. Bernard's Mission (South Providence), 104
St. Charles' Church (Providence), 142
St. Charles' Church (Woonsocket), 36, 91, 138, 139
St. Charles' School (Woonsocket), 74, 106
St. Edward's Church (Wanskuck), 105
St. James' Church (Manville), 142
St. Jean Baptiste Society, 138-139
St. John the Baptist Church (Centreville), 141-142
St. John the Baptist Church (Fall River), 34-35
St. John's Church (Providence), 104-105, 107
St. John's Church (Slatersville), 105
St. Joseph's Church (Ashton), 105
St. Joseph's Church (later renamed St. Mary's, Newport), 23, 31, 39, 62
St. Joseph's Church (Fox Point), 85, 150
St. Joseph's Church (Natick), 105
St. Joseph's Church (Pawtucket), 105
St. Joseph's Mission (Geneva, North Providence), 105
St. Joseph's School (Fox Point), 73, 74
St. Mary's Academy, Bay View, 76
St. Mary's Church (Newport), 22, 23, 31, 39, 62, 90, 150
St. Mary's Church (Pawtucket), 25, 26, 105, 140
St. Mary's Church (Warren), 85
St. Mary of the Assumption Church (Fall River), 35
St. Mary's Church (Broadway), 85, 147
St. Mary's Church (Crompton), 37, 141
St. Mary's Church (Stonington, Connecticut), 86
St. Mary's School (Newport), 62, 73, 106
St. Mary's School (Pawtucket), 74, 106
St. Mary's Seminary (Baltimore), 70, 87
St. Mary's Seminary (Providence), 70, 72, 87
St. Michael's Church (Pawcatuck, Connecticut), 86
St. Michael's Church (South Providence), 103-104, 105
St. Patrick's Academy (Pawtucket), 106
St. Patrick's Cemetery (Providence), 33-34
St. Patrick's Church (Harrisville), 86
St. Patrick's Church (Providence), 33-34, 52, 66
St. Patrick's Church (Valley Falls), 104
St. Patrick's Day, 39, 96
St. Patrick's School (Providence), 62-63, 73, 106
Sts. Peter and Paul Cathedral (Providence), 29-32, 37, 59, 60, 62, 70, 87, 105-106, 107, 109, 147, 150
Sts. Peter and Paul Church (Phenix), 85
Sts. Peter and Paul School (Providence), 62-63, 73, 74
St. Philip's Church (Greenville), 86
St. Vincent de Paul Society, 84, 123
St. Xavier's Academy (Providence), 73, 75-76, 106
Sanford, Governor Peleg, 5
Santo Domingo, 19
Sargent, Daniel, 21
Sarsfield Guards, 91
Scapular and Rosary Society, 109

Schale, Rev. Joseph A., 146-147
Scituate (Rhode Island), 12
Scotland, 119
Seekonk River, 24
Segur, Comte de, 12
Seigneuries, 133
Sentinelle Movement, 142
Seton, Mother Elizabeth, 62
Seventh Amendment (Rhode Island), 103
Shamrock Benevolent Aid Society, 123
Shannon, Rev. James, 126
Sheridan, General Philip, 90
Sinnot, Peter A., 96
Sisters of Charity (Emmitsburg), 62
Sisters of Charity (Mt. St. Vincent), 104
Sisters of Mercy, 72-76, 78-81, 87, 104, 106, 123
Sisters of St. Joseph, 62
Sisters of the Congregation of Notre Dame, 150
Sixth Amendment (Rhode Island), 98
Slater, Samuel, 24
Slatersville, 105, 137
Slavery, 90-91
Smith, Reuel, 36
Smith, Rev. James L., 105
Smithfield (Rhode Island), 35
Snow, Edwin M., 97, 119, 123
Social Manufacturing Company, 135
Socialism, 129-131
Societies, religious, 66, 67, 109, 131
Society for the Propagation of the Faith (the 'Propaganda'), 61-62, 84, 103
Society of St. Boniface, 146
Socio-Economic Mobility (Irish), 123-124, 127
South County (Rhode Island), 39, 46, 77
Spain, 1, 9, 10, 18
Sprague, Amasa, 39, 52-55
Sprague, William (1799-1856), 52
Sprague, William (1830-1915), 89, 91
Sprague Mills, 34, 37, 39, 52-54
Spruyt, Rev. Henri, 138, 141
Stang, Bishop William, 147
Staples, William R., 34
Stephens, James, 93
Stiles, Rev. Ezra, 4-5
Stonington (Connecticut), 29, 70, 86
Suffrage, 44-49, 51-52, 63, 82, 96-103
Sulpician, 16, 70
Sunday schools, 62, 74, 105-106
Survivance, 137
Synod, First Diocesan, 87

Tammany Society, 22
Taunton (Massachusetts), 22, 26, 33, 148
Taunton River, 5
Taylor, George Rogers, 29
Taylor, Rev. William, 21
Temperance, 66-68, 79, 96, 150
Ternay, Admiral Chevalier de, 12

INDEX

Thayer, Rev. John, 17, 18-19, 20
Third Plenary Council of Baltimore, 73
Third Rhode Island Regiment, 91
Tierney, Rev. Michael, 106
Timon, Bishop John, 70
Tin Top Congregational Church, 27
Tisserant, Rev. John S., 17, 19, 20
Tiverton (Rhode Island), 34-35
Tocqueville, Alexis de, 112, 113, 126, 128, 129
Tone, Wolfe, 94
Touro, Isaac, 143
Touro Synagogue (Newport), 143
Town House (Providence), 27
'Transportation Revolution,' 29
Treaty of Paris (1763), 9, 133
Trevett, Eleazar, 22
Trinity Church (Newport), 12
Truancy legislation, 78
Tucker, Rev. Hilary, 85
Tudor, William, 21
Twentieth Amendment (Rhode Island), 51-52
Tyler, President John, 46, 48, 51
Tyler, Bishop William, 26, 37, 57, 59-62, 64, 65-67, 69-70, 74, 89, 138, 148

Ultramontanism, 125, 126-127
Updike, Wilkins, 54

Van Zandt, Charles C., 97
Vatican Council (I), 89, 110-111
Vaughn, Father, 95
Vergennes, Count, 9
Verot, Bishop Augustine, 93
Verrazzano, Giovanni, 5-6
Victorian Ethic, 128

Vocations, 103
Vygen, Rev. Eugene, 138

Wallace, Rev. Michael, 104
Wallace, Senator William A., 100
Walsh, Mike, 48
Walsh, Rev. Lawrence, 138
War of 1812, 20
Warde, Mother Mary Francis Xavier, 73, 75
Warren (Rhode Island), 85, 137
Warren, Major Russell, 33
Washington, George, 10-11, 15
Warwick (Rhode Island), 3
Webster, Daniel, 21, 51
Weekly Democrat, 98
Weekly Review, 98, 111
Welsh, James, 92
West Warwick (Rhode Island), 37
Westerly (Rhode Island), 86
Wexford Rising of 1798, 113
Whaling, 143-145
Whately, Archbishop Richard (Anglican), 64
Wheeler, Robert A., 123
Whig Party, 42, 76, 77, 78, 81
Wiley, Rev. William, 33, 59, 62, 63, 66
Wilkinson, David, 25
William of Orange, 112
Williams, Roger, 1-3, 4, 6, 7
Wilson, Senator Henry, 98, 100
Wiseman, Don Josef, 19
Woodley, Rev. Robert D., 22-23, 25, 26, 36
Woonsocket (Rhode Island), 18, 22, 34, 35, 36, 67, 135-137

Yorktown (Virginia), 11, 12
Young Catholic Friends Society, 66, 68, 73
Young Ireland, 93, 115, 124, 129

173